Indian Nations of Wisconsin

Praise for

Indian Nations of Wisconsin
Histories of Endurance and Renewal
Second Edition

"In this unprecedented era of cooperation between Native Americans and non–Native Americans, a new epoch in our nation's history, we continue to enrich our understanding of our shared histories, and ultimately, our shared futures together. We are lucky. Patty Loew gives us educational treasures in *Indian Nations of Wisconsin*. The rich stories, images, and symbols in her book have all been collected and shared in partnership with the Native American Nations and communities in Wisconsin. These invaluable texts are the first steps any educator or person should take in learning about the complex 12,000-year human story of our home, the multi-ethnic and multilingual Western Great Lakes."

> —Aaron Bird Bear
>> former American Indian Academic Services Advisor, UW–Madison

"The updated information and new chapters include pertinent, timely information, making this a living and breathing history book."

> —Kanak Odekirk
>> PhD, District Administrator, School District of Wabeno Area

"Containing a plethora of primary documents, maps, archival photographs, and interviews, *Indian Nations of Wisconsin* . . . does an exemplary job of demonstrating the importance of Wisconsin's native people in Wisconsin's history, politics, and culture. *Indian Nations of Wisconsin* is a crucial resource for any school district that effectively implements the requirements of Act 31. Our First Nations Studies program at Prescott High School would not be complete without this impressive book."

> —Jeff Ryan
>> First Nations History Teacher, Prescott High School

"Patty Loew demonstrates with her research and writing that there are multiple ways of understanding the past and present. She has consulted the standard written sources, but she also took the time to interview tribal historians to learn what they had to teach based on the oral histories of each tribe. No other published work does this for Wisconsin tribes."

> —James W. Oberly
>> Department of History and American Indian Studies Program, UW–Eau Claire

Indian Nations of Wisconsin

Histories of Endurance and Renewal

Second Edition

Patty Loew

with forewords by
Paul DeMain and J P Leary

WISCONSIN HISTORICAL SOCIETY PRESS

Published by the
Wisconsin Historical Society Press
Publishers since 1855

© 2013 by the State Historical Society of Wisconsin

For permission to reuse material from *Indian Nations of Wisconsin*, 978-0-87020-503-3, please access www.copyright.com or contact the Copyright Clearance Center, Inc. (CCC), 222 Rosewood Drive, Danvers, MA 01923, 978-750-8400. CCC is a not-for-profit organization that provides licenses and registration for a variety of users.

wisconsinhistory.org

Photographs identified with WHi or WHS are from the Society's collections; address requests to reproduce these photos to the Visual Materials Archivist at the Wisconsin Historical Society, 816 State Street, Madison, WI 53706.

Printed in the United States of America

Designed by Composure Graphics

Maps produced by Amelia Janes and Mike Gallagher, Midwest Educational Graphics

Cover photo credits: top left by Charles Van Schaick, WHi Image ID 60938; top center by RJ and Linda Miller, courtesy of the Wisconsin Department of Tourism; top right WHi Image ID 35211; bottom left by Reynaldo Morales; bottom right Wisconsin Historical Museum 1942.59

Page iii: A Menominee village as depicted by Francois, Comte de Castelnau, a French naturalist and diplomat who visited the Green Bay area circa 1838; WHi Image ID 6049

Page vii, left: Members of the Ira Robinson Isham family at the Lac Courte Oreilles Reservation circa 1898; WHi Image ID 82889. Page vii, center: Menominee children photographed around 1909; WHi Image ID 23734. Page vii, right: Ojibwe picking blueberries in northwestern Wisconsin, circa 1910; WHi Image ID 78031

23 22 21 20 19   3 4 5

Library of Congress Cataloging-in-Publication Data

Loew, Patty.

 Indian nations of Wisconsin: histories of endurance and renewal / Patty Loew; with forewords by Paul DeMain and J P Leary.—2nd ed.

  p. cm.

 Includes bibliographical references and index.

 ISBN 978-0-87020-503-3 (pbk. : alk. paper) 1. Indians of North America—Wisconsin—History. 2. Indians of North America—Wisconsin—Social life and customs. I. Title.

 E78.W8L64 2013

 977.5'00497—dc23

2012033629

∞ The paper used in this publication meets the minimum requirements of the American National Standard for Information Sciences—Permanence of Paper for Printed Library Materials, ANSI Z39.48-1992.

For my mother, Alice DeNomie Loew, and the DeNomie family

Contents

FOREWORD

Have you ever wondered about those mounds just down the street? Or about that story you heard about your great-grandfather: "The Indians used to live down there, by the river; we got along fine"?

Now updated for its second edition, *Indian Nations of Wisconsin: Histories of Endurance and Renewal* by Patty Loew breathes life into our stories. With added information and new chapters for the Brothertown Indian Nation and urban Indians, Loew brings us fully across the threshold of the last century and into the new digital age, not to become extinct, not to be forgotten.

This book is interesting, intriguing, captivating. I can open it to any page and step into the pictures. I step into my family, my history, my culture—this is my state, and as Indigenous people, we became part of the earth itself long ago. Tread lightly upon us.

It is 2013, and we are engaged in another struggle in our state of Wisconsin, a state that has a progressive past and many firsts to crow about, including required reading in our schools about Indigenous populations that existed, exist, and will continue to exist into the future, with touches of Indigenous thought and wisdom. This book should be required reading for every middle-school-aged student, as well as the entire elected legislative body of the state of Wisconsin, so we don't hear things about "the bad land Indians," or "a treaty of some kind up there." We deserve better.

We careen between bulging smiles and the realization of destructive despair and often feel like the coal-miner's canary of Wisconsin's conscience. We also like to tell lots of jokes. I fondly remember the stories of Pipe Mustache, Archy Mosay, Clifford and Wilbur Blackdeer, Manny Boyd, Amos Chrisjohn, and other elders who lived in the past century, when horses went the way of trains, trains went the way of cars and freeways, and—in a whirl forward into the dizzying era of a new digital paradigm of information—we all went online. We now learn our Native languages from Facebook and other social media while explaining to our grandchildren what a rotary phone and party lines were, and while imparting the meaning of Manoomin, the sacred rice, and other sacred food sources whose harvest was preserved in treaty. This book is but one small chapter of our history, but it is a must-read if you care about people and the earth, and about those who have lived closely with and without dominion over it.

Loew's book is a rich but small window into ten thousand or more years of living history, family and social events, political upheaval, and the love and pursuit of life. But two hundred pages of Loew are worth a thousand memories to me. The pictures incite my imagination.

With each page, each photograph, each paragraph, my mind asks a hundred questions of the old ones who are now gone. Chapter upon chapter, the information takes on a life of its own, my imagination creating another new timeline to reflect upon something I thought I already knew. Each page, each face, each tidbit of our obscured history is like an opening flower with thorns—the Cahokia Mounds, the mounds of Eagle Heights, evidence of the "ancients," the migrations of the Mascouten, Texas Kickapoo, Sauk and Fox, Dakota and others, our off-reservation brothers and sisters in the hidden Indian villages throughout the woods of northern Wisconsin, and where did all our Metis blood relatives go? Fascinating, fascinating.

Open these pages and enter a world like no other, where the ancient history of Wisconsin is given birth in tiny footsteps. I once gave a presentation at a church with stories about Winaboozhoo, an Ojibwe patron half-man half-spirit, and the story of the great flood. I was asked, "You have a story about the great flood?" I answered back, "Did you think it flooded only your half of the earth?" And there is where "our" history began together and ends for the time being in *Indian Nations of Wisconsin: History of Endurance and Renewal.*

Paul DeMain, Oneida/Ojibwe
Editor, *News From Indian Country*
8558N County Road K
Hayward, Wisconsin 54843
www.IndianCountryNews.com
www.IndianCountryTV.com

FOREWORD

I have known Patty Loew for a number of years and have been fortunate to work alongside her on several occasions. I recall one summer evening, shortly after the publication of the first edition of *Indian Nations of Wisconsin*, when we sat together in a circle with educators from around the state on the grounds of the Menominee Logging Camp Museum. Patty shared some of the historical accounts that went into the book, as well her stories of collecting some of those accounts. Despite the heat, humidity, and mosquitoes, we sat spellbound throughout her talk, and she graciously answered questions, chatted, and signed books well into the evening. So many of the stories she shared were well-known in the tribal communities but largely unknown outside them. American Indian Studies Summer Institute participants and my fellow staff members who were there that night came to recognize that Patty Loew had been entrusted with those stories, making *Indian Nations of Wisconsin* a means to learn new information, to see new perspectives, and to gain valuable insights into histories that other scholars had not yet brought to the world at large.

More than a decade later, it remains clear that in both content and perspective, *Indian Nations of Wisconsin* is an invaluable book well-suited for the general public as well as for classroom use. The author, a member of the Bad River Band of Lake Superior Ojibwe, has played an important role in raising public awareness of Native issues as a journalist, documentary filmmaker, television host, and educator at the University of Wisconsin–Madison. That first edition of *Indian Nations of Wisconsin* ensured that the histories of Native peoples, and Native perspectives on those histories, were presented in a book that was informative, accessible, and enjoyable to read. This second edition builds on that contribution and is a vital resource for learning about the diverse Native peoples who call Wisconsin their home.

Our state's recent history has taught us that the lack of understanding and awareness of Native issues can incur a significant cost. The controversy, violence, and discord following 1983's *Voigt* decision, in which the Seventh Circuit Court of Appeals affirmed the continued existence of the Lake Superior Band of Chippewa Indians' right to hunt, fish, and gather within territories ceded under treaties signed in 1837 and 1842, serves as a grim reminder of the consequences of public ignorance. As the late Walt Bresette, Red Cliff Ojibwe activist, artist, and educator, noted about the Voigt decision, "No one in the state was prepared academically or intellectually for the court ruling." The ensuing public controversy, in which misunderstanding was rampant and misinformation flourished, erupted into violent conflict, often referred to as the Walleye War, that lasted over a decade.

The most immediate causes of the crisis related to education and public information. The general public had been ill-served by an education system in which Native people were invisible, excluded, or problematically presented, often in biased and stereotypical ways. Generations of Wisconsinites had never had opportunities to learn about treaty rights, tribal sovereignty, or the histories and cultures of the Native people in this state. When complex legal and historical issues emerged, racism and fear filled in gaps where accurate, authentic information was unavailable. Grassroots and professional organizations, faith communities, and others worked to complement or counter the stories available in the mass media. The best educational tools were personal and community stories, many of which were well-known in tribal communities yet largely unknown outside those settings. Though many worked diligently to develop appropriate materials to educate the general public, few were available.

One important effort to address this matter came in 1989, when Wisconsin adopted new legislation requiring all public schools to "provide instruction in the history, culture, and tribal sovereignty of the federally recognized tribes and bands in the state" as part of the state's social studies curriculum (s. 121.02(1)(L)4 Wis. Stats.). Related provisions addressed human relations education and instructional materials, required teachers to receive this instruction as part of the licensure process, and directed the Department of Public Instruction to develop curriculum on Chippewa treaty rights. Twenty years later, it might well be argued that this law, best known as Act 31, has not had the impact that tribal leaders, Native and non-Native educators, and allies of various stripes and political commitments had hoped for; yet at the time it was the most specific curriculum directive adopted to date. It represents broad recognition of the important role schools play in producing an informed populace.

Through a combination of historical research and ongoing professional work with educators and students, I have seen the continuing need for education about Native issues. I have recently begun to do an activity with groups of teachers and university students that provides an opportunity for critical reflection on their own prior learning and current knowledge about Native people. After sorting out fact from opinion and assessing the quality of the sources of information, groups are invariably stunned by several important realizations. First, they have learned only a little purportedly factual information about Native people. Second, most of their prior knowledge came from the mass media and popular culture rather than from scholarly or academic sources. Third, regardless of scholarly quality, students rarely encountered information about Native people from the perspective of a Native scholar. *Indian Nations of Wisconsin* addresses each of these gaps and provides an important balance in general and scholarly discussions.

Complex legal and historical issues continue to emerge in Wisconsin, as elsewhere, and shared understandings of those matters are critical to our shared future as Native and non-Native communities in Wisconsin. Whether the issues involve hunting, fishing, and gathering; taxation; gaming; environmental protection; or other shared concerns, we will all be well served by an educational resource that provides a Native perspective through the voice of a Native author because it will provide broader access to the knowledge and insight of tribal communities themselves. *Indian Nations of Wisconsin* brings an important balance to the knowledge base in a way that the reader will find informative, accessible, and enjoyable. It is an important resource, and I thank you, the reader, for engaging with the stories that tribal communities in Wisconsin entrusted to Patty Loew and that she shares so well.

J P Leary, Cherokee
Associate Professor in First Nations Studies, History, and Humanities,
University of Wisconsin–Green Bay

PREFACE

It's January 2013, and my Facebook page is filled with messages alerting me to public hearings and protests about a mining bill that tribal members believe could threaten the ancient wild rice beds of the Bad River Ojibwe. I'm invited to join Native listservs and directed to Native blogs. A Native TV web channel originating from the Lac Courte Oreilles Reservation offers more than a thousand livestream programs related to indigenous issues in its video library. YouTube.com offers a myriad of additional Native-themed videos.

Ten years ago, when *Indian Nations of Wisconsin: Histories of Endurance and Renewal* was first published, Facebook, YouTube, and other social media did not exist. Blogging was in its infancy, and Native newspapers existed only as hard copies. Similarly, academic articles about indigenous peoples were found primarily offline and required physical trips to libraries and archives. Today, many Native sources of news and opinion have moved online. Some tribal newspapers and newsletters exist only in electronic form. Certainly, the proliferation of electronic journals and e-books has changed the way scholars conduct their research.

Welcome to the digital world of all things Native.

Although the Internet has made it easier and more efficient to research Native topics, new questions and challenges have emerged. Who is an "expert"? What websites are credible? Whose perspectives do they reflect? And who has the right to use and interpret Native images? At this writing, an estimated 80 percent of Indian Country lacks access to broadband. Given this serious accessibility issue, it's quite obvious that many of the events, interpretations, and worldviews of Native people are not part of the cyber dialogue. It's also important to remember that despite the many new digital resources about Indians, Native cultures remain rooted in oral tradition. Face-to-face fact gathering in the form of oral interviews, story listening, and observation of Native cultural events is still essential to understanding Native people and conveying their diverse viewpoints.

Twelve years ago in the preface to this book, I wrote about the New Dawn of Tradition Pow Wow in Madison, a 1998 celebration of survival by the resident tribes of Wisconsin as well as the Sauk, Meskwaki, and Dakota nations and other Native Americans whose ancestors had been removed from the state. Along with the Potawatomi from Kansas, Kickapoo from Oklahoma, and Winnebago now living in Nebraska, for the first time in nearly 175 years, they danced together in their ancestral homelands. As I waited with other traditional women dancers to enter the arena during the grand entry, I had a deep sense of history about this remarkable event. Not since the 1825 grand council in Prairie du Chien had all the original inhabitants of Wisconsin come together. Tragically, that gathering had culminated in a treaty that presaged land cessions and removal orders—developments that would bring poverty of land and spirit to generations of Native Americans.

Initially, there had been talk among some Wisconsin tribes about boycotting the New Dawn Pow Wow. Promoted as a Wisconsin sesquicentennial event, the gathering raised the hackles of some tribal members. Native Americans asked how anyone could expect them to "celebrate" 150 years of Wisconsin statehood when it obviously came at the expense of their land and the erosion of their political rights. In the end, however, most tribal members decided to view the week—devoted as it was to Wisconsin history and culture—as an opportunity to educate

Old meets new. Jingle Dancers perform in exhibition under the shadow of a giant television monitor at the New Dawn of Tradition Pow Wow, August 1998.

Courtesy of Great Lakes Inter Tribal Council

The author in a traditional Ojibwe doe-skin dress made by her mother, Alice Loew, at the New Dawn of Tradition Pow Wow in Madison, 1998

Courtesy of Patty Loew

the white residents of this state about the injustices and triumphs of Indian people in Wisconsin. They chose to view it not as a commemoration of Wisconsin statehood, but as a celebration of Native American survival.

A year before the powwow, I had been asked by the Great Lakes Inter-Tribal Council, an umbrella organization representing the eleven federally recognized tribes in Wisconsin, to research and write text for a large, walk-through public history exhibit on Indian nations in the state. The exhibit was to be displayed during the Folklife Festival, which was scheduled to coincide with the sesquicentennial celebration. The timing was excellent; I was preparing a seminar on Wisconsin Indians as part of my teaching fellowship in the History Department and American Indian Studies Program at the University of Wisconsin–Madison. Although I had done a fair amount of research on the Ojibwe for my PhD dissertation, I knew little about the histories of other Indian cultures. I thought the experience would help me develop my seminar and nourish my personal interest in Native cultures. Over the next year, I met with tribal historians and directors of language and culture in each of the twelve Indian communities. The stories they shared with me and the materials they recommended formed the basis of the exhibit, the core of my lectures, and the genesis of this book.

As a member of the Bad River Band of Lake Superior Ojibwe, I have been frustrated by many of the books about the First People of this area. So often, Native history is filtered through white sources: missionary accounts, traders' journals, and government documents. Certainly, these have been helpful in reconstructing the past, but frequently Native voices have been absent from their own histories. In this book, I have attempted to use as many Native sources as possible: speeches delivered by chiefs during treaty negotiations, for example; origin stories; songs; legends; cave paintings; Native newspapers; and so on. I have tried to refer to the Native people in this book as they refer to themselves. For example, for the Five Nations Confederacy I use the term *Haudenosaunee* instead of *Iroquois*—a derogatory term coined by a tribe unfriendly to the Oneida. Other tribal terms include *Meskwaki* instead of *Fox* and *Anishinaabe* or *Ojibwe* instead of *Chippewa*. Although the Ho-Chunk did not formally change their name from Winnebago until the end of the twentieth century, for purposes of simplicity and consistency I refer to them throughout their history as *Ho-Chunk*.

This edition contains two new chapters: one on urban Indians, primarily in Milwaukee and Green Bay, and one on the Brothertown Indian Nation, a federally unrecognized tribe that continues to press for federal acknowledgment. Given that a majority of Indian people in Wisconsin lives in cities, the omission of a discussion about urban Indians in the first edition was a major oversight on my part.

Twelve years ago there was a paucity of information about the Brothertown—so few materials existed that I rationalized including their history in the chapter about the Mohicans, a tribe with whom they had migrated from New York in the early nineteenth century. Over the past decade, the Brothertown's complicated legal effort to "prove" their Indianness has produced considerable documentation, which provided enough material for a stand-alone Brothertown chapter. This second edition also reflects contemporary historical events and initiatives of the twenty-first century, such as the Crandon Mine struggle primarily involving the Forest County Potawatomi and Sokaogon Ojibwe and the economic, social, and environmental advancements of all twelve Native communities.

Although I have combined the very early histories and fur trade experiences of the tribes into single narratives, I have devoted separate subsequent chapters to each Indian community. From an organizational perspective, I thought it was important for the reader to understand that each tribe is culturally distinct, with its own language, ontology, and history. As much as possible, I have tried to include events and sociopolitical movements that remind us that the Indian nations that reside in Wisconsin did not relate only to white policies and pressures; they related to each other as well.

This book was much more difficult to write than I ever imagined. I was asked to write a "history book," which carried with it certain expectations that the book I delivered would "look" like a history book, that it would include dates and documented "facts" arranged chronologically. But Native people tend to organize their histories thematically, with stories unfolding in a circular fashion. Time is relative and sometimes incidental. One of my Mohican readers gently scolded me for writing that the Mohicans moved their villages every ten years. "That's so *white*," she told me. "Why don't you just say: as often as necessary." Of course, she was right.

❖

I am indebted to the tribal historians, elders, and friends in Wisconsin, some of whom not only shared their knowledge for the history project but also read portions of this manuscript, corrected errors, and suggested ways to improve it. Any mistakes in the book or errors of judgment are my fault, not theirs. Along with the tribal members who helped me with the first edition, in particular, I would like to thank David Greendeer, Janice Rice, and Anne Thundercloud of the

Oneida corn husk dolls
Wisconsin Historical Museum 1957A.978

Ho-Chunk Nation; Loretta Metoxen in Oneida; Kathleen Brown-Pérez, Richard Schadewald, and Caroline Andler of the Brothertown Indians; Eugene Shawano and Winda Collins of the Forest County Potawatomi; Dorothy Davids, Ruth Gudinas, Bernice Pigeon, Leah Miller, and the Stockbridge-Munsee Historical Committee; and David Grignon, Virginia Nuske, and Rebecca Alegria in Menominee. I owe a debt to Jeff Bowman, Butch Roberts, Craig Anderson, Lisa Poupart, David Webster, and my cousins Dave and Jim DeNomie, who read all or sections of the new urban Indians chapter and offered insights about how to improve it.

I would also like to thank and acknowledge the wise Native men and women and friends of my own nation who have guided my pen and spirit: Joe Rose and Dana Jackson at Bad River; Wanda McFaggen at St. Croix; Larry Balber and the late Walt Bresette at Red Cliff; Charlotte and the late Nick Hockings and Gregg Guthrie at Lac du Flambeau; David Bisonette, Paul DeMain, and the late Jim Schlender at Lac Courte Oreilles; and Fred Ackley, Richard Ackley, and Fran Van Zile at Mole Lake. I am grateful to everyone at the Great Lakes Indian Fish and Wildlife Commission, especially Jim Zorn, Sue Erickson, Neil Kmiecik, and Jim Thannum, who have been wonderful sources of information and support throughout the years.

This project would not have been possible without the tireless efforts of two Native graduate students, Christina Rencontre and Reynaldo Morales, who conducted interviews, collected documents, and provided photographs for this book. I am also grateful to Tim Tynan, whose digital storytelling work in Indian Country has not only inspired me but also has created an important archive of material for future researchers.

I'd like to thank two of the hardest-working men in Indian Country, journalist Paul DeMain and Dr. J P Leary, UW–Green Bay First Nations Studies, for writing introductions to this book. I've long admired Paul's work on the cutting edge of Native communications technology, and I will forever be grateful to J P for the groundbreaking work he did on Act 31 (Wisconsin's educational mandate on American Indian studies) for the Wisconsin Department of Public Instruction.

Finally, I am indebted to Rachel Cordasco and Barbara Walsh of the Wisconsin Historical Society Press, and in particular, WHS Press Editorial Director Kathy Borkowski and Senior Editor Kate Thompson for suggesting this revised and expanded edition and entrusting it to my care. *Miigwetch*.

1 EARLY HISTORY

A thousand years ago, after carefully preparing red, black, and blue-gray paints, an artist sanded the walls of a rock shelter hidden in a stand of mixed hardwoods in present-day Iowa County in Wisconsin. Satisfied that the "canvas" was properly prepared, the artist—a historian, really—began to record a remarkable story. The walls filled with painted turtles, thunderbirds, and a mythic hero who wore human heads as earrings. Supernatural athletic contests and "giant" slayings unfolded in pictographic detail.

The Red Horn composite in Gottschall Cave, Iowa County, tells an ancient Ho-Chunk story of heroes and giants. The story may relate to the arrival of the Mississippian Culture to the area.

Drawing by Mary Steinhauer; used with permission of Robert Salzer, Beloit College

Members of the modern Ho-Chunk Nation recognize this composition as the story of Red Horn, an ancient Ho-Chunk hero. This origin epic, told by generations of tribal members and preserved in a cave known today as Gottschall, testifies to the enduring power of the spoken word and the persistence of Native American oral tradition.[1] Gottschall also provides other clues to the pre-Columbian Ho-Chunk past. Along with the Red Horn paintings, the cave contains pottery shards of the Effigy Mound Builders, whose earthen works first appeared about three thousand years ago, and unusual soils associated with sacred rituals of the Mississippians, whose agriculture-based economy and impressive trade networks emerged about one thousand years ago. The connection between Ho-Chunk oral history and the physical evidence at Gottschall suggests that rather than being separate peoples, later cultures evolved from and intersected with earlier ones.

The Gottschall site, a place of obvious cultural and religious significance, is just one of more than one hundred rock art sites identified in Wisconsin, most of them in the Driftless Area of the southwestern part of the state. From simple grooves and incised geometric designs to elaborate painted birds, animals, and human forms, these cave drawings may have been created for spiritual or sacred reasons, inspired by dreams, fasts, or rituals. Perhaps Native artists carved or painted these

1

motifs to educate the young or commemorate the dead. It is likely that the ancestors of today's modern Indian nations used pictographs as mnemonic devices to help tribal members remember important events or complex ceremonies.[2]

The Anishinaabe, or Ne shna bek, a political and spiritual alliance comprising the Ojibwe, Odaawa, and Potawatomi, recorded pictographs on birch bark scrolls to help initiates remember sacred songs and sequences of the Midewiwin, or Medicine Lodge ceremonies. Each character related to a phrase in the chant, which was repeated a number of times. The integration of animal, human, and spirit figures in these scrolls illustrates how intimately the Anishinaabe synthesized the natural world with spiritual beliefs. Although most closely associated with this most important religious society, Anishinaabe picture writing was also used in more ordinary affairs of the tribe. Indeed, it became the lingua franca of diplomacy and commerce among many Native peoples.[3]

Deer Effigy Mound, a rare four-footed effigy, is contained in one of two mound groups preserved on the Mendota State Hospital grounds in Madison. Most animal effigies were sculpted with two legs, not four. The Mendota State Hospital mound cluster is one of the finest in the world. In addition to the Deer Mound, the group contains two panthers, two bears, and three bird mounds, including one with an original wingspan of over 624 feet.
WHi Image ID 4843

Wampum was another way Native American tribes communicated. Although wampum belts sometimes contained other colors, they were primarily strings of purple and white beads made from quahog shells gathered in an area near present-day Long Island, New York. For some tribes, the color of the wampum had meaning: white meant peace; purple or red sometimes meant war; black denoted sorrow or something serious.[4] Indian nations routinely used wampum belts in diplomatic relations. For example, when the Potawatomi received a dispatch in the form of a wampum belt, they sometimes referred to it as the "mouth" of the sender. After the arrival of Europeans, wampum became a form of monetary exchange.

Along with other intriguing fragments of the past, rock art, picture writing, and wampum are useful in reconstructing the experiences of Native cultures before they encountered Europeans. It is a history that encompasses a vast expanse of time. Although anthropologists believe that humans have occupied the Great Lakes region for at least twelve thousand years, contemporary tribal historians resist such efforts to date human occupation of the area. According to the origin stories of most Indian nations in Wisconsin, the tribes have been here "from the beginning of time."

Early Native Americans adapted to a landscape dramatically different from the one we recognize today. Twelve thousand years ago, at the end of the Ice Age, small communities of hunters and gatherers searched for food in coniferous forests that grew in the paths of the retreating glaciers. They encountered fragments of tundra, spongy plains, and large lakes. Over the next five thousand years, they learned to shape copper into useful and ornamental objects that they could trade to other communities. They began to cultivate certain crops, such as beans, squash, sunflower, and corn, selecting and sowing seeds that had the most desirable characteristics.

Postglacial erosion, however, created wildly fluctuating lake and river levels. At various times until 1500 BP (before present), some of Wisconsin's landscape may have been an uninhabitable bog. Interestingly, the Ojibwe and Potawatomi recall a time long ago when the people forgot the teachings of the Midewiwin, the spiritual foundation of the Anishinaabe, and as punishment were forced to leave their homes and travel east. Like nearly every other Great Lakes tribe, they tell stories about water once covering the earth.

In the Ojibwe story of Winneboozho and the Great Flood, for example, the Creator purified Mother Earth with water. Then Winneboozho—half spirit, half man—found himself, along with the animals, clinging to a log. Winneboozho and the animals took turns diving under the water to try to bring up some earth. After better divers failed, Muskrat gave his life in a successful effort to retrieve a few grains of sand. From that bit of matter, Winneboozho created a New World, which Turtle offered to carry on his back. In honor of Turtle's sacrifice, some Native people today refer to North America as Turtle Island.[5]

The Oneida have a similar story of how the world began. Their version, however, begins in the Sky World after the Tree of Life is uprooted, leaving a gaping hole between the sky and a watery world below it. Sky Woman slips into the hole, but as she falls, she manages to grab a twig from the tree. Birds carry her safely to the watery world, where Muskrat dives to retrieve some earth and Turtle offers her back to hold the spreading world. With seeds from the Tree of Life, Sky Woman begins to plant and creates Mother Earth. Contemporary Native Americans believe that flood stories such as these are evidence that their ancestors occupied the Great Lakes region during the end of the last Ice Age.[6]

Thunderbird Petroglyph, Twin Bluffs. The thunderbird is one of the most consistent images in Wisconsin rock art. The Thunderbird Clan is the largest clan among the Ho-Chunk and a significant clan among the Menominee.

Photo by Charles Brown; WHi Image ID 34556

Physical evidence of early human presence, such as stone tools, spear points, and pottery, along with campsites and refuse pits, also helps us to understand what life was like in ancient times. These fragments of the past suggest that the earliest Native people subsisted mainly on a diet of plants and small mammals—rabbits, raccoons, and squirrels—as well as larger ones such as deer and elk. From spear points embedded in the buried bones of now-extinct mammoth and mastodon, we also know they once hunted these larger mammals. They learned to supplement their diet with fish and freshwater clams and mussels.

From the stories and songs passed down to present generations of Native Americans, we can make inferences about the relationships early inhabitants had with the animals and plants that sustained them. The Ho-Chunk, for example, sing about their reverence for deer and a hill near present-day Black River Falls where their ancestors used to hunt. It was here that deer would beckon Ho-Chunk hunters by singing to them songs of love: "If he is there, let him come. If he is there, let him come," the deer would call. "An old man fasted there," the Ho-Chunk remember. "They took pity on him—that hill, the deer, and Earthmaker. Whatever that was sacred, they could bestow on him, they did." The hill remains a spiritual place where tribal members fast and pray.[7]

The Ojibwe's appreciation for animals is evident in Fisher Goes to the Sky World, a story about four animals who stole the sun and brought seasons to the earth. In this story, Mother Earth was dark and cold because the Sky People had captured the sun and all its warmth. Fisher, aided by his friends, Otter, Lynx, and Wolverine, dug a hole into the Sky World and tried to capture the sun. As the sun's rays escaped, the earth began to transform itself. The snow melted and plants and trees appeared. By the time the Sky People discovered Fisher, he and his friends had dug a hole large enough for the sun to warm the earth half the year. Such stories reinforce the notion that ancient Native people viewed animals not as inferior creatures intended solely for human exploitation, but as helper beings with their own spirits and purposes.[8]

Plants, too, are imbued with human qualities and presented as helper spirits in Native American songs and stories. Potawatomi oral tradition hints at the strong connection earlier Native people may have had to the plants that nourished them—especially corn. Five mysterious strangers visited a young woman who was spared after the Creator "lifted up the whole world and dropped it in a lake." The first visitor was tall and wore a green blanket, which turned into tobacco leaves. The second, who was short and round, rolled on the ground and became a pumpkin. The third and fourth visitors became beans and squash. The fifth was a handsome man whom the young woman married. After their wedding, the husband revealed himself to be the leader of the corn nation. Rain blessed their union and produced an abundance of growing things. "The woman and the corn chief gave thanks to the Good Spirit," the Potawatomi remembered, "and taught their children how to pray and offer their thanks for corn, pumpkin, beans, squash, and tobacco."[9]

Whereas non-Indian anthropologists explain the tribes' increasing reliance on agriculture as an evolution from hunting and gathering, some Native elders and historians view their origin stories as proof that they have always had agriculture. However, advocates of both theories agree that the preeminence of agriculture represented a marked change in community life. With a more reliable food supply, tribal populations increased and Native Americans began to live in larger, more permanent villages. They developed more sophisticated political structures and traded more extensively. They devoted more time to artistic and religious expression, evidenced by the pottery that began to emerge and the effigy mounds that began to dot the landscape.

About twenty-five hundred years ago, Native people began constructing earthen effigies, including turtles, bears, and humans. Some of the mounds were massive. A bird effigy near Muscoda in present-day Richland County, for example, had a

Double Panther Mound, near Lake Winnebago in Calumet County. Sometimes described as a water spirit effigy, this mound was photographed in 1915 but has since been destroyed.
WHi Image ID 34544

wingspan of more than a quarter mile. Although many of the effigies contained human remains, some did not. It is likely that water held a special attraction for mound builders, since many of the earthen effigies were located near lakes and rivers. Intriguingly, in southern Wisconsin some of the mound groups correspond to Ho-Chunk clan divisions: eagles and thunderbirds from the Sky World and bears representing the Earth World. Some mound clusters include water panthers, which are symbolic of the underground spirits. There is some evidence that the tails of panther effigies often point to underground springs—entrances to the underworld, in the Ho-Chunk oral tradition.

Some researchers surmise that these mounds are the key to understanding the cosmology of the culture that built them—the people the Ho-Chunk call "ancestors." There is speculation that mound groups may symbolize the clan structures of some contemporary tribes. Others suggest they may be gargantuan maps or, perhaps like the Mayan pyramids, calendrical or astronomical devices. There is no question that for the people who built them, these monumental cultural expressions were a form of communication.

About a thousand years ago, an entirely different cultural group entered the region. Unlike the effigy mound builders, the Mississippians had not emerged from the Great Lakes area but rather had migrated to the region from the south. They belonged to a powerful nation of people whose principal city, Cahokia, near present-day St. Louis, supported a population of at least thirty-five thousand. The Mississippians appear to have had a complex belief system that emphasized the interaction of the sacred and the secular.

The Mississippians developed an impressive trade network that extended from the Atlantic to the Rocky Mountains and from the Gulf of Mexico to the Great Lakes. Trade most likely led them to establish the village known today as Aztalan, considered one of Wisconsin's most significant archaeological sites, near present-day Lake Mills in Jefferson County. The palisade that surrounded the village suggests that these tall residents of Aztalan did not always live in harmony with their neighbors. Could they have been the "giants" slain in the Red Horn story?

From excavated refuse pits, we know that the residents of Aztalan grew considerable quantities of corn, beans, and squash. Their basic meat staple was venison, although they also ate duck, fish, and mussels. The site they chose for their village, along the west bank of the Crawfish River, provided lush bottomland for farming and easy access to fish and waterfowl. For some reason, however, Aztalan did not succeed as a permanent settlement. Within ten generations, the inhabitants abandoned their village and the Mississippians faded from the cultural landscape.[10]

A Late Woodland pot excavated in the 1930s in Clam Lake, Burnett County
Courtesy of the Milwaukee Public Museum; neg. 71951

Well before the arrival of Europeans, the Indian cultures that we recognize today lived in present-day Wisconsin: Siouan-speaking Ho-Chunk and Dakota (Sioux) in the north and west and Algonquian-speaking Menominee, Ojibwe, and Potawatomi in the northeast, central, and south. As could be expected from peoples sharing the same woodland environment, these tribes shared some characteristics. They lived in wigwams made from bent saplings sheathed with bark. They shared a similar diet. They hunted deer, rabbit, and waterfowl; fished for sturgeon, pike, lake trout, and catfish; gathered nuts, wild rice, berries, edible plants, and shellfish; and planted corn, beans, squash, tobacco, and sunflowers. Communities farther north, such as the Ojibwe, who were limited by shorter growing seasons, were less dependent upon agriculture than the Ho-Chunk and Menominee. Because of their reliance on hunting and trapping, the Ojibwe lived in smaller, more mobile bands. The Ho-Chunk and Menominee tended to inhabit larger villages.

Gathering Wild Rice, as depicted by Seth Eastman. A mapmaker and illustrator for the US Army, Eastman made many paintings and drawings of Native American life.

Engraving after a drawing by Seth Eastman, from the *American Aboriginal Portfolio* by Mary H. Eastman, 1853; WHi Image ID 9023

Each tribe organized itself into clans, providing "a framework of government to give them strength and order," in the words of Edward Benton-Banai, a contemporary Anishinaabe medicine man. In the Ojibwe O-do-daym-i-wan (clan system), there were seven original clans: Crane, Loon, Fish, Marten, Deer, Bear, and Bird. The Crane and Loon Clans contributed the chiefs, and their shared leadership provided important checks and balances. From the Fish Clan came the intellectuals and the mediators; from the Marten Clan, the warriors; from the Deer Clan, the poets. Bear Clan people served as protectors: some policed the village while others learned about medicines and used their knowledge to heal people. Finally, the Bird Clan provided the spiritual leaders. Marriage within a clan was forbidden.[11]

The Menominee and the Ho-Chunk divided their clans into two groups, representing either the earth or sky. Among the Menominee, the earth clans, including the Bear Clan, supplied the peace chiefs. The sky clans, such as the Eagle Clan, produced the war chiefs.[12] In Ho-Chunk culture, the roles of the clans were reversed: sky clans were responsible for leadership during times of peace; earth clan chiefs led their communities during war.

The Ho-Chunk tell a story about the origin of the Buffalo Clan, an earth clan, which produced many fine warriors. A long time ago, an evil water spirit was terrorizing the Ho-Chunk who lived near Da Cesik—meaning Green Lake in east-central Wisconsin. Buffalo challenged the Water Spirit to a fight, and the two struggled in the cold, dark, "bottomless" lake. "The waters churned and churned and suddenly the Buffalo rose to the surface and lifted his head. He was victorious over the Water Spirit, and thus began the Buffalo Clan."[13]

Let the Great Spirits Soar, an effigy tree sculpture by Ho-Chunk artist Harry Whitehorse in Madison near Lake Monona. The sculpture, originally dedicated in 1991, was carved in wood from a hackberry tree struck by lightning. After wind and rain took their toll, in 2009 a replica in cast bronze was rededicated and installed at the same location.
Courtesy of Peter Patau

Two-Tailed Turtle Mound is located on Observatory Hill on the University of Wisconsin–Madison grounds. The turtle, also identified as a Water Spirit, was one of several mounds in a group that included a bird effigy that spanned more than 130 feet, along with a panther and a linear mound. The bird and turtle effigies are all that remain.
WHi Image ID 34547

It is worth noting that clan leaders, or chiefs, did not "rule" in the manner of European royalty but rather led by consent. Tribal members expected their chiefs to be generous and to put the interests of the community above their own interests. They especially appreciated leaders who were both shrewd negotiators and accomplished orators, useful skills in brokering treaties and forming alliances.

Many Indian nations created confederacies that still exist today. The best known of these is the Five Nations Confederacy, which includes the Oneida, one of the New York tribes that immigrated to Wisconsin Territory in the 1820s. Centuries earlier, the Oneida joined the Mohawk, Cayuga, Onondaga, and Seneca to form the Five Nations, or Great League. After the Tuscacora joined the league in the 1720s, it became known as the Six Nations Confederacy. According to oral

tradition among Oneida still residing in New York, the league began during the month "when the corn was ripe and the grass was knee high" (August) and when the "sun went dark during the day" (a solar eclipse).

Based on the number of Thatatàlho (presiding chiefs) since the confederacy was ratified, researchers at the University of Toledo estimated that the birth of the confederacy occurred sometime in the twelfth century. Of the eight solar eclipses that occurred during that time period, only one was visible in central New York during the month of August. In 1999, on the basis of this oral history, mnemonics, mathematics, and astronomical evidence, researchers concluded that the Oneida and their allies formally became the Five Nations Confederacy on August 31, 1142.[14] In Wisconsin, however, Carol Cornelius, a Wisconsin Oneida and tribal historian, cross-referenced the number of Thatatàlho to historical stories within her tribe's oral tradition and arrived at a much earlier date. Cornelius cautioned that Wisconsin Oneida do not accept any founding date, other than "a long time ago."[15]

For Native Americans, research that combines oral history, mnemonics, and physical evidence represents a new approach to reconstructing the past. Had archaeologists not collaborated with Ho-Chunk elders, the priceless Red Horn composite at the Gottschall site might have remained an indecipherable mystery. The ancient songs, stories, and art of Native people are filled with symbolism and wisdom. In order to understand the cultural meaning of the people, places, and events that shaped their lives, we must not only *read* history, but also *listen* to it.

2 EUROPEAN ARRIVALS

In the summer of 1634, the Ho-Chunk, Menominee, and Potawatomi near present-day Green Bay awoke to a strange sight: a light-skinned visitor who arrived at their villages by canoe, bearing gifts and displaying metal objects the Ho-Chunk later described as "thunder sticks." The visitor was Jean Nicolet, a French trader sent by the governor of New France in North America, Samuel de Champlain, to negotiate peace between the Ho-Chunk and the Odaawa. Champlain hoped to expand his fur trade into the western Great Lakes area; however, hostilities between the Ho-Chunk and Odaawa had thwarted his plans. Nicolet's "thunder sticks" were, of course, firearms, and their introduction into Native culture would forever change the Indian nations.[1]

Some Native American prophecies had foretold the arrival of the "light-skinned hairy ones." The Ho-Chunk chiefs who met Nicolet in the village they called Moga-Shooch, or Red Banks, for example, welcomed him as their prophecies had instructed—by sprinkling tobacco on his head as a sign of honor and respect. Rumors that the pale-skinned people had actually arrived in eastern North America, however, likely had reached the inhabitants of the western Great Lakes long before Nicolet's visit. Indigenous trade networks, which kept the various tribes in regular contact, had existed for centuries.

Even before their actual arrival in the western Great Lakes region, Europeans had already touched the lives of the Native peoples. Intense competition between the French and their Algonquian friends and the Dutch and their Five Nations allies had led to open warfare and caused massive migrations. Refugee tribes fleeing the violence steadily encroached upon the lands of the Ho-Chunk and Menominee. The Sauk, Mascouten, Potawatomi, and Kickapoo moved west and north from around the southern edge of Lake Michigan. The Ojibwe, Odaawa, Meskwaki (Fox), and Iroquois-speaking tribes outside the Five Nations Confederacy pressed westward along the northern boundaries of Ho-Chunk and Menominee territory. For the Ho-Chunk, these northern encroachments were especially threatening, since the intrusions pushed them southward toward the enemy tribes of the Illinois Confederacy.[2]

The tension between the Odaawa and the Ho-Chunk was especially fierce. Sometime before Nicolet's arrival, the Ho-Chunk had killed a delegation of Odaawa that had attempted to explore trade possibilities. The antagonism may have stemmed from attempts by the Odaawa to trade with the Sioux and other tribes the Ho-Chunk considered enemies. Whatever promises Nicolet elicited from the indigenous people of the western Great Lakes, peace was shattered a year after his visit, and the Ho-Chunk and Menominee were plunged into a cycle of continuous warfare with the refugee Algonquian tribes. Disease, perhaps brought by Nicolet and his party, further crippled the two nations. Amid the chaos, the Ho-Chunk and Menominee suffered tremendous hardship.

In the years immediately following Nicolet's visit, the Ho-Chunk focused their attention on those they perceived to be the most immediate threat: the Meskwaki. One Ho-Chunk story tells of a massive war party that traveled by canoe across Lake Winnebago to attack the Meskwaki. A storm arose, and hundreds of Ho-Chunk warriors drowned. Fearing reprisal, three separate Ho-Chunk communities, a total of twelve thousand people, drew together in a single village to defend themselves. Unfortunately, a "yellow sickness," as the Ho-Chunk described it, descended upon the village and claimed the lives of one-third of the Ho-Chunk population.[3]

Jean Nicolet arrives at Mogo-Shooch (near present-day Green Bay) in 1634. Although Nicolet is credited with being the first white man to visit the area, there is evidence that Étienne Brûlé may have explored the upper Great Lakes more than a decade earlier.
Painting by E. W. Deming, 1904; Wisconsin Historical Museum 1942.187

Animosities between the Ho-Chunk and the Illinois Confederacy also escalated. During the 1640s, a major offensive by confederated tribes resulted in the near destruction of the Ho-Chunk. In 1665, when the French fur traders Nicholas Perrot and Jesuit Claude Jean Allouez arrived in Green Bay, along with four hundred members of a Huron-Odaawa trading party, they found only five hundred Ho-Chunk survivors in a village wracked by starvation and disease.

With less than 10 percent of their pre-Nicolet population surviving these decades of war and disease, the Ho-Chunk approached Algonquian families and offered their sons and daughters as spouses. By extending kinship to those who had encroached on their territory, they were able to survive and begin the process of rebuilding their nation.

The Menominee, who were strong allies of the Ho-Chunk, experienced similar distress. The influx of refugee tribes after 1660 strained the resources of the area. The demands of an expanding population and constant warfare scattered and depleted the game. There were fights over fishing grounds. One such quarrel escalated into a regional war after the Menominee constructed fish traps on one of their rivers, preventing sturgeon from reaching Ojibwe villages located upstream.

When their protests went unheeded, the Ojibwe attacked a large Menominee village. The Menominee, with help from the Sauk, Meskwaki, and Potawatomi, retaliated. This sporadic warfare between the Ojibwe and the Menominee reflected territorial encroachments and shifting alignments.[4]

Augustin Grignon, a prominent fur trader and patriarch of the Menominee Nation
WHi Image ID 4170

The arrival of the French in the Great Lakes region did not have the same immediate effect that British and other European settlers had had on tribes in the East. Whereas the Massachusetts colonists wanted land for farming and viewed the indigenous tribes as nuisances, the French were primarily interested in trade and looked upon the Great Lakes tribes as potential partners. Some French trading families sent their sons to live in the communities of their Indian trading partners so that they could learn the language and establish kinship ties. There was a great deal of cultural absorption by the French, who adopted Native foods, medicines, dress, and customs. Voyageurs, the French traders who traveled along the waterways of the Great Lakes, adapted Native modes of transportation, such as snowshoes and canoes, to suit their needs. Many traders married Indian women and assimilated themselves into Native communities. Together, the French and their Indian allies created what came to be called a

"Middle Ground," where a mutually accepted system of borrowed and blended customs emerged.[5] Today, hundreds of tribal members carry the surnames of early French traders—among them Grignon, Corbine, Denomie, and Cadotte—a reflection of how intertwined the two cultures became.

The introduction of European trade goods and the absorption of French culture profoundly affected the indigenous people of the Great Lakes as well. Initially, the change strengthened tribal identities. Tribes whose economies were tied to agriculture, such as the Ho-Chunk and Menominee, became better farmers with metal hoes, axes, and tools for clearing the land. Copper kettles, knives, and utensils made domestic chores more tolerable. Hunting tribes, including the Potawatomi and Ojibwe, became better hunters with flintlock rifles, lead ammunition, and metal traps. On the other hand, firearms made warfare deadlier and potentially more catastrophic.

The seductive nature of European goods created irresistible incentives for Native communities to embrace an economic system that essentially exploited them. The value of finished trade goods always exceeded the value of the raw materials needed to produce them. Indian hunters provided an ever-increasing supply of pelts in exchange for lesser quantities of the manufactured items they desired. It was a system that fostered dependency. Tribes that willingly embraced it ultimately discovered that it depleted their natural resources and impoverished their people.

The demand for fur produced fundamental changes in both intertribal and intratribal relationships. When Indian hunters depleted the supply of fur-bearing animals in their own areas, they sometimes encroached on the hunting grounds of neighboring tribes. This produced friction and sometimes outright skirmishing. The political and social structures of Indian communities evolved to accommodate this new emphasis on hunting. Tribes that may have lived in larger villages prior to European contact, such as the Ho-Chunk and Potawatomi, separated into smaller bands in order to track game and harvest pelts more efficiently.

These changes had a pronounced effect on the role of Native women. The absence of male hunters for longer periods of time meant that women in larger communities, whose hunter husbands ranged far from home, undoubtedly found themselves doing more work—constructing and repairing lodges, gathering firewood, butchering game, and similar heavy work in which they usually were assisted by men. With most of the village men away, women had a greater responsibility in providing food for their families. Agriculture became more important. In addition to planting and gathering, women and children probably engaged in more subsistence hunting and fishing.

Brass kettle once owned by John Priest, grandson of the Ho-Chunk chief Little Priest
Wisconsin Historical Museum
1954.1769

Potawatomi fur ornament
Wisconsin Historical Museum
1950.8910

**An artist's rendering of a
Menominee sugaring camp**

Enagraving by Mary Irvin Wright,
circa 1896; WHi Image ID 5224

Women whose tribes fragmented into smaller bands as well as extended family units may have seen their political influence diminish. According to Ne shna bek oral tradition, each Potawatomi village had a woman's council, or W'okamakwe, made up of the eldest sisters of the male clan chiefs. These "honored women" were expected to lead their clan families "in paths of goodness" or be impeached and stripped of any power. New laws went first to the W'okamakwe and then to the men's council.[6]

After European contact, Potawatomi men relied less on female counsel. With the primary focus on hunting, decision making most likely fell to the leaders of these hunting expeditions—traditionally men, upon whom the safety and survival of the smaller bands depended. Furthermore, European notions about gender roles influenced the Indians with whom they traded. Exploration, trade, and politics were the domain of men in European societies. French traders expected to deal with Native men, not women.

From the French perspective, the tribes' loosely organized political structures were exasperating. There were no kings among the tribes of the Great Lakes and no central authorities with whom political and economic power resided. Tribal chiefs and headmen, chosen on the basis of heredity or proven experience, led by consent, not by coercion. With no single entity authorized to speak for Indian communities, the French sometimes took to designating their own Indian "chiefs." In a pattern adopted by the English and later by the Americans, French traders staged ceremonies and presented flags and medals to Indians based on their friendliness and their ability to provide furs. By favoring these individuals with attention and giving them trade goods that could be distributed to other members of the tribe, the French undermined the basic political structures of tribes. This practice created deep divisions within the tribes, producing, in the words of one nineteenth-century Ojibwe historian, "jealousies and heart-burnings."[7]

The introduction of alcohol to Indian communities was another debilitating aspect of the fur trade. Simon Pokagon, a Potawatomi chief, described its arrival in his village as "the midnight of my soul." Fermented beverages were previously unknown to the tribes of the Great Lakes. French traders quickly exploited the weakness some Indians had for whiskey and rum and used it to gain advantage in trade negotiations. Pokagon, who lost two children to alcohol, asked how a race that had accomplished so much could have unleashed "'tchi-maw-tchi gi-go'—that great devil-fish upon the sea of human life."[8] In some cases, alcohol intensified the problems created by the need to accommodate a new economic system. Its effect was an increase in abuse, neglect, and violence. In other cases, alcohol dulled the pain of population losses resulting from disease and warfare associated with the fur trade. Although drunkenness in Indian villages was probably no more intense or frequent than it was in white communities on the frontier, alcohol, like the fur trade itself, fostered dependency among Native Americans.

In addition to European trade goods, the introduction of Christianity had profound effects on Native cultures. In 1661, Father René Menard, an itinerant Jesuit missionary, ventured into the Chequamegon Bay area with Huron and Odaawa fleeing from the Haudenosaunee. Although Menard died before completing his mission, four years later another Jesuit, Father Claude Jean Allouez, arrived at La Pointe on present-day Madeline Island and established the Saint Esprit Mission for the Ojibwe. In 1671, Allouez also founded the St. Francis Xavier Mission on the Oconto River to serve the Menominee, Ho-Chunk, Sauk, Meskwaki, and Potawatomi.[9]

In 1665, the Jesuits established Saint Esprit Mission on the shores of Chequamegon Bay, creating religious divisions between the Christian converts and adherents of the traditional Midewiwin religion.

The Missionary, a wood engraving by H. F. Higby based on a Frederic Remington illustration published in *Harper's Monthly*, April 1892; WHi Image ID 95722

The Jesuits achieved varying success in converting the Great Lakes tribes to Catholicism. Disease, warfare, and chaotic change in the late seventeenth century made tribal members vulnerable to Christian promises of salvation and deliverance from sorrow, especially when traditional medicines often proved powerless against European diseases. Even as epidemics raged through Indian villages and devastated entire communities, the Jesuits, with their European immunities, often stayed healthy.

The Ojibwe had mixed feelings about the Muk-a-day-i-ko-na-yayg, or "Black Coats," as they called the Jesuits. At times they considered them to be helpful. For the most part, however, they found them less respectful of their ways than the French traders with whom they interacted. Anishinaabe medicine man Edward Benton-Banai has blamed the Jesuits for turning tribal members away from the Midewiwin, the traditional Medicine Lodge religion, and for promoting factionalism between the Christian and Mide followers. According to Banai, Christian Indians were encouraged to "resent and reject" those who followed the Midewiwin way.[10]

The collapse of the Huron Confederacy in 1649 had immediate consequences for the tribes of the Great Lakes. The Huron had acted as a middleman for the resident nations. The tribe's virtual annihilation by the Five Nations Confederacy left the French fur trade in shambles. The only option available to the Great Lakes tribes was to bring their furs to Montreal, a dangerous proposition that took them into areas controlled by the Five Nations. Only the Ojibwe, Odaawa, and Potawatomi attempted the difficult journey, usually organizing massive canoe flotillas that could fight their way past enemy warriors.

In 1659, the arrival of two unlicensed traders—Pierre Esprit Radisson and his brother-in-law, Médard Chouart, Sieur des Groseilliers, a French nobleman—offered the Great Lakes tribes a new trading opportunity. Radisson and Groseilliers paddled into Chequamegon Bay after exploring the south shore of Lake Superior and the Keweenaw Peninsula. Following a year of furious trading with the Lac du Flambeau and Lac Courte Oreilles Ojibwe and the Santee Sioux, they returned to Quebec, only to have their substantial cargo of furs and other trade items confiscated by the Crown. However, word of their success spread, and soon unlicensed traders were pouring into the Great Lakes region.

For the tribes, these *coureurs de bois*—"woods runners"—were a welcome relief. Their presence enabled Indian communities to conduct exchanges closer to home without exposing themselves to the Five Nations threat. For the French, however, the *coureurs de bois* represented a dilemma. On the one hand, they extended French influence into previously unexplored areas. On the other, they paid no royalties to the Crown. In addition, the Jesuits complained that the *coureurs de bois* indiscriminately supplied Indians with liquor and generally debauched them. A more serious concern, however, was that the uncontrolled trading they promoted created a glut of furs. This lowered prices and contributed to the overall economic and political instability of the area. When King Louis XIV of France officially forbade the tribes to trade with the *coureurs de bois*, Indian traders simply ignored the order.

The French responded by closing outlying forts and relocating their official traders to consolidated trading centers such as Detroit. They hoped this would entice their Indian partners living in Green Bay to move. Some of the refugee tribes did, in fact, resettle near Detroit, enabling the Menominee and Ho-Chunk to reoccupy the lands they had inhabited at the time of European contact. But overall, the French resettlement policy was a dismal failure. Relocation produced infighting among the tribes and opened the door to British traders, who were more than happy to fill the void left by the French exodus from the western Great Lakes.

In the 1740s, British traders began moving into the Ohio Valley. The shifting loyalties that marked intertribal and intratribal politics during the years of the French intensified with the arrival of the British. The French responded by building or reopening a string of forts, including one at Green Bay and another at Michilimackinac (present-day Mackinac Island).

Fort Mackinac, circa 1812. Mackinac, or Michilimackinac as it was originally known, was the site of two major battles involving pan-Indian forces. In 1763, under the ruse of a lacrosse game, Anishinaabe warriors attacked and took the fort, hoping to return it to French rule. In 1812, Anishinaabe supporting Tecumseh and his British allies led a successful attack against American forces at the fort.

From *The Pictorial Field-Book of the War of 1812*, Benson J. Lossing, 1869; WHi Image ID 9527

In 1775, Charles de Langlade, a Green Bay fur trader, and a contingent of Anishinaabe Indians defeated British general Edward Braddock in defense of Fort Duquesne (modern-day Pittsburgh) during the French and Indian War. In this painting by Edwin Deming, Langlade is pictured in the foreground directing the attack. A young George Washington, a major in Braddock's army, is holding the bridle of Braddock's horse.

Painting by Edwin Willard Deming, 1903; Wisconsin Historical Museum 1942.488

Between 1753 and 1759, the French and their allies clashed with the British and their allies in what is known in America as the French and Indian War. Ultimately, the British prevailed when in 1759 General James Wolfe defeated the main body of the French army outside Quebec. Montreal surrendered a year later. Although most of the Great Lakes Indian nations officially declared themselves neutral in the fighting, individual Indian warriors, especially Anishinaabe, hired themselves out as mercenaries. Members of the Denomie family from the Ojibwe community at La Pointe, for example, were listed as scouts for French General Joseph de Montcalm's troops in the battle for Quebec.[11] Charles de Langlade, the son of a French trader and an Odaawa woman, was one of the strongest French allies. In 1752, Langlade led a force of Ojibwe, Potawatomi, and Odaawa against Old Briton, a Miami chief and British ally, at Pikawillany along the Miami River in Ohio. Three years later, Langlade and his warriors also ambushed and helped defeat General Edward Braddock's British army as it marched on Fort Duquesne, near present-day Pittsburgh.[12]

The tribes of the Great Lakes reacted differently to the arrival of the British. Among the Anishinaabe, who enjoyed kinship and most-favored-nation trade status with the French, there was great uneasiness. Among the Menominee and Ho-Chunk, who resented the favoritism shown the Anishinaabe and found the French trading system exasperatingly inefficient and disorganized, there was considerable optimism. The two factions did agree that English trade items were less expensive and generally of better quality than French items.

From the beginning, English trade practices were substantially different from those of their predecessors. Whereas the French lavished gifts upon their Indian partners, the British offered no such presents. Sir Jeffrey Amherst, the commander in chief of British forces in North America who directed military actions from the East, dismissed gift giving—an essential part of tribal culture—as bribery. Instead he adopted a diplomatic strategy based on fear and reprisal. The French had usually extended credit to their trading partners, supplying them with ammunition for hunting and food during particularly harsh winters. Amherst ordered the commanders of his western forts to intentionally keep the Indians short of ammunition. Further, he insisted that all trading be conducted inside the fort in order to control the exchange of alcohol, weapons, and ammunition. Amherst's high-handed decrees produced wholesale resentment in Indian communities. When Pontiac, the son of an Odaawa chief and an Ojibwe woman, organized a pan-Indian military effort to oust the British, all but the Menominee and Ho Chunk nations in the western Great Lakes enthusiastically offered their support.

In April 1763, Pontiac organized a war council along the Aux Ecorces River attended by four hundred chiefs and warriors. They agreed that on a certain day in June, they would rise up in unison and attack the British forts in their areas, including Michilimackinac, a principal trading fort for the Great Lakes tribes. Beginning in early June, Indian warriors, including Ojibwe, Potawatomi, Sauk, and Meskwaki, rose up against fourteen British forts and eventually managed to take most of them. At Michilimackinac, the Ojibwe organized a lacrosse game outside the fort, ostensibly for the amusement of British troops inside the fort, who were celebrating the king's birthday. Posing as spectators and participants,

Fort Crawford, in Prairie du Chien, was a major trading center for the Ho-Chunk, Menominee, Ojibwe, Potawatomi, Sauk, Meskwaki, and Dakota people.
WHS Archives, Album 12.24a;
WHi Image ID 4512

the warriors had given their weapons to their women, who hid them inside their blankets and clothes. After the ball was launched toward the gates of the fort, the warriors grabbed their weapons, rushed in, and overwhelmed the garrison. Sixteen soldiers were killed outright and twelve others taken captive.[13] Elsewhere, confederated warriors lay siege to Forts Detroit and Pitt and forced the British to flee Fort Edward Augustus in Green Bay.

When the British abandoned their fort in Green Bay, they entrusted its care to the Menominee, a tribe that had no interest in seeing French influence restored in the area. Menominee warriors, who had been coerced into fighting for the French during the French and Indian War, returned with smallpox and ill will toward the French. During the winter of 1759, they revolted and killed twenty-two French soldiers. In retaliation, the French seized some of the warriors who had participated in the uprising and executed them in Montreal. As a result, the Menominee did not join Pontiac's Rebellion. In fact, after the Ojibwe captured Michilimackinac, the Menominee helped ransom British prisoners from the fort.

Although the rebellion failed to permanently oust the British, it did force important concessions. The British issued the Proclamation of 1763, which forbade their American colonists from settling west of the Appalachians. This decree, however, failed to stop westward expansion. The British Crown expanded trade, relaxed restrictions on the sale of guns and ammunition to the tribes, and restored the French practice of gift giving. At Michilimackinac, the British began using French traders to deal with the Ojibwe. The result was a gradual shift in Indian loyalties from the French to the British. By the time of the American Revolution (1775–1783) and the War of 1812, most of the Wisconsin tribes fought on the side of the British, not the Americans.[14]

3 MENOMINEE

The Menominee call themselves *Omeaqnomenewak*, an Algonquian word meaning "People of the Wild Rice," invoking a resource that became a feature of their identity and "shaped their understanding of the seasons and the landscape around them."[1] Menominee identity is also rooted in the white pines and towering sugar maples of the western Great Lakes. The forest sustained the tribe before Europeans arrived on the continent, and to this day the forest continues to provide cultural and economic sustenance to the Menominee. As a present-day Menominee descendant explained, "We *are* the forest."[2] The struggle to preserve this critical resource, however, nearly cost the Menominee both their land and their identity as an Indian people.

The years following the arrival of the French in the mid-seventeenth century were ones of great change and adaptation for the Menominee. Tribal members experienced considerable cultural stress because of increased warfare, disease, and political and economic instability. Overhunting of Menominee land by refugee tribes fleeing the Five Nations strained the area's resources. The environmental pressure outsiders placed on the forest was a theme that would repeat itself throughout Menominee history.

The American Revolution brought more changes for the Menominee. Tribal members not only provided the British with canoes, furs, and other supplies, but some joined the British in battles against the Americans in New York, Ohio, Missouri, Pennsylvania, and Indiana.[3] Most, including the Menominee war chief Tomau, chose to stay out of the fray.[4] "We have considered you and the Americans as one people," he told the British. "You are now at war; how are we to decide who has justice on their side?"[5] Even after the Treaty of Paris (1783) transferred control of the region to the Americans, the British maintained their presence in Menominee country. Despite a

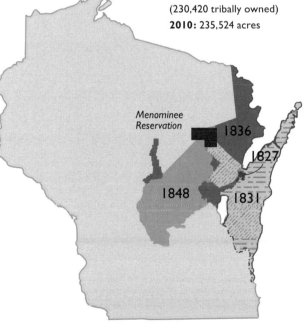

MENOMINEE
2010 population: 8,720
1854 Treaty: 276,480 acres
1856 Treaty: 232,400 acres
1961–1973: Tribal status terminated
1999: 236,548 acres
(230,420 tribally owned)
2010: 235,524 acres

Menominee
Reservation

1836

1827

1848

1831

series of Trade and Intercourse Acts between 1790 and 1802 that attempted to restrict commercial contact with tribes to traders licensed by the American government, few American traders ventured into Menominee country. British traders and the old resident French traders continued to conduct their business without interference from the new American government.

Events taking place farther east, however, eventually drew the Menominee into the War of 1812. American settlers began trespassing on Indian lands in the Ohio Valley in violation of federal laws that forbade settlement west of the Appalachians. In response, Tecumseh, a Shawnee warrior, amassed a pan-Indian military alliance and began raiding the illegal settlements. Tecumseh argued that it was only a matter of time before the Americans threatened the nations of the Great Lakes as well. The Menominee, however, were convinced that war with the Americans

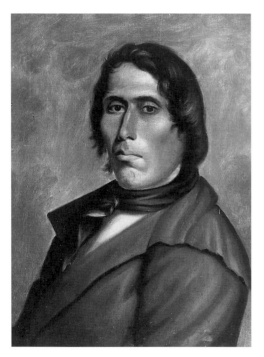

Tecumseh, Shawnee war leader and brother of Tenskwatawa, the Shawnee Prophet. After the United States declared war on Great Britain in 1812, the Menominee joined Tecumseh's military alliance.

Courtesy of the Field Museum of Natural History, Chicago

was irrational and could not be won. As a result, the Menominee stayed neutral during these border wars (1783–1812). It was not until Tecumseh's battles merged with those of the British in the War of 1812 that the Menominee entered the fighting.[6]

In July 1812, about forty warriors, including the seventeen-year-old Oshkosh, joined British officer and trader Robert Dickson and a contingent of Ho-Chunk and Sioux in taking Fort Michilimackinac without firing a shot. After the war, and under the tutelage of Tomau, Oshkosh became an influential figure in the Bear Clan, the clan from which the Menominee select their speakers and leaders. Oshkosh rose to prominence within his clan just as the Menominee began facing major land crises.

Pressure in the Oneida homeland led a Christianized group of New York Indians—the Oneida, Stockbridge, Munsee, and Brothertown—to seek land in the west. In August 1821, they approached the Menominee and Ho-Chunk Nations and expressed interest in the territory of the two tribes. Under pressure from the American government, the Menominee and Ho-Chunk supposedly agreed to "joint tenancy" with the New York tribes along an eighteen-mile strip straddling the Fox River north of Lake Winnebago. In September 1822, during a second council between the Menominee and the New York Indians, negotiators purportedly increased the size of the land in question to the "whole of the Menominee country East and North of Winnebago Lake." In exchange for this right to share the land, the New York tribes offered the Menominee five thousand dollars in goods.

There are conflicting accounts of the events surrounding the negotiations between the Menominee and the New York Indians. "Principal chiefs of the Menominee nation were not present at this treaty and did not sign it," according to Menominee tribal historian David Grignon. "When they heard about it, they refuted the treaty as invalid."[7] The treaty also angered traders and white citizens of Green Bay, who feared that they would lose their landholdings, "which they maintained by permission of the Menominee."[8] Another complication was that the interpreter the government regularly used in discussions with the Menominee was in Chicago at a different treaty session. His substitute, who accidentally invited the Ho-Chunk to the negotiations, did not even speak Menominee.[9]

From the Menominee perspective, the New York Indians, some of whom had been educated in white schools, used their sophisticated understanding of property issues to unfair advantage in the Menominee land negotiations. Although the Menominee understood the agreements to mean that they would *share* land with the New York Indians—a concept compatible with their own traditional view of the land—white negotiators and the New York tribes increasingly framed the arrangement as a land *cession*. Furthermore, the Menominee argued that land cessions arranged by anyone other than an agent authorized by the president of the United States violated both the US Constitution and the Trade and Intercourse Acts. The arrival of a small group of Stockbridge Indians in 1822 and a sizable contingent of Oneida, Mohican, and Brothertown immigrants in 1824 produced considerable anxiety among the Menominee.

In 1825, US officials invited all the tribes residing in present-day Wisconsin to a Grand Council at Prairie du Chien. They explained the gathering as an opportunity to sign a "peace and friendship" treaty that would end intertribal warfare in the region, most notably between the Ojibwe and the Dakota. In the process, the leaders of the attending nations were pressured to declare their boundaries, an exercise that proved to be the crucial first step in alienating the tribes from their land. Within a few years of the treaty, US negotiators began approaching each nation to arrange land cessions.

The Menominee were reluctant to declare their boundaries, not only because of the disputed Oneida land sale, but also because of a vacuum in leadership. The tribe's principal chief, Tshekatshakemau ("The Old King"); Tomau; and several other respected elders had passed away and the Menominee relied upon a council of clan leaders to guide them through a difficult decade. "It is a long time since we have had any Chief," they informed the commissioners.[10] Because the Menominee were underrepresented at the Council (four times as many Ojibwe as Menominee signed the treaty), US officials agreed to discuss the boundaries issues with them

Oshkosh, Menominee clan leader and protégé of the war chief Tomau. Oshkosh was one of the principal negotiators during the crisis years when federal officials threatened to remove the Menominee to lands west of the Mississippi.

Painting by Samuel Marsden Brookes, 1858; Wisconsin Historical Museum 1942.59

again at Butte des Morts two years later. Oshkosh, the grandson of Tshekatshakemau, was a logical successor. At age thirty-two, Oshkosh not only had hereditary claims, but also had been a protégé of Tomau, the powerful war leader. In 1827, when Treaty Commissioner Lewis Cass hung a peace medal on Oshkosh, he acknowledged the will of the Menominee people.[11]

In 1827, at Butte des Morts, the US officials insisted that the Menominee declare their boundaries between their land and that of the Ojibwe. Later, in the Treaty of 1831, the Menominee were pressured into giving up a portion of that land to be set aside for the New York Indians. At the request of Oshkosh, Chief Grizzly Bear, a celebrated speaker of the Menominee Council, represented the tribe at the negotiations.[12] He told the commissioners that his people understood that the Oneida had come "not to purchase land, but to procure the grant of a small piece to sit down upon, that they might live with us like brothers."[13] Unwilling to come to terms with the New York Indian claims, the Menominee delegation agreed to allow President John Quincy Adams to settle the disputed claim.

Later that year, when fighting broke out between white settlers and a band of Ho-Chunk led by Red Bird, a company of Menominee, along with some Oneida and Stockbridge Indians, served with the US Army. A decision on whether the Menominee would engage their traditional allies was averted when the Ho-Chunk surrendered Red Bird to US officials. The next Menominee service to the Americans came in 1832 when Black Hawk's band of Sauk Indians resisted resettlement and attempted to return to their homes in present-day Illinois. A battalion of 250 Menominee, under the leadership of Feather Shedder, protected the white citizens of Green Bay who lived in fear of a Sauk attack.

Oshkosh, meanwhile, had narrowly avoided life in prison. In 1830, he found himself facing murder charges in a white court. He and two other Menominee were accused of fatally stabbing a Pawnee Indian who had killed a member of the Menominee Nation. Menominee law held that Oshkosh was within his rights to take the man's life, but a territorial jury found him guilty of manslaughter. Judge James Doty, however, reviewed the case, reasoned that Menominee law should apply on Menominee land, and ordered that all charges be dropped. Given his prominence within the Bear Clan, the clan authorized to speak for the Menominee and conduct negotiations, Oshkosh may have represented someone whose good will Doty hoped to cultivate. Following the Treaty at Butte des Morts, pressure on the Menominee to give up land escalated. In 1831, tribal representatives signed a treaty in Washington, DC, in which the Menominee ceded three million acres in exchange for $146,500 over twelve years. The area ceded included 500,000 acres "for the benefit of the New York Indians." The US Senate, however, amended the treaty by adding an article that changed the boundary lines of the land set aside for the New York Indians. The Menominee refused to ratify the new document, arguing that the changes adversely affected their trade routes. Negotiators redrew the boundary lines, and in 1832 the Menominee reluctantly signed the amended treaty.[14]

Four years later, the Menominee were pressured into ceding the eastern half of their remaining territory; in 1848 they were forced to cede the remaining western half. As Wisconsin statehood loomed, the Menominee were ordered to exchange their lands for a 600,000-acre reservation in Minnesota. Government officials were so confident in Menominee relocation that they prematurely printed maps of Minnesota Territory with what would have been the new Menominee homeland. Two years later, a group of Menominee clan leaders, including Oshkosh, reluctantly led an exploratory expedition to the Crow Wing River area in Minnesota. When they returned, they told tribal members that Crow Wing was unsuitable for the Menominee. Oshkosh announced that "the poorest region in Wisconsin was better than the Crow Wing," adding that constant fighting between the Dakota and Ojibwe threatened the safety of his people.[15] He and other clan leaders followed their visit to the Crow Wing area with a trip to Washington, during which they met with President Millard Fillmore and persuaded him to temporarily rescind the removal order. Over the next several years, the Menominee council filed petitions and used delaying tactics to resist removal. The tribe's persistence paid off. In the Treaty of 1854, the Menominee were allowed to reserve 276,000 densely forested acres along the Wolf and Oconto Rivers for a permanent home.[16]

Two years later, the Menominee were forced to sign one final treaty in which they ceded two townships in the southwestern portion of their reservation to the Stockbridge and Munsee Tribes "at the rate of sixty-cents per acres." The

Grizzly Bear, Menominee clan leader and negotiator in the Menominee treaties

Sketch by George Catlin, circa 1831; courtesy of Smithsonian American Art Museum, DC/Art Resource

treaty stipulated that the money would be used to "promote the improvement of the Menomonees."[17]

After the Menominee were settled, they struggled to protect their timber from "small-scale thieving entrepreneurs" and a large-scale assault by Philetus Sawyer, a powerful lumber baron. After Sawyer's election to Congress, he introduced two bills: the first would have sold Menominee land at public auction; the second would have sold their timber. In 1871, the Menominee insisted they were "unwilling to part with any portion of our lands" and instead asked for and received permission to cut and sell their timber on their own terms.[18] Not only did the plan reflect the tribe's strong moral value, in that it set aside 10 percent of the profits for the sick and needy, but it also demonstrated the Menominee environmental ethic. Oshkosh, who was distressed by the clear-cutting practices of white loggers around the reservation boundary, advised tribal members to begin selectively cutting mature trees in the east, working toward the west. When they reached the reservation boundaries, the trees in the east would be ready for them to harvest again.

The decision to focus on sustainable logging, instead of farming, allowed the Menominee to escape the fate of other Wisconsin tribes, whose lands were divided and privatized under various allotment efforts, epitomized by the General Allotment Act of 1887. Allotment was part of a multifaceted government effort to assimilate Indians and economically exploit Native lands and resources. Government officials expected that as forested lands were cleared, Indians would turn to farming and become self-sufficient. Government officials decided not to allot the Menominee reservation because the logging operation had already brought the tribe a measure of self-sufficiency.

Tribal members could not escape the government's other efforts to assimilate them. Indian agents had absolute authority over the education of Indian children. The Browning Ruling, a policy in effect from 1896 to 1902, explicitly stated that "Indian parents have no right to designate which school their children shall attend."[19] Some Menominee children were sent to government boarding schools in Wisconsin—Lac du Flambeau, Tomah, and Hayward—and as far away as Flandreau, South Dakota, and Carlisle, Pennsylvania. Others remained on the reservation and attended either St. Joseph's Catholic School or the government boarding school in Keshena. In these schools, educators forbid Menominee from speaking

Logging on the Menominee Reservation, 1909
WHi Image ID 95683

their native language or engaging in Menominee cultural practices. The imposition of white culture upon entire generations of Menominee caused profound cultural confusion and contributed to a deep sense of loss that continues to this day.

At the turn of the twentieth century, some Menominee continued to hunt, fish, and gather on a subsistence basis. However, many tribal members found jobs in the timber industry. By 1905, at an annual cut rate of 20 million board feet, the Menominee had harvested nearly 300 million board feet of timber. That year, however, a tornado blew down 40 million board feet. The Menominee, accustomed to floating white pine down the Wolf River to private sawmills in the area, could not do this with much of the blown-down timber, which consisted primarily of hardwood trees that would not float. To better enable the Menominee to process the extra logs, Congress authorized construction of three temporary sawmills on reservation land. The tribe was supposed to get bids from outsiders to build the mills, which the Menominee would operate themselves. The bids, however, failed to materialize. Two years later the sapwood was gone and the hardwoods had begun to decay.[20]

At the request of the Menominee, US Senator Robert M. La Follette of Wisconsin successfully introduced a bill and gained passage of legislation directing the US Forest Service, in cooperation with the Interior Department, to organize logging on the Menominee Reservation on a sustained yield basis. La Follette's legislation was consistent with the tribe's own vision. It was designed to ensure that the Menominee would continue to selectively cut only mature trees—an estimated 20 million board feet annually—along with the trees affected by the blow-down.

Sustainable forestry was a radically different approach to forest management than the philosophy of clear-cutting advocated by commercial loggers and most government foresters. Forest Service officials, who "knew nothing and cared less" about selective cutting, simply ignored La Follette's mandate.[21] Instead of constructing three small temporary mills that could be dismantled after the downed timber was logged, forestry officials authorized one large sawmill capable of sawing 40 million board feet annually—double the volume authorized by Congress.

As a result, the Menominee were saddled with an oversized sawmill, paid for with tribal funds, which in order to be profitable had to process twice as much timber as tribal foresters thought appropriate. Despite the protests of the tribe and local foresters appointed by the Interior Secretary, entire sections of the Menominee Forest were clear-cut. The practice continued until 1926, when the Interior Department wrenched control of the Menominee logging operations from

The Menominee Forest, one of the planet's healthiest forests, has sustained the Menominee for thousands of years.
Photo by David Nevala, for climatewisconsin.org

the Forest Service. Over the next twelve years, cutting was scaled back from 70 percent of the salable timber to just 30 percent.

In 1934, the Menominee filed suit in the US Court of Claims, alleging that the Forest Service had mismanaged their resource. Evidence revealed that more than 10 percent of the reservation—half a billion board feet of timber—had been clear-cut. Furthermore, according to expert witnesses called by the tribe, federal foresters had failed to replant the cutover as promised and "abandoned" proper slash disposal. This "indifference" led to forest fires that further damaged the resource.[22] The court awarded the Menominee Nation $8.5 million.

This judgment, which finally came in 1952, made the Menominee attractive candidates for termination, an ill-conceived federal effort of the 1950s to dismantle the reservation system. Termination reflected a dramatic departure from Indian policy of the previous fifteen years. Under the 1934 Indian "New Deal," assimilation programs, such as allotment, had ended. Most Indian boarding schools had closed. Many Indian nations, including the Menominee, reorganized their tribal governments and adopted constitutions. Indian self-determination had its critics, however, who wanted to "free" Indian people from government paternalism and integrate them into mainstream society. Termination also "freed" the government from the cost of its obligations to protect Indian people and their property and the trust responsibility to the Menominee people, a direct abrogation of the treaties.[23]

In 1953, Congress passed House Concurrent Resolution 108, which laid out the goals of termination and its companion policy, relocation, which was intended to move Indian people from rural reservations to urban areas. Among the enticements were job training programs and housing assistance. Unfortunately, most Menominee who opted for relocation received only one-way bus tickets to Chicago, Milwaukee, or St. Paul. Unfamiliar with city life, many felt rootless and disconnected from their families and customs. Inevitably, without proper support systems, many languished in these cities.

The leading proponent of termination, Senator Arthur Watkins of Utah, searched for tribes that might have the financial wherewithal to fend for themselves.

By white standards, the Menominee were poor. However, with $10 million in their trust account, the Menominee were one of the wealthiest tribes in the country.

The Menominee General Council voted to distribute a per capita payment from the claims settlement—$1,500—to each member of the tribe. After Wisconsin Congressman Melvin Laird and Senator Joseph R. McCarthy introduced a bill in Congress authorizing the Interior Department to set aside the money for that purpose, Watkins, who sat on the Senate Committee on the Interior, held up the appropriation, demanding that the Menominee first submit a termination plan. Watkins pressured the Menominee to support termination, telling them that if they did not agree to the principle, within three years Congress would terminate them anyway. During a visit to Wisconsin, the senator insisted on a tribal vote that tied the issue of termination to the per capita payment. Fewer than 6 percent of the 3,200 tribal members were at the meeting. Of the 174 voters who cast ballots, only five voted against termination. Two days later, when they understood the full implications of termination, however, the Menominee took another vote and this time voted unanimously to oppose termination.[24] Unfortunately, Congress ignored the second vote and in 1954 passed Public Law 399, better known as the Menominee Termination Act.

In an effort to preserve their tribal identity and their land base, the Menominee voted to become a separate county. In July 1959, Governor Gaylord Nelson signed a bill creating Menominee County. After the per capita payments were made, the tribe had $7 million with which to create a county infrastructure, including roads, schools, law enforcement, courts, parks, and recreation. By 1961, when the tribe was officially terminated, this so-called "wealthy" tribe was losing about a quarter million dollars a year and

As Menominee tribal leaders look on, Wisconsin Governor Gaylord Nelson signs a bill establishing the former Menominee Reservation as the state's seventy-second county in July 1959. This Menominee response to termination was an effort to protect the tribe's land base. Watching are, from left to right, Gordon Dickie, Bernard Grignon, Hilary Waukau, Attorney General John W. Reynolds, James Frechette, and Al Dodge.

Capital Times photo; WHi Image ID 45289

had become the poorest among Wisconsin's seventy-two counties. That Congress forced the Menominee to pay for the expenses associated with termination was an added insult.

The Menominee, with plenty of solicited and unsolicited help from state and federal legislators, Bureau of Indian Affairs (BIA) representatives, and tribal attorneys, created Menominee Enterprises Incorporated (MEI) to oversee the tribe's financial interests. Each tribal member received one hundred shares in MEI, which featured a complicated organizational structure including a board of directors and two trusts. The Voting Trust, comprising four Menominee and three non-Indians, elected the MEI board of directors. The Menominee Assistance Trust held the proxy votes for children, incompetent tribal members, and prisoners. The BIA appointed First Wisconsin Trust Company as guardian of the Assistance Trust, for which it received $214,000 annually. First Wisconsin represented nearly half the certificates and always voted its shares as a bloc. The resulting structure ensured that the Menominee would not control their own tribal operations.

Termination carried a tremendous quality-of-life cost. Previously, the Menominee had provided 100 percent of the funding for a Catholic hospital on the reservation. Shortly after termination, the Voting Trust ordered the hospital closed, and tribal members were without medical care. The tribal rolls were closed, the tribal courts dissolved, and the land reverted to fee status and became taxable. The tribe had often overemployed its mill, believing it was more important to provide jobs than increase profits. Under a board of directors controlled by white financial interests, the emphasis shifted to the bottom line. To become more efficient and profitable, MEI began modernizing equipment and laying off workers. Menominee began to leave the reservation for jobs in the city, an exodus that further diminished the tribe's tax base. The board of directors looked to different solutions to attack the tribe's insolvency. It voted to lease some of the tribe's finest land along the Wolf River to the state of Wisconsin for a public campground and to offer long-term leases to tourists for summer homes.[25]

In 1968, MEI formed a corporation, Lakes of the Menominees, and entered into a partnership with a real estate developer to connect nine reservation lakes and create a vacation area known as Legend Lake. The original plan was to carve just under 2,700 waterfront and off-shore lots that would be offered to Menominee and non-Menominee long-term lease holders. Property holders without direct access to the water were given interest in one of forty-one "beach clubs" so that residents without waterfront property could enjoy the beaches. However, corporate planners quickly determined that leases would not generate enough money and instead began selling the lots outright, promising MEI $6 million in sales and $2 million in shared profits.

The decision to sell the lots infuriated many tribal members. A grassroots activist group, Determination of Rights and Unity for Menominee Shareholders (DRUMS), led by James Washinawatok and Ada Deer, emerged in the late 1960s and began to educate tribal members about the trust situation and the need to change the financial structure of MEI. It sent Deer—who was then a student at the University of Wisconsin and would later become Assistant Secretary of the Interior—to Washington to lobby Congress in the hopes of repealing termination and restoring the tribe. "The feeling was we'd already given up ten million acres a hundred years ago," recalled tribal historian Dave Grignon. "Why did we have to give up any more?"[26]

DRUMS members organized a march from Keshena to the state capitol in Madison. They filed suits in federal court claiming that the dams required for the project would inundate streams and marshes, adversely affect wildlife habitat, and destroy burial grounds and archaeological sites. Menominee elders lay down along the highway leading to the real estate office to prevent land sales. In 1972, after nearly two thousand home sites had already been sold, MEI terminated its agreement with the corporation and land sales ended. A year later, Congress passed the Menominee Restoration Bill, which restored official status to the tribe.

During the late 1960s and early 1970s, Menominee tribal members staged protests and marches in an effort to regain tribal control of Menominee Enterprises Incorporated and halt the sale of Menominee land.

Milwaukee Journal photo, © Journal Sentinel, Inc.

Compared to the neighboring tribes in Wisconsin, the Menominee Nation has been able to assert more sovereign control over its reservation. During the restoration process, the Menominee successfully petitioned Congress to be exempt from Public Law 280, a measure passed in 1952 that transferred civil and some criminal jurisdiction from the federal government to five states with large Indian populations, including Wisconsin. The Menominee reasoned that, as a result of termination, they already had police and courts equipped to handle disputes. Consequently, tribal police or federal marshals handle crimes involving tribal members on the Menominee Reservation. In contrast, Indians who commit crimes on all other reservations in Wisconsin fall under county and state jurisdiction.

Jurisdictional issues, particularly those involving Legend Lake, however, continue to be a problem for the Menominee. Just 1 percent of Menominee County land is taxable and nearly all of that taxable land is in the Legend Lake and surrounding lakes area, where 1,838 private parcels held mostly by non-Menominee landowners generate 95 percent of the county's taxes.[27] Although the tribe contributes toward the cost of providing county services, residents complain that they are underserved. The Menominee, who were able to acquire unsold lots after restoration, have placed 815 lots in trust, meaning that these parcels are not taxable. They have also leased some of these untaxed home sites to individual tribal members for recreational or residential use. Fewer than half the taxable lots have homes on them, with only two hundred occupied by permanent residents. The rest are used for seasonal housing, camping, or other recreational uses.

These tangled interests—tribal and nontribal, permanent and seasonal, taxed and nontaxed residents, all within an area of overlapping jurisdictions—have created a monumental administrative challenge for the tribe and their non-Indian neighbors. The Menominee County Taxpayers Association (MCTA), representing for the most part nontribal property owners, has fought all efforts by the tribe to reacquire Legend Lake property, arguing that it would increase the tax burden of the remaining property owners.[28] In 1995, MCTA petitioned the state legislature for permission to merge Menominee County with Shawano County, a move that infuriated the tribe. "There's no way in the world that we Menominees are going to sit idly by and let someone strip us of our reservation," Menominee vice chair Louis Dickson stated. "They want to deprive the Menominees of the land that's part of our ancestral heritage."[29]

In 2008, the tribe attempted to purchase seven lots from the Legend Lake Property Owners Association (LLPOA). That Menominee would like to repurchase all of the land lost within their reservation is no secret. "If I could buy that property back, I would in a heartbeat," Menominee chair Lisa Waukau said in a 2009 interview. "However, we don't have the kind of money to do that."[30] The LLPOA not only refused the tribe's offer to purchase the lots, but in June 2009 it adopted a "restrictive covenant" that attempted to prevent land sold or transferred to the tribe from being placed into trust.[31] The Menominee called it an attack on their sovereignty and questioned the legality of the covenant. "A property owners association will not trump a sovereign nation," Waukau told tribal members.[32] Some believe that the issue will eventually be litigated. Given the federal government's role in terminating the Menominee and facilitating the land loss, one possible solution is for the state, tribe, and LLPOA to pressure the federal government to provide "payment in lieu of taxes," a strategy that has been used elsewhere.

Another post-termination historical event that deeply affected the tribe and its relationship with its non-Indian neighbors was the 1975 New Year's takeover of the Alexian Brothers' Novitiate. The novitiate, located about five miles south of the reservation in Shawano County, had stood empty since 1968. A group calling itself the Menominee Warrior Society muscled its way past a caretaker into the complex and demanded that it be turned over to the Menominee tribe for use as a hospital. The Warriors, some of whom had taken part in AIM's occupation of Wounded Knee two years earlier, insisted that their actions were justified under a US code that stated that when a religious organization that had received a land patent to minister or educate Indians no longer functioned, its property reverted to the tribe.[33] Reeling from the effects of termination, 75 percent of Menominee were unemployed and half lived below the poverty level. The Warriors told reporters they just "wanted to start the New Year out right for the poor people."[34]

The takeover revealed fundamental divisions within the tribe. Although the Menominee had just passed a new constitution and bylaws, they had not yet elected a tribal legislature and were operating under the leadership of the Menominee Restoration Committee (MRC) headed by Deer and two other women who denounced the takeover as illegal. The Warriors believed the MRC was not responding quickly enough to the

Menominee Crystal Caldwell wrapped herself in a US flag during the 1975 takeover by the Menominee Warrior Society of the Alexian Brothers Novitiate in Gresham, Wisconsin. Governor Patrick Lucey summoned the National Guard during the monthlong protest.

Courtesy of the Shawano Leader

National Guard troops stand ready outside the Alexian Brothers Novitiate in Gresham. On December 31, 1974, the Menominee Warrior Society took over the abandoned facility and occupied it for thirty-four days before negotiating a withdrawal.

WHi Image ID 83076

suffering of Menominee tribal members and did not reflect traditional Menominee leadership. The takeover was further complicated when prominent AIM members, including Russell Means and Dennis Banks, joined the occupation. By this time, then-governor Patrick Lucey had called out the National Guard, which had surrounded the facility. Many white Shawano County residents grew impatient with the occupation and wanted the soldiers to storm the complex. When the governor refused, they organized vigilante groups that tried to engage the Warriors in gun battles.

Thirty-four days later, after the Alexian Brothers agreed to deed the property to the Menominee, the Warriors withdrew. There were allegations that the occupiers had "trashed" the buildings; however, it was revealed that the authorities' decision to cut off services to the complex had caused the pipes to burst, resulting in thousands of dollars' worth of damage. In the aftermath of the occupation, the leaders of the takeover stood trial in Juneau County, where the proceedings had been moved because of pretrial publicity and concerns that the Warriors could not receive a fair trial in Shawano County. Although some Warriors were acquitted, others were convicted and received prison sentences, and the Menominee Nation never took possession of the novitiate. The incident created hard feelings and divisions within the Menominee, some of which still have not completely healed.[35]

The willingness of tribal members to pick up arms in defense of their communities is a familiar theme throughout Indian Country, but nowhere does it dominate as much as in the Menominee Nation. At least 125 Menominee volunteered during the Civil War, most of them in Company K, First Brigade, and Thirty-seventh Regiment, which lost one out of every three men.[36] An estimated three hundred, including nine women, served in World Wars I and II.[37] During the Korean War, 165 men and three women were in the military. An estimated four hundred Menominee men and women, many of them enlistees, served during the Vietnam War.[38] High enlistment rates continued throughout the Gulf Wars, the Iraq War, and the war in Afghanistan. "On a per-capita basis," according to a 2008 analysis by the *St. Louis Post-Dispatch*, "Menominee County provided more soldiers to the Army over the last four years than any other county in the nation without a major Army installation."[39] Although dire conditions on the reservation, especially during the Korean and Vietnam Wars, may have encouraged disproportionate numbers of Menominee to enlist, economics was just part of the reason. "There's a warrior spirit," J. Boyd, a Menominee Vietnam veteran, explained. "And when it's time to go, a lot of young people figure it's their time to go, like their fathers and uncles and grandfathers have before them."[40]

The Menominee who remained or returned to the reservation after termination have struggled to rebuild their economy. Following passage of the National Indian Gaming Act in 1988, the tribe opened a casino, bingo, and hotel complex in Keshena. In 2010, despite a plunging bond market and recession, the tribe managed to complete an ambitious multimillion-dollar renovation and expansion project.[41] Today, the Menominee Casino Resort features thirteen thousand square feet of conference space, banquet accommodations for six hundred, and a 103-room remodeled hotel. Reflecting Menominee history and culture, the décor of the complex features the Ancestral Bear, the Five Clans, and a traditional woodland aesthetic. In addition to the casino, the tribe also operates the Thunderbird, a satellite complex that includes a supper club, mini casino, convenience store, and gas station located about nine miles east of the resort. The Menominee also hope to build an off-reservation casino in Kenosha, site of the former Dairyland Greyhound Racetrack. The $800 million project, first proposed in 2004, met resistance from the Potawatomi, whose Milwaukee casino is just twenty miles away from the Kenosha site, and rejection from the BIA. However, in 2011 the BIA withdrew its rejection and agreed to review a revised application.

One of the most anticipated developments in Menominee Nation was the long-awaited opening of the tribe's grocery store. In fall 2011, the 11,600-square-foot Save-A-Lot opened for business. Tribal officials promised that in addition to budget-friendly basic items, the store would offer locally produced goods including wild rice, maple syrup, and organic produce. Store plans included grocery delivery service for elders and tribal members with disabilities.

Gaming dollars have also enabled the Menominee to expand and improve their tribal clinic. After its hospital closed down in 1961—a casualty of termination—the tribe was without any health-care services on the reservation until 1972, when it opened a makeshift health center in the basement of the Neopit Community Center. Five years later it built the Menominee Tribal Clinic, the first Indian-owned and -operated health-care facility in the United States. Since 1977, it has expanded three times and provides comprehensive medical services, including emergency, dental, optometry, and pharmacy.[42]

The tribe also operates College of Menominee Nation (CMN), one of two tribal colleges in Wisconsin. CMN offers fifteen associate degrees, five technical degrees, and four certificates. In 2013, CMN graduated its first class of students receiving bachelor of science degrees in teacher education. Future four-year degree programs include public administration, forestry, and business. More than six hundred students, nearly 80 percent of them Native American, attend

College of Menominee Nation, Keshena

Courtesy of Dale Kakkak

John Teller teaches the Menominee language to kindergarten children at the Menominee Tribal School in Neopit.

Photo by Patty Loew

classes on the main campus in Keshena or at CMN's urban campus in Green Bay. Since opening its doors in 1993, the college has experienced tremendous growth and expansion. In 2006, it unveiled new classrooms, laboratories, lounge areas, and conference space. By 2007, it had negotiated agreements with a number of schools, including five within the University of Wisconsin system, to allow CMN students with associate degrees to continue toward bachelor's degrees. In 2008, the college completed the first phase of an eighteen-thousand-square-foot environmentally friendly library with geothermal features that heat and cool the main and upper floors of the building. That year it also broke ground on a new cultural learning center.

Cultural revitalization remains a key priority for the Menominee. Like many Indian nations, the Menominee are very concerned about losing their language. Each summer, they hold a culture camp, during which tribal members learn or refresh their language skills, express themselves through traditional arts and crafts, and play traditional games like lacrosse and chaha, a stick game for women.[43] The weeklong camp is also an opportunity for younger Menominee to learn new songs and practice their drumming. "It gives them the opportunity to experience Menominee language, culture, and history," Grignon said. "It helps their self-esteem and helps them identify themselves as Menominee people."[44]

One of the most uplifting contemporary events in the Menominee Nation has been the return of the sturgeon, a fish central to the Menominee creation story and the essence of the Nation's cultural calendar. For thousands of years, the Menominee relied on this prehistoric fish—their "lifeblood"—to replenish them after a long winter.[45] Their return in the spring was cause for joy and ceremony. However, when dams erected on the Wolf River in the 1890s and 1920s blocked the sturgeon run, the Menominee lost this important resource and their sturgeon ceremonies went dormant.

In 1994, the Menominee Nation, US Fish and Wildlife Service, and Wisconsin Department of Natural Resources began restocking thirty thousand sturgeon from Wolf River strains on reservation lakes. By 2005, the population had rebounded enough to allow the first tribal harvest in more than a century. Because of the dams, sturgeon from Lake Winnebago are still unable to make their way up the Wolf. However, the tribe is gifted each year with a small number of sturgeon taken from below the dam for ceremonial use. There is growing pressure within many environmental groups to remove the manmade barriers. "When the dam is gone," David Grignon, director of the Menominee Historic Preservation Office, stated, "they will be with us here again."[46]

There have been other environmental success stories in Menominee Nation. In the 1980s, the tribe found its ancestral lands targeted for a high-level radioactive waste disposal site. Alarmed at the lack of nuclear waste storage space, the Energy Department created a list of twelve potential sites in the eastern United States for the repository, including the Wolf River Batholith near the Menominee Reservation. In April 1986, Menominee tribal chair Gordon Dickie angrily wrote to DOE Secretary John Herrington expressing the tribe's "shock and disappointment" and questioning a process that he felt was "totally skewed" against Native interests. "We do not think it is an accident that the 12 areas so far designated include five federally recognized Indian reservations."[47] Two months later, he restated the tribe's position in testimony before a Senate Energy Subcommittee in Washington. Although by then the DOE had announced it had indefinitely postponed the search for the site of a new repository, Dickie again complained about the process by which the Menominee received only $26,000 to review five years of highly technical documents in order to defend themselves. The postponement, he told the committee, left the Menominee in "a very uncomfortable state of limbo," wondering if DOE would someday return and "will the Tribe again have to fight DOE on every point?"[48]

Dickie represented a community united in its opposition to the nuclear waste dump. Dickie's daughter, Rebecca Alegria, remembered that when DOE representatives came to Menominee High School for a public hearing, elders including

The Wolf River, a federally designated Wild River, flows through the Menominee Reservation.
Photo by RJ and Linda Miller, courtesy of the Wisconsin Department of Tourism

Helen Wynos, Johnson Awanohopay, Mary Dowd, Jane Dowd, and Menominee environmental activists "chased them out of the meeting."[49] The Menominee tribal legislature unanimously approved several resolutions, including one stating its "Total Opposition to the development of any nuclear waste facility within the sovereign borders of the Menominee Nation."[50] Anxiety in the community ran so deep, even Menominee schoolchildren wrote letters to Washington expressing their fears and concerns.

```
Dear Sirs:
     No one wants you to put that junk under
our houses and our trees. Our kid's kids
will die and also our fish,plants and animals
We want our town to grow and our cities. So
So please don't put your nuclear waste under
our buildings and streets. I feel that it
is not right to do this.

                              Sincerely
                              Kevin Warrington


Dear Sirs:
     I'm writing to tell you how I feel
about a nuclear waste dump on our reservation
It could kill us, and kill our animals.

                              Sincerely,
                              Cheryl Maho
```

Children from Menominee Tribal School wrote dozens of letters to Washington protesting the government's listing of the Wolf River Batholith as a potential site for a high-level nuclear waste repository.

Courtesy of Rebecca Alegria

Just as the Wolf River threat subsided, a new environmental challenge surfaced—the Crandon mine project. Seeds for the controversy had been sown in the mid-1970s, when Exxon Minerals began exploratory work on a plan to extract fifty-five million tons of primarily copper and zinc from an ore body located five miles south of Crandon, Wisconsin. In 1986 the company withdrew its application, citing depressed metal prices. Seven years later Exxon formed a partnership with Rio Algom Limited to create the Crandon Mining Company (CMC) and in 1995 applied for permits to construct the mine.[51] CMC's original plan was to discharge treated wastewater from the mine into the Wolf River. Anticipating the return of Exxon, however, in 1988 the Menominee led a coalition of environmental groups that successfully won an "outstanding water resource" designation for the Wolf, a distinction that eliminated the possibility that Swamp Creek, a tributary of the Wolf, could be used by Exxon as a dumping point for treated mine effluent. Elders, like Hilary "Sparky" Waukau, emerged as strong leaders. "My last breath I want to be considered as for the environment, Wolf River and my people."[52] For the remainder of his life, until his passing in 1995, Waukau traveled the state, galvanizing support among Native and non-Native citizens for environmental awareness. "When Hilary speaks at public hearings," George Meyer, then secretary of the Wisconsin DNR, said, "the room quiets down and everyone shows respect, whether or not they agree with him."[53]

When the plans were rewritten to divert the effluent instead to the Wisconsin River, the Menominee, led by Waukau, continued to lobby against the mine and supported the Mole Lake Ojibwe, whose wild rice resource the mine threatened. The Menominee and a coalition of Wisconsin environmental groups successfully pushed for a mining moratorium, passed by the state legislature and signed into law in 1995. The Menominee breathed easier when the Mole Lake and Potawatomi purchased the mine in 2003.

The deep spiritual and cultural connection the Menominee have to the Wolf River extends also to their forest. Although commercial forests are managed to maximize profits, the Menominee have resisted that approach. "We could really push the red oak right now," Marshall Pecore, Menominee Forest manager, told a group of tribal journalists touring the forest in 2003. "That would bring in a lot of money."[54] Instead, however, they let the soil, not market factors, determine which trees they'll plant. Pecore explained that Menominee elders know

Hilary "Sparky" Waukau, Menominee elder and environmental advocate
Courtesy of Rebecca Alegria

The Eagles Soar: 2004–2005 Menominee Boys Basketball Team

Legendary.

Sometimes a sports team accomplishes what political and economic sages cannot. In victory, it suspends time and unites the community in a blur of excitement and pride. In winter 2004–2005, the Menominee High School boys' basketball team wrote itself into the annals as the most successful team in school history, winning the Division C regional championship. Most of the boys had played together since they were five or six years old and had bonded over basketball. "These were good kids with good family support," Menominee athletic director Chuck Raasch said. "A special team" is how assistant coach Dave Wynos remembered them.

The 2004–2005 Division C regional champion Menominee High School basketball team. Front row (left to right, players only): Mo-wa-sa Beauprey, P-ne-ci Thunder, Mike Waupoose, Jordan Corn, Alan Waukau. Back row: Coach Dave Wynos, Aaron Waukau, Vincent Grignon, Daniel Peters, Roman Haack, Meyakenew Kakkak, George Johnson, Coach Brad Nunway, Coach Robert Webster. (The ball boys in the front row are Coach Webster's sons.)

Courtesy of *Menominee Nation News*

continued on page 43

Stacked lumber, Menominee Tribal Enterprises, Neopit
Photo by David Nevala, for climatewisconsin.org

that certain species grow with particular plants, like ferns. This traditional ecological knowledge (TEK), as well as contemporary scientific soil analysis, informs the tribe's sustainable management plan. Despite economic pressures that forced the tribe to lay off fifty people in 2002 and a severe recession beginning in 2008, the Menominee continue to heed the wisdom of their ancestors and cut selectively. At so many critical moments—the early reservation years, termination, and during the creation of Menominee County—the Menominee were given the option of liquidating all or part of their forest. Each time they resisted.

Today, the Menominee Forest has become a laboratory for sustainable forestry and is considered one of the most beautiful and healthiest forests on earth. Forest managers from all over the world visit it, marveling at its diverse species and mixed ages, including four-hundred-year-old hemlocks. A space shuttle astronaut once remarked that from outer space, the forest looked like a "jewel." It's so visible from space that satellites use the forest edges to focus their cameras.[55] Along with sustainability has come productivity. The Menominee have harvested nearly two billion board feet of timber since they signed the treaty that established their reservation. An estimated one and a half billion board feet stands today—the same amount that stood in 1854.

continued from page 42

With each game, excitement grew. Through conference and regional play, cheering, sign-waving Menominee crowded the high school gym each week. At sectionals, more than a thousand tribal members packed the gym in Antigo to see their boys take on Amherst High School. There was a personal record at stake, too. In the middle of the second quarter, Meyakenew Kakkak drove to the hoop and banked a shot, putting him over the one-thousand-point mark for his high school career. With Amherst's approval, officials stopped the contest and awarded him the game ball.

It was a close back-and-forth game that Amherst eventually won, but as one fan impressed with the team's tenacity and sportsmanship put it, "There are other paths to victory." After the game, Wynos told the boys to enjoy what they had accomplished. "The community is proud of you," he told them. "In twenty years, they'll still be talking about you." On March 17, 2005, the Menominee tribal legislature awarded the players and coaches eagle feathers, proclaiming that "the Menominee Eagles' achievements will go down in tribal history, not just for their athleticism, but for how they instilled in the community a deep sense of pride."[1]

1. Chuck Raasch, athletic director, Menominee Indian School District, phone interview with the author, October 10, 2011. See also "Eagles Finish Strong at Sectionals," *Menominee Nation News*, March 28, 2005.

4 HO-CHUNK

The Ho-Chunk people express their remembered past in the songs, stories, effigy mounds, rock art, and place names that dot the landscape of their ancestral home. For thousands of years, the Ho-Chunk have lived in the western Great Lakes region, south and west of present-day Green Bay. The Ho-Chunk, or Hochungra, formerly were known as the Winnebago, which came from the Meskwaki word *Ouinipegouek*, meaning "People of the Stinking Water." This appellation was not intended to be an insult. It referred to the waters of the Fox River and Lake Winnebago, which were turbid and rich in algae at certain times of the year. The French truncated it to "Stinking People," which, for obvious reasons, made it a name the Ho-Chunk people never appreciated.

Hochungra, the name by which the Ho-Chunk describe themselves, translates to "People of the Big Voice" or "People of the Sacred Language."[1] This refers to the Ho-Chunk belief that they represent the original people from whom all Siouan-speaking people sprang. The Ho-Chunk are most closely related to the Iowa, Oto, and Missouri tribes, which were part of the Ho-Chunk Nation at one time. According to oral history, the four tribes split apart shortly before European contact.

Ho-Chunk are also related linguistically to the Osage, Quapaw, Omaha, Kansas, and Ponca peoples, as well as the Mandan in North Dakota and Siouan-speaking people in the southeastern United States. The fact that the Ho-Chunk are situated in the geographic center of all these people lends weight to the Hochungra contention that they are the "original people" and explains why the Iowa, Oto, and Missouri tribes refer to the Ho-Chunk even today as "grand-fathers."

Although Ho-Chunk culture today is patrilineal, meaning descent and clan membership derive from

Ho-Chunk
2010 population: 6,563 Ho-Chunk tribal members
1962: 554 acres
1978: 3,673 acres (individually owned homesteads)
1999: 4,325 acres (918 tribally owned)
2010: HCN Trust Land Acreage – 3,535
HCN Fee Simple Acreage – 5,328

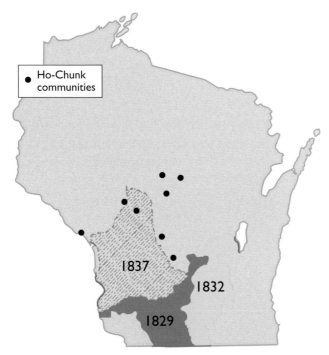

- Ho-Chunk communities

1837

1832

1829

the father's side, some anthropologists believe that the Ho-Chunk originally were matrilineal. They speculate that this shift may have been the result of extensive intermarriage with neighboring patrilineal tribes in the seventeenth century and involvement in the fur trade, which emphasized male activities. Clans descend from two major divisions, or moieties: an earth division comprising eight clans, and a sky division with four clans. The earth division includes the Bear Clan, from which war chiefs were selected. The sky division includes the Thunderbird Clan, which traditionally produced the peace chiefs. Together, these leaders governed with the help of a council made up of principal members of each clan. They guided day-to-day activities in the large villages the Ho-Chunk inhabited at the time of European contact. Their closest neighbors were the Menominee, who were also their closest allies, and the Illinois, who were sworn enemies.

Yellow Thunder (c. 1774–1871), Ho-Chunk chief who resisted removal efforts in 1840. He eventually succumbed to pressure and was relocated along with his people to Iowa but returned to Wisconsin and received forty acres of land under the Indian Homestead Act.

Painting by Samuel D. Coates; Wisconsin Historical Museum 1942.1

The Ho-Chunk believe they originated at Moga-Shooch (Red Banks), on the south shore of Green Bay, the deep notch between thumb and fingers on today's map of Wisconsin.[2] They were the most powerful tribe in the area, with homelands that extended from upper Michigan to southern Wisconsin. Sometime during the century that preceded European contact, the Anishinaabe (Ojibwe, Potawatomi, and Odaawa) began moving into Ho-Chunk territory along the shore of Lake Huron to the confluence of Lakes Michigan and Superior. The Anishinaabe migration displaced the Menominee and the Ho-Chunk. One theory is that the loss of territory, combined with a growing population, created enough environmental stress that the Ho-Chunk began moving southward, which created antagonism with the tribes of the Illinois Confederacy (Kaskaskia, Peoria, and Illinois). With no place to expand, the Ho-Chunk split apart. Sometime around the year 1570, a tribal faction that would evolve into the Iowa, Oto, and Missouri left the main body of Ho-Chunk and headed west down the Wisconsin River to present-day Iowa, where they separated and evolved into three distinct tribes. The weakened main body of Ho-Chunk concentrated into large villages near Green Bay in order to defend their homeland against the encroaching Anishinaabe from the north and the Illinois Confederacy from the south.

The population decline and economic dependence on European trade goods that accompanied Ho-Chunk participation in the fur trade left the tribe vulnerable to encroachment by white settlers, especially miners who were attracted to the rich lead deposits of the Upper Mississippi Valley. The indigenous people of the area had mined galena, the grayish lead ore, for at least eight thousand years. Women of the Sauk, Meskwaki, and Ho-Chunk Nations worked the lead deposits every spring and fall, gathering enough of the mineral for personal use and sometimes collecting enough to trade with other Indians. The Ho-Chunk melted galena and used it as body paint, reserving the finest pieces for burial with their dead.

After the American Revolution (1775–1783), lead eclipsed fur as the principal means of exchange between the Ho-Chunk and white traders. In 1788, neighboring Sauk and Meskwaki formally leased a portion of their mineral lands to Julian Dubuque, a French miner who hired Native women, including Ho-Chunk, to work the mines. Soon this region, known as the Fever River Valley, was producing up to forty thousand pounds of lead bars, sheets, and bullets a year. As word spread of the richness of the deposits, the Ho-Chunk witnessed a steady stream of white miners pour into their territory "like wolves in the Plains to the dead buffalo," as Old Grayheaded Decora, a Ho-Chunk leader, described them. "They spread out in every direction and began to dig and find and carry off lead on the Winnebago lands."[3]

When the United States dramatically expanded its territory with the Louisiana Purchase (1803), the Ho-Chunk discovered that their homeland, once at the edge of American territory, was now in the middle of it. As war with Britain loomed, the Fever River Valley took on more importance as a strategic source of lead for ammunition. The federal government encouraged white encroachment by offering miners generous leases in exchange for 10 percent royalties. Alarmed by the number of lead miners trespassing on their territory, the Ho-Chunk responded to the pan-Indian call to arms by Tecumseh, who was trying to repel white encroachment into the Ohio Valley. Enthusiastically endorsing the religious exhortations of Tecumseh's brother—Tenskwatawa, the Shawnee Prophet—the Ho-Chunk became one of the most militant members of Tecumseh's alliance. By 1809, the Ho-Chunk had established a permanent Hochungra village near Prophetstown (Tippecanoe) in present-day Indiana.

In 1811, Tenskwatawa disregarded his brother's orders not to provoke the Americans and, during Tecumseh's absence, attacked William Henry Harrison's troops. In what became known as the Battle of Tippecanoe, the Ho-Chunk and other members of the alliance suffered a tremendous defeat. The Ho-Chunk, furious, took Tenskwatawa prisoner for several weeks. It was only Tecumseh's return that saved Tenskwatawa from being killed. With assistance from the Ho-Chunk,

Tecumseh was able to put his alliance back together. When the War of 1812 began, the united tribes threw their support behind the British.[4]

The Ho-Chunk played a prominent role in that war. Along with the Sauk, Meskwaki, and Potawatomi, they besieged Fort Madison in Illinois and forced the Americans to abandon it. They also fought at the battles of Maumee in Ohio and the River Raisin in Michigan. Even after Tecumseh was killed in battle in Ontario in October 1813, the Ho-Chunk continued to help the British repel an American attack at Fort Michilimackinac.

Following the Treaty of Ghent (1814), which ended the War of 1812, a portion of the Ho-Chunk signed a peace treaty with the Americans in St. Louis. The pact did not include land cessions, although some Ho-Chunk correctly feared that a land grab was inevitable, and many remained hostile to the American intruders in their homelands and even charged them a toll to travel through their country.

By 1825, more than ten thousand miners had illegally invaded the area. Hoping that an agreement with the federal government would firmly establish their boundaries, the Ho-Chunk and numerous other tribes signed the "Peace and Friendship Treaty" at Prairie du Chien.[5] However, two years later nothing had changed. "There are a great many Americans on our land, working it without permission," Four Legs, a Ho-Chunk chief, told a council at Butte des Morts. "And I want you to tell our Great Father to stop it, to reach out his long arm and draw them back."[6]

Ho-Chunk anxiety heightened in June 1827 with rumors that several of the tribe's warriors had been executed at Fort Snelling in the Minnesota Territory. Red Bird, a Ho-Chunk war chief, retaliated by attacking the home of white squatters south of La Crosse and killing several family members. Later, he attacked a barge carrying miners and mining supplies near Prairie du Chien. For three months, the Ho-Chunk resisted pressure to turn over Red Bird to white authorities, but eventually they prevailed on Red Bird to surrender. In September 1827, he gave himself up to Major William Whistler, pleading to be executed then and there. "I am ready," he told Whistler. "I do not wish to be put in irons. Let me be free. I have given away my life."[7] Despite his pleas, Red Bird was shackled and led away.

Red Bird's resistance had made him a hero to many Ho-Chunk, and his honorable surrender had

Yellow Thunder (second from right) and a contingent of Ho-Chunk in Washington, circa 1880
WHi Image ID 34543

Black Hawk (1767–1838), Sauk warrior. Black Hawk's refusal to relocate his band to Iowa touched off the Black Hawk War in 1832. The US Army and militias pursued Black Hawk's band throughout southwestern Wisconsin and massacred them near the Mississippi at the mouth of the Bad Axe River.

From *History of the Indian Tribes of North America*, 1848; WHi Image ID 25690

even earned the grudging respect of many white officials. Still, it came as a surprise to many that a Ho-Chunk delegation to Washington was able to obtain a release and a presidential pardon. Unfortunately, it was too late. In February 1828, the war chief died of dysentery while imprisoned in Prairie du Chien.

The Ho-Chunk mission to Washington and Red Bird's ill-fated pardon proved costly to the tribe. In order to secure his release, the Ho-Chunk had agreed to give up their lead-rich lands in Illinois. A year later, they learned that US officials wanted all their mineral lands south of the Wisconsin River. "Do you want *our* Country? Yours is much larger than ours," said the Ho-Chunk speaker Little Elk to the government's negotiators. "Do you want *our* wigwams? You live in palaces. My fathers, what can be your motive?"

The Ho-Chunk problems intensified in 1829 when national attention turned to a neighboring Sauk war chief whose lands near present-day Rock Island, Illinois, had been ceded in a fraudulent treaty twenty-five years earlier. When US officials informed Black Hawk that he must abandon his village, he initially refused. Eventually he agreed to move to the Iowa side of the Mississippi River, only after officials promised to replace the corn his people had planted. When the corn arrived, the Sauk discovered it to be inferior in both quality and quantity. Later, Black Hawk remembered that his band was forced to sneak over in the night "to steal corn from their own fields . . . where they were discovered by the whites and fired upon."[8]

In 1832, Black Hawk's band sought refuge in Illinois with White Cloud, a Ho-Chunk prophet of Sauk and Ho-Chunk ancestry, who invited them to plant their corn in his village. As Black Hawk crossed the Mississippi and led his people northeastward toward White Cloud's village, regular army troops and several ragtag militias moved to intercept him. Lacking widespread support from the Ho-Chunk and disappointed that help from the British did not materialize, Black Hawk attempted several times, unsuccessfully, to surrender. For sixteen weeks, his warriors created diversions while the main body of Sauk—exhausted, starving, reduced to eating tree bark—fled from the militia. Eventually Black Hawk's retreat ended in the so-called Battle of Bad Axe in August, which was little more than a massacre of Sauk men, women, and children as they attempted to cross the Mississippi south of La Crosse. Black Hawk's band, once numbering 1,200, had been reduced to 150 people.

The Black Hawk War divided the Ho-Chunk. Some enthusiastically supported the Sauk war chief. Most remained neutral. Others, who had been terrorized by the Sauk, joined the Americans. White Crow, for example, agreed to fight against Black Hawk only after a coercive meeting with Henry Dodge, a Missouri miner and slave owner who arrived in 1828. Dodge, who commanded a militia of lead miners and later would become Wisconsin's first territorial governor, threatened that if the Ho-Chunk allowed Black Hawk to camp with them, it would be interpreted as an act of war. In the summer of 1832, he told a delegation of Ho-Chunk chiefs: "You will have your country taken from you, your annuity money will be forfeited, and the lives of your people lost."[9]

Following the Black Hawk War, the Ho-Chunk were forced to cede their lands south of the Wisconsin and Fox Rivers to the Rock River, encompassing their cornfields, hunting grounds, and other significant sites, including De Jope (Madison) and Neesh (Wisconsin Dells), in exchange for lands in western Iowa. Five years later, twenty individual Ho-Chunk ceded the tribe's remaining lands east of the Mississippi River and agreed to move to lands set aside for them in Iowa. Tribal leaders protested in vain that of the signers, only two were from the Bear Clan—the only clan authorized to conduct land negotiations.[10]

In this portrait taken in Black River Falls circa 1894, Susie Kingswan (HeNuKah) wears a pair of appliqué beaded Ho-Chunk moccasins. Her son Fred Kingswan (MaHeNoGinKah) wears traditional leather leggings (waguca) and beaded garters.

Photo by Charles Van Schaick; WHi Image ID 60862

The 1820s signaled the beginning of the removal period for the Ho-Chunk. In 1837, the Americans offered the Ho-Chunk land they described as more desirable than the Iowa tract and told them they had eight years to prepare for their move. (It was only after the tribe received a written copy of the agreement that it learned that the treaty actually read eight *months*.) The new land was in present-day northern Minnesota near Long Prairie. In the view of US negotiators, the Ho-Chunk were to act as a buffer between enemy factions of Dakota and Ojibwe—an unfortunate role for the displaced tribe. Tribal leaders pressured federal officials for new lands.

Some Ho-Chunk, however, refused to leave their homelands, and others traveled to Iowa and Minnesota and returned. The Wisconsin Ho-Chunk today are the descendants of the "renegades" or "rebel faction," as twenty-first-century tribal member

Lance Tallmadge describes them, "who refused to move out west as the reservations were established for them."[11]

In 1855, the Ho-Chunk in Long Prairie exchanged their lands for a reservation near Blue Earth, in south-central Minnesota. The reservation was not very large, but the land was fertile and the Ho-Chunk farmed successfully. Life was improving when the Civil War broke out in 1861. Many Ho-Chunk enlisted in the Union Army, joining regiments from Minnesota, Nebraska, and Wisconsin. While they were away, the Sioux Uprising (1862) claimed the lives of nearly five hundred settlers. Although the Ho-Chunk were not part of the revolt, terrified whites demanded that the Ho-Chunk be removed from the area along with the Sioux. As a result, the government forced the Ho-Chunk to cede their lands at Blue Earth for lands on the Crow Creek in South Dakota. The Ho-Chunk chief Baptiste visited the proposed site and bluntly reported: "It is damn cold country . . . no wood . . . damn bad country for Indians."[12]

In the winter of 1863, the government ordered the Ho-Chunk to move, ignoring Baptiste's objections and his pleas to wait for better weather. The chief's worst fears were realized when a quarter of the tribe—more than 550 of the nearly 2,000 tribal members—died en route to South Dakota. Many Ho-Chunk became ill from the rancid pork and rotten vegetables the government provided to the émigrés. Despite all this hardship and despair, however, the Ho-Chunk continued to resist removal. Of the 1,382 survivors, more than 1,200 fled in canoes down the Missouri River and took refuge among the Omaha in Nebraska. In 1865, the so-called treaty-abiding Ho-Chunk signed a treaty in which they purchased a portion of the Omaha reservation. There they remain to this day, a tribe politically distinct from the Ho-Chunk of Wisconsin.

The "renegades," the tough survivors who hid out in Wisconsin or returned from reservations in the west, were rounded up again and again and on one occasion were put into boxcars and shipped to Nebraska. Again, they made their way home. In 1874, as a little girl, Mountain Wolf Woman heard her mother's account of the last of the government's forced removal of the Wisconsin Ho-Chunk. There was "much rejoicing" at the train station when her

In this circa 1907 portrait, Mountain Wolf Woman, also known as Stella Blowsnake Whitepine Stacy (HayAhChoWinKah), holds her two daughters, Josephine Whitepine Mike (AhHooGeNaWinKah), left, and Lena Whitepine Shegonee (HaCheDayWinKah).
Photo by Charles Van Schaick; WHi Image ID 9385

family reunited with Nebraska relatives. However, by spring their joy had turned to fear when "great numbers" of Ho-Chunk began to die. She recalled in an interview in 1958 how her mother was frightened and disoriented by the tribe's removal to Nebraska: "Why do we stay here? I am afraid because the people are all dying. Why do we not go back home?"[13]

Within a year of their removal in 1874, about 650 of the 1,000 Wisconsin Ho-Chunk sent to Nebraska, including Mountain Wolf Woman's family, had gone home. Some who returned found leadership under Chiefs Dandy and Yellow Thunder, who had managed to secure a homestead in Wisconsin. Other Ho-Chunk followed suit, and in 1881 Congress passed special legislation allowing the Wisconsin Ho-Chunk forty-acre homesteads. Although the lands were inferior, most Ho-Chunk eked out an existence hunting, gathering, fishing, and gardening and occasionally hiring themselves out as farmhands.

The 1881 legislation, however, carried a provision that the homesteads, which numbered more than six hundred across ten Wisconsin counties, would remain tax-free for just twenty-five years.[14] In 1906, when the land became taxable, few Ho-Chunk understood their tax liability and many did not pay their taxes. Land companies began buying up Ho-Chunk parcels that lapsed into foreclosure, and the majority of Ho-Chunk homesteads were lost.

By the turn of the century, the Ho-Chunk had moved into the commercial cranberry market. Where once tribal members had gathered cranberries extensively

Yellow Thunder, Ho-Chunk chief, circa 1880. Yellow Thunder is believed to be the first Ho-Chunk who took up a homestead in western Wisconsin.
Courtesy of Jolley's, Portage City, Wisconsin; WHi Image ID 27886

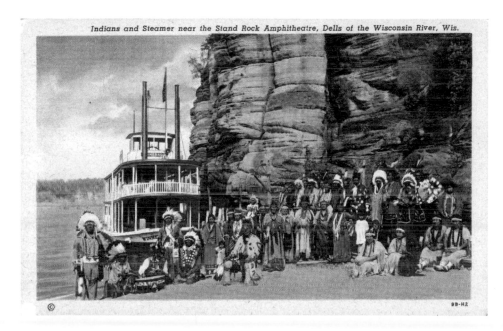

Indians and Steamer near the Stand Rock Amphitheatre, Dells of the Wisconsin River, Wis.

Ho-Chunk tribal members in Wisconsin Dells, circa 1915. Postcards produced as early as 1890 suggest that the Ho-Chunk took an active role in Dells tourism.
WHi Image ID 34535

for trade and personal use, now fences and private property signs marked their ancestral fields as belonging to white growers. Many Ho-Chunk went to work in the cranberry industry, only to be classified as migrant farmworkers by the federal government. This was another stroke of bad luck for the Ho-Chunk. During the Great Depression of the 1930s, after government reformers instituted Social Security, Ho-Chunk elders who had worked for decades in the fields were ineligible for retirement benefits because their employers had not withheld Social Security payments from their paychecks.[15]

Tourism also played an important role in the lives of Ho-Chunk members, especially in the area known today as the Wisconsin Dells. In the early 1900s, tourists and vacationers who had seen and heard of the unsurpassed natural beauty of the river and its sandstone outcroppings began to arrive by train from Chicago, Milwaukee, the Twin Cities, and elsewhere. The Ho-Chunk were hired to entertain the tourists with traditional songs and dances at the Stand Rock Ceremonial and sold souvenirs: wood carvings, picture postcards, and distinctive baskets woven of black ash.

Like other Indians in Wisconsin, the Ho-Chunk faced intense pressure to assimilate. Christianity had been introduced as early as 1670 when French Jesuit Claude Jean Allouez established a mission at the mouth of the Oconto River. Other Catholic missions followed in Prairie du Chien and Polonia in Portage County. In 1878, the Evangelical Reformed Church began a mission school near Black River Falls. Six years later, Norwegian Lutherans established a mission and boarding school a few miles from Wittenberg in Shawano County. Tension between these contending Protestants and Catholics eventually led to a reorganization of the Indian boarding school program. The government phased out subsidies to sectarian schools and opened more of its own boarding schools, including the Tomah Indian Industrial School. Present-day Ho-Chunk literature suggests that economic interests also played a part in this missionary fervor: "The missionaries vied with each other for souls, and for Indian school contracts."[16]

A government school opened at Tomah in January 1893 with seven employees and six students, all of them Ho-Chunk. Until 1934, when it closed, the Tomah School provided both an academic curriculum and manual training, along with music, athletics, religious instruction, and military training. By 1901, it had grown to two dozen teachers and 173 students—23 over capacity. Of all the government boarding schools in Wisconsin, Tomah had perhaps the best reputation. Its superintendent, Ludley M. Compton, was a member of the Indian Rights Association and made a practice of hiring Indian staff, including teachers. But despite the relatively tolerant culture Compton established, school officials discouraged

Ho-Chunk children from speaking their Native language and expressing their traditional culture. Often children as young as six were placed in the Tomah School and prevented from returning home until after they graduated from high school. Inevitably the experience resulted in family and community disassociation. A century later, many Ho-Chunk still wonder: was the education worth the price?[17]

In 1934, when under the Indian Reorganization Act (IRA) tribes were offered the opportunity to create constitutional governments, the Ho-Chunk declined. An effort in the US Court of Claims in 1928 to obtain redress for past wrongs had failed, and many Ho-Chunk were unwilling to accept IRA funds until their claim against the United States was settled. In 1946, tribal members elected a committee to bring suit with the Nebraska Winnebago under the Indian Claims Commission Act. This panel evolved into the Acting Wisconsin Winnebago Business Committee (WWBC), which focused on meeting the health, education, housing, and welfare needs of tribal members. There was some question whether a nonreservation tribe such as the Ho-Chunk was even eligible for the IRA benefits of a constitutional government. However, in 1961 a sympathetic official in the administration of President John F. Kennedy found an obscure Ho-Chunk homestead that had been declared tribal trust land. "We formed [as a tribe] under forty acres of land that was underwater—almost swampland," recalled WWBC member Richard Day. "That's all the tribe had—forty acres that nobody owned, but the tribe did."[18]

With the encouragement of most Ho-Chunk and the assistance of Indian advocacy groups such as the National Congress of American Indians, the committee began work on a Ho-Chunk constitution, which established four branches of government: an Executive Council, a Legislative Council, a Judicial Council, and a General Council composed of all adult tribal members. The democratic ideals of the Ho-Chunk Nation are reflected in the sweeping powers delegated to the General Council, whose members can vote to set policy, reverse legislation and judicial policy, call special elections, and dis-enroll or reenroll members by a two-thirds majority vote.[19] In a referendum conducted in January 1963, Ho-Chunk from as far away as California overwhelmingly ratified the document. The tribal land base expanded in the 1960s when the Evangelical Reformed Church (now United Church of Christ) gave the

Civil War veteran James Bird (WeeJukeKah or MaKeSucheKaw), photographed circa 1900. The arrow emblem on his hat was the insignia of a Civil War Indian scout. James Bird was a private with Company A of the Omaha Scouts, a Civil War outfit comprising six white officers and seventy-two Ho-Chunk soldiers.

Photo by Charles Van Schaick; WHi Image ID 60634

Ho-Chunk its original church and mission property in Black River Falls. These 150 acres became the core of tribal trust land.

Then in 1974, the Ho-Chunk won a $4.6 million judgment from the Indian Claims Commission to compensate the tribe for its lands lost through fraudulent treaties. For elders, such as Bernadine Tallmadge, this compensation was too little and the resolution too dear: "Four point six million dollars, and you divide that among the Winnebago population. What did we get?" she asked. "We just sold our birthright."[20]

Today approximately 7,100 members of the Ho-Chunk Nation hold title to nearly 8,800 acres of land scattered across twenty Wisconsin counties.[21] Despite the difficulties of providing service to a far-flung population, the Nation operates scores of tribal programs, including health clinics, Head Start centers, and economic development activities in each of its communities. Much of the tribe's economic success has been fueled by profits from its six gaming facilities—in Lake Delton, Nekoosa, Black River Falls, Tomah, Wittenberg, and Madison. These in turn have allowed the Ho-Chunk to expand their enterprises to include hotels, restaurants, convenience stores, and gas stations, all of which contribute significantly to the local, tribal, and state economies.

In 1993, the Ho-Chunk reintroduced a small herd of bison to tribal trust lands along the Wisconsin River near Muscoda and later established a second herd on an organic ranch in Tomah. The Nation expanded the operations when it received a gift of twenty-five surplus animals from Badlands National Park. The herd grew to nearly 150 animals before concerns about the economy, the "fractured nature of the existing Ho-Chunk land base," and the animals' overall well-being led the Nation in 2010 to suspend its bison operations and sell its remaining stock. The Nation remains a member of the InterTribal Bison Cooperative and has not ruled out a return to bison ranching in the future if conditions become more favorable.[22]

Many Ho-Chunk members believe the greatest challenge facing the tribe remains their lack of a land base. In 1998, the Ho-Chunk applied to the General Services Administration (GSA) for acquisition of land surrounding the "mothballed" Badger Army Ammunition Plant near Baraboo—one of the most contaminated sites in Wisconsin.[23] The Ho-Chunk hoped the federal government would return nearly half of the 7,354 acres of surplus land around the

Harry Whitehorse, Ho-Chunk master carver and sculptor

Photo by Skot Weidemann Photography, courtesy of Whitehorse Gallery site, which the tribe intended to restore to prairie and use for bison habitat. However, other entities, including the US Department of Agriculture and the Wisconsin Department of Natural Resources, also requested portions of the land. In March 2007, the Ho-Chunk signed an agreement with the GSA to accept just over 1,500 acres. In 2011, tribal leaders were devastated when the Bureau of Indian Affairs (BIA) announced that it would not accept the parcel on behalf of the Ho-Chunk because of the contamination. "As a land claimant for excess federal land, we [the Nation] did everything right," Ho-Chunk president Jon Greendeer said in a statement. "We are extremely disappointed in the BIA's decision to deny the return of this important ancestral land to the Ho-Chunk Nation." In announcing that the Nation would give up its land claim, Greendeer commented on the relationships the nation had built with other units of government and stakeholders and promised to continue to support the "key values" of the reuse plan. "These include joint management of the BAAP, advocate for the highest quality cleanup, and protection of the natural resource," Greendeer said.[24]

Ho-Chunk ribbon appliqué adorns a black broadcloth skirt.
Wisconsin Historical Museum 1954.929

In 2001, the Ho-Chunk Nation drafted a ten-year strategic plan that identified self-determination and self-sufficiency as its two most important goals of the next decade. The plan called for a "viable, strong and balanced economic infrastructure" and a "decentralized decision-making approach." The plan, drafted by fourteen steering committee members through a series of surveys and public hearings, identified six long-term goals, including acquisition of an adequate tribal land base, elimination of tribal unemployment, and "generation of revenues by non-gaming tribal enterprises equal to or greater than those generated by gaming enterprises within five (5) years." Other goals included economic stability, funds for social services, and a focus on culture, history, and language.[25]

The Ho-Chunk have an unquestionable impact on the regional economy. The Nation operates casinos, bingo halls, several hotels, a convention center, and a six-plex movie theater, among other enterprises. Tribal government and the nation's economic ventures employ more than 3,300 Ho-Chunk and non-Ho-Chunk individuals, nearly 3,000 of them full-time, making the Nation one of the largest employers in Wisconsin.[26] In 2001, the Nation's payment to food, transportation, and other service vendors in Sauk County alone was nearly $4 million.[27]

Health continues to be a challenge for the Ho-Chunk Nation, which has the daunting responsibility for providing services to members flung out across twenty Wisconsin counties. It does this through two full-service health clinics in Black

Annual powwows on Memorial Day and Labor Day weekends draw hundreds of visitors to Andrew Blackhawk Memorial Pow Wow Grounds in Black River Falls.
Courtesy of Hocak Worak

River Falls and Baraboo; satellite health offices in LaCrosse, Tomah, Wittenberg, and Nekoosa; and a food distribution center in Black River Falls. Older Ho-Chunk members in particular have unique health challenges. A 1998 health study indicated that nearly half of Ho-Chunk over age fifty-five have type 2 diabetes. The number one reason for a visit to the tribe's health care center in Black River Falls, for example, is diabetes or diabetes-related problems.[28] The Nation is attempting to address these needs, not only through expanded health programs but also through five "nutrition sites," senior centers that offer balanced meals onsite as well as a home delivery program.[29]

Housing—another need identified in the tribe's ten-year strategic plan—saw sharp improvement in the 1990s, with the average number of new homeowners skyrocketing from nine in 1994 to eighty-eight in 2002.[30] In late summer 2005, the Nation held a ribbon-cutting ceremony at a thirty-six-unit apartment complex near Baraboo. The $5 million affordable housing project was just one of several that opened between 2000 and 2011.

In setting forth its long-term goals, the Nation paid particular attention to the needs of two groups: elders and veterans. In January 2008, tribal officials opened two new centers for the elderly in Wittenberg and Tomah. Each facility offered 7,300 square feet of meeting space, a kitchen and dining room, and a fitness area. Future plans to serve elders include two-bedroom assisted living units. Addressing the needs of the Nation's warriors, in September 2010 the Ho-Chunk Nation set up the Veterans Home Ownership program to provide housing to its veterans. The tribe established a $4 million restricted fund to augment dollars received from other state and federal veterans' programs.

The ability to leverage tribal dollars with outside grants to create a multiplier effect has brought positive change to the Nation. The period between 2007 and 2009 saw a 50 percent increase in grant awards, from just under $55 million to nearly $83 million. The grants paid for housing, social service programs, and education, among other needs.

The Ho-Chunk take particular pride in the educational achievements of their youth but still see room for improvement. According to a 2001 census, nearly 79 percent of tribal members have a high school diploma and more than 37 percent have graduated from college. However, like most other American Indian nations, the Ho-Chunk are alarmed by increasing dropout rates and declining literacy levels.[31] The strategic plan identified the need for more parental involvement as well as adult education that includes child care for nontraditional adult learners.

At the core of the Ho-Chunk long-range vision is a belief that culture and language can strengthen the Nation and prepare its members to meet the challenges of the future. The language "embodies the Tribe—its historical, cultural, and spiritual essence," as a former director of the language program stated.[32] Despite a 1994 study that found that only 9 percent of Ho-Chunk members were fluent in their language, and nearly all of those were elders over the age of sixty, the tribe is optimistic that revitalization efforts, based on models such as those developed by the Maori in New

Raising the Flags

Each Memorial Day, the Ho-Chunk honor both Native and non-Native veterans with a special flag-raising ceremony at Andrew Blackhawk Memorial Pow Wow Grounds in Black River Falls. Family and friends, each assigned a flagpole, slowly and reverently raise the colors to remember a warrior who has "walked on." Sometimes family members place a photograph, dog tags, or memorabilia at the base of their pole. In 2010, more than a hundred flags were raised, along with consciousness about the sacrifice veterans have made.

Each Memorial Day the Ho-Chunk Nation invites the families of Native and non-Native veterans to raise flags in their honor. A traditional powwow follows the ceremony.
Courtesy of *Hocak Worak*

The powwow that follows the flag-raising ceremony is usually one of the largest in Wisconsin. In 2010, nearly 450 dancers and twenty-five drum groups participated. In the grand entry that marks the beginning of the powwow, the American flag and Eagle Staff enter the arena first, along with the prisoner-of-war, missing-in-action, and tribal post flags. The first

continued on page 58

continued from page 57

dance is reserved for veterans, both Native and non-Native. Many of the dancers incorporate symbols of military service into their regalia— "semper fi" beaded into a belt; dog tags pinned onto a ribbon shirt; a breechcloth made of camouflage, and so forth. The Ho-Chunk have special songs honoring each branch of service.

The Ho-Chunk Nation sponsors another annual powwow on July 4, also known as Mitchell Red Cloud Day, to honor a tribal member who sacrificed his life to save his unit during the Korean Conflict and posthumously received the Medal of Honor. In 1957, the US Army renamed the headquarters of the Second Infantry Division in Korea Camp Red Cloud, and in 1999, the US Navy launched a ship bearing his name, the USS *Red Cloud*.[1]

Corporal Mitchell Red Cloud Jr.
Military Sealift Command

1. Patty Loew, *Way of the Warrior*, PBS documentary aired nationally in November 2007 and May 2011. For more on the flag-raising ceremony, see "2010 Memorial Day Traditional Pow Wow," *Hocak Worak*, June 11, 2010, 1.

Zealand, can save its language. In 2006, the Nation unveiled a promising "master-apprentice" program in which five teams, each made up of one teacher (usually an elder) and one learner, worked together for forty hours a week. The project was successful enough that five more apprentices were added the following year, and by 2012, a total of fourteen apprentices were in the program.[33]

Some of the elders and apprentices teach Ho-Chunk language courses in four school districts. The classes, taught in high schools in Black River Falls, Tomah, and Wisconsin Dells and at a charter middle school in Nekoosa—are open to both Ho-Chunk and non-Ho-Chunk children. Ho-Chunk speaker Henning Garvin believes that learning a language not one's own exposes students to other cultures and broadens their view. "When you learn another language, you really get to see another perspective on the world," he said. "I think that's vitally important in today's age."[34]

5 OJIBWE

The Anishinaabe remember a time when they lived "on the shore of the Great Salt Water in the East." In the words of Ojibwe medicine man Edward Benton-Banai, their numbers were so great that "if one was to climb the highest mountain and look in all directions, they would not be able to see the end of the nation."[1] This eastern domain, however, had not always been their home. According to oral tradition, their original homes were in the Great Lakes region, where long ago the Creator, Gichi-manidoo, had placed them on the last of the Four Worlds he created. He taught them everything they needed to know and gave them medicines to keep them healthy.

Over time, however, the people lost their way and began to quarrel among themselves, so Gichi-manidoo told them to leave.

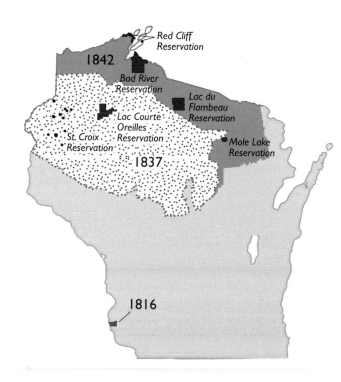

OJIBWE

RED CLIFF
2010 population: 5,312
1854 Treaty: 7,321 acres
1978: 7,267 acres (5,122 tribally owned)
1999: 7,962 acres (6,181 tribally owned)
2010: 14,541 acres (6,404 tribally owned)

BAD RIVER
2010 population: 7,000+
1854 Treaty: 124,332 acres
1978: 41,802 acres (8,235 tribally owned)
1999: 56,283 acres (20,166 tribally owned)
2010: 125,000+ acres

LAC DU FLAMBEAU
2010 population: 3,415
1854 Treaty: 70,000 acres
1978: 50,479 acres (25,152 tribally owned)
1999: 44,947 acres (30,507 tribally owned)
2010: 86,600 acres (39,403 tribally owned)

LAC COURTE OREILLES
2010 population: 7,275
1854 Treaty: 70,000 acres
1978: 30,529 acres (3,945 tribally owned)
1999: 47,944 acres (22,869 tribally owned)
2010: 76,465 acres (24,364.89 tribally owned)

ST. CROIX OJIBWE
2010 population: 2,909
1934 Land Grant: 1,700 acres
1978: 1,817 acres (1,200 tribally owned)
1999: 2,712 acres (2,712 tribally owned)
2010: 4,689 acres (2,126 tribally owned)

SOKAOGON (MOLE LAKE)
2010 population: 1,377
1934 Land Grant: 1,700 acres
1978: 1,700 acres (1,700 tribally owned)
1999: 1,731 acres (1,731 tribally owned)
2010: 4,904.2 acres (Reservation: 1,930 acres)

They migrated east and were gone so long they forgot the way home. Sometime later, speaking through a prophet, Gichi-manidoo told them it was time to return. They were to follow a Sacred Shell that would lead them to seven stopping places and, ultimately, to the "food that grows on water."

Perhaps as early as 1500 BP, the Anishinaabe, an alliance that includes the Ojibwe, Potawatomi, and Odaawa, left their homes along the Atlantic seaboard and traveled west. Among their stopping places were Gichi-gakaabikaang—a powerful place of "water and thunder" known today as Niagara Falls—and Bawatig, an excellent fishing area, which the French later renamed Sault Ste. Marie. The Anishinaabe continued on to the site of present-day Duluth to a place known as "Spirit Island" and explored the south shore of Lake Superior. There, according to oral tradition, they found Manoomin, meaning wild rice, the "food that grows on water." They also found their final resting stop: an island they called Mo-ning-wun-a-kawn-ing, translated as either "the place that was dug" or "the place of the gold-breasted woodpecker." In 1792, the eldest daughter of White Crane, the hereditary chief of the Crane Clan, married French fur trader Michel Cadotte and took the Christian name Madeleine. The Ojibwe renamed the island in her honor.

According to a copper plate belonging to Chief Tagwagane of the Crane Clan, the Ojibwe had arrived on Madeline Island well before Columbus encountered the New World. Tagwagane's ancestors had carved a notch with each passing generation. By 1844, nine indentations had been incised on the copper plate. Using a conservative life expectancy figure of 40 years, approximately 360 years had passed since the Ojibwe had established a village on Madeline Island. According to this same medallion, the Ojibwe had encountered—or at least heard about—whites a decade or more before Jean Nicolet arrived in present-day Green Bay in 1634. Near the third notch, someone from that generation had etched the figure of a man in a large hat. The figure may have been Étienne Brûlé, who is believed to have explored Lake Superior in 1622.[2]

The Ojibwe enthusiastically embraced the French people who arrived after Brûlé and Nicolet. These European traders brought the Ojibwe marvelous new items: metal axes, iron cooking kettles, bright-colored cloth, and glass beads. They also introduced them to guns, which not only enabled the Ojibwe to become more efficient hunters but also gave them an advantage over their enemies, especially the Bwaanag, as the Ojibwe referred to the Dakota, with whom they fought for control of the rice beds.

Life among the Ojibwe bands, then as now, was organized around the seasons. In early spring the Ojibwe processed maple sugar or syrup. The sap began to run when the temperatures turned warm: still freezing at night, but forty or fifty degrees during the day. The Ojibwe tapped the trees and collected the liquid in buckets made of birch bark. They slow-boiled the sap over a fire until it turned to sugar, which was eaten alone, mixed into other foods, or stored for use throughout the year. A month and a half to two months later it was time to spear fish. Although the Ojibwe speared different kinds of fish, walleye were among the favorites. After the female fish laid their eggs in the gravelly shallows and returned to deeper water—usually when the water temperature was between forty-two and forty-five degrees—the males spread their milt and lingered near the shoreline, making them a readily available food source.[3] The Ojibwe ate them fresh, dried them for later use, and often shared them with elders or saved them for feasts and other community gatherings.

In summer, Ojibwe men fished intensively and hunted minimally, while the women gathered nuts, berries, and other foods and planted gardens in which they grew corn, beans, squash, and potatoes. In late summer, the Ojibwe gathered to prepare the wild rice beds. A few weeks before the harvest in some communities, Ojibwe families marked a section of the bed as belonging to a particular family. Although there was no formal system of private property, families returned to the same sections of rice beds year after year and reseeded their areas so they would have a crop the next year. Others respected the right of each family to harvest in a particular place.[4]

It appears that Ojibwe women traditionally did most of the ricing, although in 1942 a Lac Courte Oreilles elder insisted that "in the old days" men were responsible for the harvest. After the rice ripened, the Ojibwe paddled their canoes to the rice beds. With one person poling

A Chippewa (Ojibwe) sugar camp as depicted by Seth Eastman around 1850

Sketch by Seth Eastman, from *The Indian Tribes of the United States*, edited Francis S. Drake, 1881; WHi Image ID 9829

Ojibwe spearfishing in winter

WHi Image ID 95718

or slowly paddling through the beds, the other, using two lightweight sticks, gently "knocked" the rice kernels from the stalks into the floor of the canoe. The Ojibwe then spread the rice on woven mats for a day or two to remove the moisture.

From there the Ojibwe either dried the rice on scaffolds over slow-burning fires or parched it on hot stones in fire pits. Men or boys in clean moccasins then undertook the strenuous task of "dancing" the rice—treading on it in clay-lined tramping pits—in order to loosen the chaff from the kernel. Finally, the Ojibwe placed the rice in shallow birch bark winnowing baskets to separate the broken husks from the kernels. Wild rice—technically not rice at all, but rather an aquatic grass—was used in soups, stews, pancakes, and jerky. Nutritionally, it was vital to the Ojibwe diet. Spiritually and culturally, it was the embodiment of their covenant with the Creator, who had led them to the Food that Grows on Water.[5]

During the wintertime, the Ojibwe hunted white-tailed deer and trapped for beaver, fisher, otter, and other fur-bearing animals. Pelts, maple syrup, processed rice, and crops from their gardens became principal trade items, binding the Ojibwe to the voyageurs, who moved between Indian communities and brokered items between the tribes and the French.

The affection between the French and the Ojibwe was so unqualified that the Ojibwe assimilated the French into their communities and adopted them into their families. They encouraged intermarriage, even absorbing the children of these unions into the tribe's warrior clan, the Marten Clan. As animosities between the French and English crept farther west into the western Great Lakes region, the Ojibwe—bound by friendship and kinship—offered the French their military support. Throughout the seventeenth century the Ojibwe fought alongside their allies against the English and their confederates, the Five Nations, or Haudenosaunee.

Madeline Island, with its major trading post at La Pointe, according to oral history was not only the economic headquarters of the Ojibwe Nation but also its spiritual center.[6] The Three Fires, as the Anishinaabe referred to their religious alliance, returned to the island at various times of the year to conduct Midewiwin, or Grand Medicine Lodge ceremonies. The Midewiwin, through its songs, stories, and rituals, embodied the spiritual heritage of the Anishinaabe and offered a code of conduct to keep them culturally rooted and physically and spiritually healthy.

After Nicolet's visit, Jesuit missionaries began visiting the island, and in 1665 Father Claude Jean Allouez established his Saint Esprit Mission near there, most likely near present-day Washburn. Although

Ojibwe beaded buckskin moccasins
Wisconsin Historical Museum 1954.241,A

the "Black Coats," as the Jesuits were called, tried to convert the Ojibwe to Christianity, these early efforts were largely unsuccessful. Pressures, perhaps caused by an expanding population and the depletion of natural resources, led various bands of Ojibwe to leave the island in search of fish, game, and wild rice. These were the ancestors of the distinct Ojibwe bands that exist in Wisconsin today.

As the fur trade depleted the fur-bearing animals along the south shore of Lake Superior, the Ojibwe began pushing farther inland in search of pelts. This brought them into increasing conflict with the Sac and Fox and the Dakota. With guns acquired from the French, the Ojibwe had a distinct advantage over these two tribes, who still relied primarily on war clubs and bows and arrows. Each winter, the Ojibwe traveled west to the St. Croix and Chippewa River Valleys to hunt deer, moose, elk, and other fur-bearing animals in the game-rich forests. Each spring they returned to La Pointe for Midewiwin ceremonies.

The Ojibwe had an intense relationship with the Dakota, sometimes warring with them, sometimes coexisting peacefully. During periods of amity, Ojibwe men and women intermarried with the Dakota. Today their descendants, along the east and west banks of the Mississippi River, reflect the intermingling of cultures. Often, however, the two nations fought bitterly. Throughout the French and English fur trade periods, the Ojibwe and the Dakota viewed each other with suspicion. By the early nineteenth century, diplomacy between the two tribes had broken down to the point that attacks and reprisals were almost continuous. In 1825, the United States invited the Ojibwe, Dakota, and other Indian nations in what would become the state of Wisconsin to meet at Prairie du Chien, ostensibly to negotiate a treaty of "peace and friendship." In actuality, the federal government was interested in stabilizing the area for western expansion and acquiring land from various Indian nations. However, before it could begin cession treaties, it first had to establish tribal boundaries. Ojibwe-Dakota enmity was a convenient pretext for the acquisition of Ojibwe land.

Entering into treaties with the Ojibwe was no easy task. Because of the autonomous nature of the bands, the Ojibwe did not have one principal chief with whom federal officials could negotiate. Unlike a European monarchy, each Ojibwe band had several leaders and headmen who "governed" by consent of the people rather than by authority. "I do not speak altogether of my own mind," the young St. Croix war chief Lone Man told the assembly at Prairie du Chien, "but listen to the words of the collected chiefs." The 1825 treaty itself is clear evidence of the decentralized nature of Ojibwe politics. No fewer than forty-one Ojibwe "chiefs" and headmen signed the document.[7]

View of the 1825 treaty negotiation held at Prairie du Chien, September 1825

Sketch by J. O. Jewis, from Thomas L. McKenney's *Sketches of a Tour to the Lakes, 1827,* WHi Image ID 3142

Although it is not clear that the Ojibwe leaders who signed the treaty at Prairie du Chien in 1825 were aware of the government's motives at the time, within twelve years they began to understand the full implications of entering into treaties with the United States. In 1830, President Andrew Jackson signed the Indian Removal Act, by which the United States claimed to have the authority to move tribes east of the Mississippi River to lands set aside for them in the West. The Ojibwe nervously watched as dozens of tribes, including other Anishinaabe—the Potawatomi—were forcibly removed from their homelands.

Federal negotiators used not-so-subtle means of coercing concessions from the Ojibwe. A year after the Prairie du Chien council, federal negotiators met the Ojibwe at Fond du Lac. Before the talks began, soldiers, who drilled, paraded, and demonstrated their firepower for the Ojibwe, provided a clear message. "You have never seen your great father's arm [the military]," one commissioner told the Ojibwe, "only a bit, and a very little bit, of his little finger." In addition to their weak military position in comparison to the federal government, the Ojibwe understood how their decentralized political structure placed them at a disadvantage: "We are a distracted people," Naudin (The Wind) told territorial governor Henry Dodge, "and have no regular system of acting together."

The treaty meeting at
Fond du Lac, 1826
Sketch by J. O. Jewis, from
Thomas L. McKenney's
*Sketches of a Tour to the
Lakes, 1827*; WHi Image
ID 95720

In the treaties of 1837 and 1842, the Ojibwe were forced to concede vast acres of land: nearly two-thirds of present-day northern Wisconsin, a portion of central Minnesota, and much of Michigan's Upper Peninsula. Historian David Wrone estimated that the Ojibwe gave up 170 billion board feet of timber, 150 billion tons of iron ore, and fifteen thousand lakes, as well as rivers, ports and power sites.[8] In exchange for the land given up in the two treaties, the Ojibwe received $19,000 in annuities, $67,000 in goods and services, and $115,000 for mixed-blood Ojibwe.[9] It is revealing, but perhaps not surprising, that the lion's share of payment in the two treaties, including $75,000 in the 1842 treaty, went to claimants associated with John Jacob Astor's American Fur Company. Treaty commissioner Robert Stuart, a former employee of the company, "used heavy-handed tactics to secure the treaty" and award funds to Astor, his former employer and close friend.[10] There is evidence the Ojibwe believed they were merely leasing the land, not selling it. In 1864, an Ojibwe delegation to Washington delivered its written version of the 1837 treaty negotiations, in which the Ojibwe insisted they had sold the timber rights, not the rights to the land itself: "From the usual height of cutting a tree down and upwards to the top is what I sell you, I reserve the root of the tree." In the 1837 treaty minutes, Chief Ma-ghe-ga-bo declared: "Of all the country that we grant you we wish to hold on to a tree [maple] where we get our living, & to reserve the streams where we drink the waters that give us life."[11]

PICTOGRAPH. A.   Pl. 60

SYMBOLIC PETITION OF CHIPPEWA CHIEFS,
presented at Washington, January 28ᵗʰ 1849, headed by Oshcabawis of Monomonecau. Wisconsin.

Nineteenth-century petition from Ojibwe clan chiefs. The animal figures represent clan leaders, the thick line represents Lake Superior, and the four small ovals represent the rice beds. This petition indicates that the Ojibwe are of one mind and one heart and do not wish to be removed from their wild rice beds near Lake Superior.

From *Historical and Statistical Information Respecting the History of the Indian Tribes . . .* , Vol. I, Henry Rowe Schoolcraft, 1851; WHi Image ID 1871

The Ojibwe negotiators were also concerned about protecting the interests of future generations. In both the 1837 and 1842 treaties, the Ojibwe clearly reserved the right to hunt, fish, and gather on the land they ceded the United States government. Article 5 of the 1837 treaty stated: "The privilege of hunting, fishing and gathering the wild rice, upon the lands, the rivers and the lakes included in the territory ceded, is guarantied [*sic*] to the Indians, during the pleasure of the President of the United States." Likewise article 2 of the 1842 treaty states: "The Indians stipulate for the right of hunting on the ceded territory, with the other usual privileges of occupancy, until required to remove by the President of the United States." The Ojibwe had been promised they would not be removed as long as they did not "misbehave." As they were to learn a mere six years later, this was a hollow promise.

By 1848, rumors that the Ojibwe would be removed to Minnesota had reached tribal leaders. From La Pointe, Chief Buffalo sent out runners to see if there had been any transgressions—to ask if the Ojibwe had, in fact, committed any "depredations" and broken the terms of the treaty. No such infractions were reported.

On February 6, 1850, at the urging of Commissioner of Indian Affairs William Medill, President Zachary Taylor signed the dreaded removal order. Although government officials insisted that they could better protect the Ojibwe from "injurious contact" with whites by moving them to Minnesota Territory, there were other motivations. Western expansionists believed the peaceful Ojibwe could be used as a buffer between white settlers and the more unpredictable Sioux. Minnesotans eagerly eyed the patronage jobs that accompanied Indian agencies, along with Indian annuities that sustained a corrupt network of white politicians, traders, and businessmen.

In an effort to coerce the Ojibwe to move, federal officials ordered that the 1850 annuity payments, normally paid at La Pointe—the centrally located heart of the Ojibwe Nation—instead be made at Sandy Lake, Minnesota. Of the estimated 5,500 Ojibwe who traveled hundreds of miles to claim those annuities, more than 150 died at Sandy Lake in the late fall and winter of 1850, mostly from measles, dysentery, or exposure. Another 250 died on the return trip.[12] "Our women and children do indeed cry, our Father, on account of their suffering from cold and hunger," Chief Buffalo dictated in an 1851 letter sent to the Commissioner of Indian Affairs. "We wish to . . . be permitted to remain here where we were promised we might live, as long as we were not in the way of the Whites."

For the next two years, Ojibwe chiefs and headmen begged Washington officials to reconsider the removal order. In spring 1852, Chief Buffalo, who was then ninety-three years old, traveled by foot, canoe, and railroad to Washington to plead his people's case. Buffalo managed to get an audience with President Millard Fillmore and persuaded him to smoke the peace pipe. He and Chief

Annuity payment to the Ojibwe at La Pointe on Madeline Island, circa 1852
WHi Image ID 48581

Chief Buffalo, Principal Chief of the Ojibwe. In 1852, Buffalo traveled to Washington, DC, and persuaded President Millard Fillmore to rescind an earlier order removing the Ojibwe to Sandy Lake, Minnesota. Buffalo was instrumental in securing four of the six Ojibwe reservations in Wisconsin.

WHi Image ID 3957

Ozhoge explained that the Ojibwe had been told in both the 1837 and 1842 treaties that the government was interested not in the land, but only in the pine and minerals. In their minds they had never ceded the land itself. It is unclear whether Fillmore himself rescinded the removal order or told the delegation that Minnesota governor Alexander Ramsey would rescind it.[13] However, the Ojibwe believed that they explicitly had been told that removal would not happen and that the process of setting up permanent reservations for the Ojibwe would begin. Buffalo, Ozhoge, and the four other members of their party returned by rail and steamship to St. Paul, Minnesota, and then went overland to Lake Superior. Along the way, they spread the news to various Ojibwe bands, which "caused great rejoicing." The celebration continued the following year, when the new administration, headed by Franklin Pierce, reinstated annuity payments at La Pointe.[14]

In 1854, although there was excitement and relief, the Ojibwe were wary. Chief Na-gon-ab no doubt spoke for many when he told the commissioners that the Ojibwe felt that they were misled by the 1837 and 1842 treaties. "Does the great father tell the truth?" he asked. "Does he keep his promises?" Na-gon-ab, a noted orator and principal chief of the Fond du Lac Band, told the assembly that the Ojibwe had committed the treaty to memory and had kept faithfully to it. Their memorized version differed from the written version—the "black marks," as he put it:

> You go to your black marks and say this is what those men put down; this is what they said when they made the treaty. The men we talk with don't come back; they do not come and you tell us they did not tell us so. We ask where they are? You say you do not know or that they are dead and gone.

During the 1854 negotiations—the final treaty that Ojibwe in Wisconsin would sign with the United States—tribal leaders were insistent on two provisions: first, that they establish reservations at "different points of the country that would suit their convenience," and second, that the needs of future Ojibwe generations be met.[15]

As a result of the negotiations, the Ojibwe created four reservations in Wisconsin: Bad River (124,332 acres), Lac Courte Oreilles (70,000 acres), Lac du Flambeau (70,000 acres), and Red Cliff (originally 2,560 acres but later expanded by

Congress to 7,321). Of the millions of acres that represented the original Ojibwe homeland, after the 1854 treaty fewer than 275,000 acres remained. As they had in the earlier treaties, the Ojibwe in the 1854 negotiations insisted on the right to hunt, fish, and gather in the land they had ceded: "And such of them as reside in the territory hereby ceded, shall have the right to hunt and fish therein, until otherwise ordered by the President." The wisdom of the Ojibwe leaders in reserving this right for future generations would become evident more than a century later.

The signature page of the 1854 treaty reflects the shifting political identities of the Ojibwe bands and is significant not only for which names appear, but also for *where* the names appear. Leaders of the St. Croix, including Ayaabens (Little Buck), and the Sokaogon, represented by Gichi-waabizheshi (Great Marten), were listed under the Lac Courte Oreilles section.[16] Another Sokaogon delegate, Nigig (The Otter), signed under the Lac du Flambeau section. The confusion may partially explain why both bands failed to secure reservations in the 1854 treaty and would remain landless for nearly eighty years. By reducing the Ojibwe to just four reservations in Wisconsin, the federal government attempted to consolidate the Ojibwe and impose new generalized identities on tribal members. In this vision of containment, the residents of Yellow River, Mud Lake, and Old Post did not have distinct band identities but rather became simply Lac Courte Oreilles.

The size of the Bad River Reservation suggests that federal officials may have expected that the Ojibwe who were left out of the treaty, including the scattered bands along the St. Croix River, would attach themselves to the Ojibwe at Bad River. Although some of the distinctiveness that then marked each band has been lost to time, it is important to understand that differences did exist and sometimes shaped how the bands responded to historical challenges, especially in regard to their treaty rights.

The bands did share the pain of common experiences, such as forced assimilation through allotment and Indian boarding schools. In 1887, Congress passed the General Allotment Act by which reservation land was divided in severalty and allotted to individual tribal members in eighty-acre parcels. In actuality, the act had little relevance to the Indian Nations in Wisconsin, most of which had already received their allotments. To ensure that the new Native landowners would be exposed to the supposed "civilizing" effects of the Christian work ethic, Indian lands that remained after federal officials completed the allotment process were sold to whites. Although Indian land was supposed to be held in trust for twenty-five years, during which time Native people could not sell their allotments, the government made exemptions for Indians judged "competent"—meaning they could read and write English and make informed decisions about their property.

FIRST PEACE COUNCIL EVER HELD BETWEEN CHIPPEWAS AND SIOUXS, "BUFFALO BILL" PEACE MAKER.

William "Buffalo Bill" Cody in Ashland in 1896, during negotiations for the "Peace Treaty" he helped arrange between the Ojibwe and the Sioux
WHi Image ID 95716

During the trust period, a surprising number of Ojibwe became "competent" enough to lose their land. By the time allotment ended in 1934, the allotment policy had reduced the Ojibwe land base in Wisconsin from 271,653 to 160,561 acres—a loss of more than 40 percent.

The boarding school experience did to Ojibwe culture what allotment had done to Ojibwe land. As early as 1856, Ojibwe children were taken from their homes and placed in government boarding schools, where school officials discouraged them from speaking their language or practicing their traditional religions and customs. Through much of the late nineteenth and early twentieth centuries, Ojibwe parents had no say in which schools their children would attend. Most Ojibwe children went to one of three government-run schools, in Hayward, Tomah, or Lac du Flambeau. Some went to parochial schools, such as St. Mary's School, run by the Franciscan Sisters of Perpetual Adoration on the Bad River Reservation. Other children were sent as far away as the Carlisle Indian School in Pennsylvania, where they received instruction in a quasi-military atmosphere. Most of the schools in Wisconsin patterned themselves after the Carlisle model, providing a half-day of academic instruction and a half-day of manual training. As one critic complained in 1914, "When an Indian is 14 years of age and enters a white school, he is practically only as far advanced as a child who would be in knickerbockers."[17]

To be sure, some Ojibwe were able to rise above the mediocrity of Indian board-ing schools and enter professional fields. The vast majority, however, became part of a growing underclass of young Indian adults with marginal skills. Indian men became hired farmhands or laborers. Indian women entered domestic service. A formal system of exploitation, known as the "outing system," solidified this mar-ginalization. Instead of returning to their homes during summer vacation, board-ing school students worked for exploitive wages in white homes. "For the present I will pay her $1.25 per week as I consider that this is all she is worth to me," said Mrs. J. T. Martin of Lucy, an eighteen-year-old Ojibwe girl from the Lac du Flam-beau School. "I think the Indian girls naturally slow and this of course is a hard fault to overcome." For that dollar and a quarter—less than half the wage paid to white Midwestern domestics—Lucy was expected to work twelve hours a day, six days a week.[18]

Throughout the difficult years of forced assimilation, the Ojibwe struggled not only to construct their identities as new Americans, but also to maintain their identities as Native Americans and members of their distinct bands. It is a remark-able achievement and a tribute to the persistence of culture that six Ojibwe com-munities survived the intense pressure on their lands and traditional teachings to maintain their tribal identity in Wisconsin.

LAC COURTE OREILLES

In about 1745, three brothers of the Bear Clan led their families to Odaawa Zaaga'igan, an abandoned Odaawa (Ottawa) camp on the east shore of Lac Courte Oreilles near present-day Hayward, and established a permanent village. There are two versions of the story. In one, the clan traveled to the large lake, where they found the frozen body of an Odaawa Indian. Believing this to be a powerful sign, they pitched their lodges not far from the spot and established their village. In the other, more accepted version, a young member of the clan died during the winter. Unable to bury the child because of the hardness of the ground, the griev-ing family stayed with the body to protect it from wolves and scavengers. Spring turned to summer, and the clan decided to make the area its permanent home. Additional Ojibwe families gravitated to the area, settled on the west fork of the Chippewa River, and named their settlement *Bakweyawaa*, a geographical term to describe a bay or lake on a river. To the French, however, *Bakweyawaa* was known as *Lac Courte Oreilles*—"Ottawa Lake." The term "Courte Oreilles" (short ears) is an old French Canadian slang term for the Odaawa.[19] From Lac Courte

Indian veterans return to the Lac Courte Oreilles Reservation following World War I. The Ojibwe joined twelve thousand Native soldiers who volunteered for service even though they were not citizens.
WHi Image ID 35070

Logging on the Lac Courte Oreilles Ojibwe Reservation, 1909
WHi Image ID 39615

Oreilles, the Ojibwe pushed farther west to the Mississippi River and established other Ojibwe settlements along the St. Croix River.

Before the 1854 treaty, which established the Lac Courte Oreilles Reservation, Chief Akiwenzii (The Old Man) was said to have walked the perimeter of the lands he had chosen for his people's reservation, taking great care to choose those that contained the most productive rice beds. The band's precious resource, however, soon fell victim to competing interests: logging, flood control, and the desire for hydroelectric power. Soon after the Ojibwe land cessions, timber companies began cutting down the pine forests near the Lac Courte Oreilles Reservation. After allotment, the Bureau of Indian Affairs granted contracts to lumber companies to cut timber on the reservation itself. Since it was cheaper to float the logs than to transport them overland to sawmills downstream, lumber companies and even some Ojibwe constructed dams to control the water flow along the Chippewa River and its tributaries.

The need for flood control and hydroelectric power grew with the lumber towns and farming communities that sprang up along the Chippewa River downriver from the Lac Courte Oreilles. Beginning in 1912, the Wisconsin-Minnesota Light & Power Company (W-MLP) began acquiring the permits and property necessary to build a massive dam that would flood 5,600 acres of reservation land, inundating maple groves, cranberry bogs, wild rice beds, cemeteries, and the village of Pahquahwong itself.

The company promised to move Indian graves to an upland site and build a new village on higher ground. It also promised to replant the rice beds and compensate the Ojibwe for the loss of their annual harvest. The Lac Courte Oreilles vehemently objected. Over the next decade, tribal leaders used every legal and administrative means possible to block the dam. On

August 8, 1921, however, the Federal Power Commission, over the objections of the tribe, granted a fifty-year license to build and operate the dam.

Two years later, the floodgates closed and reservation lands began to fill with water. By late summer of 1923, twenty-five feet of water covered the village of Pahquahwong and the resources that had sustained it for nearly two centuries. The company had broken its promises. When the remains of hundreds of deceased Ojibwe began washing ashore, a horrified community learned that seven hundred Indian graves were left behind. Further, the water level in the newly created impoundment fluctuated dramatically, making it impossible to sustain new rice beds. The Ojibwe learned a sad truth about the reservoir that became known as the Chippewa Flowage: "The food that grows on water" could not grow on this water.[20]

Children at the drum during the Winter Dam Protest at Lac Courte Oreilles, 1971. LCO members, aided by members of the American Indian Movement (AIM), took over the dam to protest a lease extension for Northern States Power Company. The occupation ended with NSP granting concessions to the LCO tribe.
WHi Image ID 35211

LAC DU FLAMBEAU

Sometime before 1745, Zhedewish, a chief of the Crane Clan, led his extended family to the headwaters of the Wisconsin River, near Lac Vieux Desert. After the Ojibwe pushed the Meskwaki Indians west, Zhedewish's son, Giishkiman (Sharpened Stone), continued his father's mission. In their lightweight birch bark canoes, Giishkiman's band followed the river south, paddling and portaging to the maze of interlocking lakes and streams near present-day Minocqua. They established their village where the Bear River exits Flambeau Lake.

Girls at the Lac du Flambeau Boarding School, circa 1890
WHi Image ID 55938

WOJB Radio: "The Voice of the Ojibwe"

Jordan Gokey, WOJB development director and host of *Native Tuesday*
Photo by Patty Loew

On April 2, 1982, its first transmission was a blessing in Ojibwe. WOJB-FM was the first Native-owned and operated radio station in Wisconsin. "The Voice of the Ojibwe," as it was known in its early days, broadcast Native news and public affairs from the community and around the world. From traditional powwow music to works by contemporary artists, it introduced a generation of listeners to a broad range of multicultural issues and musicians. Over the years, through a network of hosts and volunteers, it widened its scope and evolved into a listener-supported community radio station. Tune in weekdays to 88.9 on the FM dial and you might learn about Indian sovereignty on *Native America Calling*, or listen to a recent Afro-pop or reggae release. On weekends, it might be National Public Radio's *Weekend Edition*; Native affairs and language; or honky-tonk, big band, and jazz.

Oral tradition tells of a nearly blind old man who taught the Ojibwe how to "fire hunt" for fish. At night, by the light of pitch-filled birch bark torches, the Ojibwe speared pike, suckers, and muskellunge, which became an important part of their diet. The Ojibwe called the fire hunters Waswaagan, and the community became known among the other bands as Was-waagaming. French fur traders who witnessed the spearing ritual called the village Lac du Flambeau, meaning "Lake of the Torches."

Lac du Flambeau remained an important center for trade, first for the French and then for the British, who established a year-round outpost on the lake in 1792. After the War of 1812, the American Fur Company moved in and continued to maintain a presence at Lac du Flambeau until 1842. After the 1854 treaty, federal officials surveyed the land and set aside three townships for the reservation, adding a fourth in 1866. The next twenty years brought railroad and stagecoach service. Soon, loggers, settlers, and entrepreneurs pushed into the region, drawn by its rich forests and myriad clear lakes.

By 1894, the Flambeau Lumber Company was cutting 30 million board feet of white pine timber annually on the reservation. In letters to Washington, tribal leaders continually complained that the company capriciously cut timber that did not belong to them and did not always honor the lumber contracts they had signed with tribal members. Furthermore, their Indian agent controlled their allotment money and allowed them just ten dollars a month in the form of a coupon redeemable only at Flambeau Lumber's "company store." The store itself, and the system it represented, created hardships for the tribe. At a US Senate hearing in 1909, Charles Headflyer, a Lac du Flambeau shop owner, told investigators that he sold flour for "ten cents cheaper than they were selling it at the company store" yet still could not compete. "I have a little store, trying to make a living, and all I got in the way of orders is $5 this whole summer."[21]

Much of the tribe's attention at the turn of the century was focused on the government boarding school, which was built in 1895 and was notorious for its heavy-handedness toward Indian children. Albert Cobe, who attended the school, recalled a small jail located behind the school near the road. Cobe remembered a mustached disciplinarian beating him with a length of garden hose after he tried to run away. A friend of his, who also tried to escape, was taken to the basement and ordered to crawl about on his hands and knees. Apparently, the mustached

Indian baseball team, Lac du Flambeau Indian Boarding School, 1925. During the boarding school era, Indian youth were discouraged from playing traditional games like lacrosse and encouraged to play more "civilized" sports like baseball. Nearly every Indian boarding school had baseball, basketball, and football teams.
WHi Image ID 2106

man forgot about the boy. "When morning came, we all filed downstairs for the shower, and found him on the floor, crying," Cobe remembered. "His hands and knees were all bloody."

The first few decades of the twentieth century were difficult ones for the Lac du Flambeau. Twin assaults on Ojibwe land and culture had weakened the band. When tourism replaced timber as the area's leading industry, some Ojibwe men found employment as hunting and fishing guides. Lac du Flambeau women earned income selling beadwork, weavings, and baskets to appreciative visitors. However, most tribal members found it difficult to eke out a living. By a variety of means—foreclosures, skullduggery, and their own naiveté—the Lac du Flambeau had lost much of their land base. White vacationers and resort owners now owned most of the tribe's prime waterfront property. More and more, the Lac du Flambeau found themselves outsiders on their own reservation.[22]

Old Abe the War Eagle

"Old Abe," the beloved mascot of the Eighth Wisconsin Regiment during the Civil War, was a bald eagle with strong ties to the Ojibwe. In spring 1861 Chief Sky of the Lac du Flambeau found two eaglets near the headwaters of the Flambeau River in Chippewa County. He traded one of them to a white farmer for a bushel of corn, and a few days later, the farmer sold him to Company C of the Eighth, which was mustering out of Eau Claire. The men of Company C, who chipped in ten cents apiece to buy him, built him a perch and in battle raised him along with the American flag.

"Old Abe" became the mascot of the Eighth Wisconsin Regiment during the Civil War. This card was sold to raise money for Soldiers' Home, a recuperation and housing facility for veterans in Milwaukee.
WHi Image ID 79111

Old Abe became a legend, inspiring the men of the Eighth and accompanying them into thirty-nine battles. Although he and his bearers became special targets of the Confederates (one of his bearers was killed), Old Abe was wounded just once—shot through the wing—

continued on page 77

RED CLIFF

Ojibwe who remained in the vicinity of Madeline Island after the Ojibwe diaspora in the mid-eighteenth century became known collectively as the La Pointe Band, named after the primary village on the island. Although most La Pointe Ojibwe did not permanently reside on the island, Madeline remained the "center of the earth" for them. The La Pointe Ojibwe actually represented more than a dozen bands that lived along Lake Superior's south shore and traveled back and forth to trade and to attend Midewiwin ceremonies.

Missionary activity among the Ojibwe, especially by Roman Catholic priests, intensified during the early nineteenth century. Some chiefs, including Buffalo, converted to Christianity. However, a majority of Ojibwe chiefs and headmen continued to follow the old ways. The 1854 treaty allowed the two factions to solidify a division that had been evolving for decades. The Christianized Ojibwe, under the leadership of Chief Buffalo, took up permanent residence near the red cliffs of Buffalo Bay adjacent to the tribe's traditional fishing grounds. The other group established themselves at Bad River, where the Ojibwe had planted gardens every year. Despite this physical separation, the two groups maintained cordial relations.

Buffalo's band settled on the 7,321 acres their chief had negotiated under terms of the 1854 treaty. The community relied heavily on fishing. Ojibwe women fashioned large gill nets from basswood, nettle, and other natural fibers. Men carved cedar floats and stone sinkers. Ojibwe fishermen, in birch bark canoes, set their nets on deepwater reefs far offshore. As early as 1830, tribal fishermen were providing the American Fur Company with lake trout and whitefish on a commercial basis. By 1837, the enterprise was producing more than two thousand barrels of fish a year.

With their small boats and handmade nets, the Red Cliff Ojibwe found it difficult to compete with the large commercial fleets that were attracted to the rich fishing waters of Superior's south shore. By the 1880s, the tribe's small fishing operation had fallen on hard times, and more and more tribal members worked for non-Indian fishing interests in nearby Bayfield.

In 1873, tribal logging began on the Red Cliff Reservation. After the commissioner of Indian Affairs approved construction of a sawmill, members of the Red Cliff Band began cutting timber for frame houses. In 1896, the Indian agent awarded a contract to the Red Cliff Lumbering Company, which harvested nine million board feet of white and Norway pine, hemlock, and spruce the following year. Many Red Cliff tribal members found employment as loggers, scalers, and millworkers. Within a decade, however, nearly all the timber was gone. Poor logging practices had left many thousands of acres littered with slash piles that were vulnerable to fire. The prohibitive cost of stump removal made the ravaged landscape expensive to clear and difficult to farm.

After the mill burned down in 1906, it was never rebuilt. Red Cliff Ojibwe found themselves on the downside of timber's boom-and-bust cycle. Some tribal members went to work for mining companies, mostly as woodchoppers and loaders. Others loaded and unloaded freighters for Great Lakes shipping companies. A few returned to fishing. Others supported themselves by working in non-Indian shops and factories or by hiring themselves out as farmhands.

By 1929, few Red Cliff Ojibwe even felt the effects of the Great Depression. Their economy had already been depressed for years. Ninety-five percent of tribal members had sold or lost their lands to foreclosures.[23]

continued from page 76

Ahgamahwegeszhig (Chief Sky), the Lac du Flambeau Ojibwe leader who found Old Abe as an eaglet
WHi Image ID 78915

but recovered fully. One of his bearers remembered that whenever generals, including Ulysses S. Grant and William Tecumseh Sherman, reviewed the troops and passed Old Abe, they would doff their caps, a gesture that elicited wild cheers from the regiment and screams from Old Abe. The mascot returned home safely and resided at the state capitol until his death in 1881. Were it not for a first-person account of Old Abe's exploits during the Civil War, we would not know that the legend of this original "Screaming Eagle" began in Lac du Flambeau.[1]

1. The first person account was delivered by David McLain, who bore Old Abe through many Civil War battles, to a meeting of the Dunn County Old Settlers Association at the turn of the twentieth century. The original manuscript, "That 'War Eagle' Had Quite a Record," was handed down through McLain's family and reprinted by the *Eau Claire Leader-Telegram* on July 4, 1976. http://users.ap.net/~chenae/oldabe4.html.

Environmental Warrior
Walter Bresette (1947–1999)

Walter Bresette (Red Cliff Ojibwe), author, journalist, environmental activist, and co-founder of the Wisconsin Greens and Midwest Treaty Support Network
Courtesy of the Great Lakes Indian Fish and Wildlife Commission

He was an author, a journalist, and a visionary. Walter Bresette mobilized Native and non-Native people around environmental issues and empowered them to organize themselves. Among the groups he founded or cofounded were the Wisconsin Greens, Lake Superior Greens, Midwest Treaty Network, Great Lakes Indigenous Network, Anishinaabeg Millennium Project, and Woodland Indian Craft Cooperative. Bresette found his voice during the Ojibwe treaty rights struggle and became one of the best-known proponents of tribal self-determination. Born and raised in Red Cliff, Bresette founded Witness for Nonviolence, a group that observed and documented civil rights abuses during the boat landing protests and whose presence was credited with helping to keep the peace. Bresette wrote about the group's involvement in *Walleye Warriors*, a book he coauthored with Rick Whaley.

continued on page 79

Joe Stoddard ricing on the Bad River Reservation, 1941
WHi Image ID 34567

BAD RIVER

When the so-called pagan La Pointe chiefs chose their 120,000-acre reservation site under terms of the 1854 treaty, they selected an area that contained 16,000 acres of high-quality wetlands, including the rich rice-producing Kakagon and Bad River Sloughs along Lake Superior's south shore. This was the area that had sustained the Ojibwe for generations. They called their settlement simply Odanah—the Ojibwe word for "village."

Simon Edward DeNomie (1895–1980), top right. The author's grandfather, Private "Ed" DeNomie (Bad River Ojibwe), 127th Infantry, Thirty-second "Red Arrow" Division, saw action in all seven major battles in which American Expeditionary Forces fought during World War I.
Wisconsin Veterans Museum

The attempt to separate themselves from their Christian relatives was not successful. In 1856, federal officials agreed to pay the American Board of Commissioners for Foreign Missions, which had established an ecumenical mission at Odanah some years earlier, $900 to educate eight boys and eleven girls. In a letter to the board, J. M. Gordon wrote: "An Indian needs to be taught subjection to authority, love of labor, and systematic industry in some useful employment to make a civilised man of him. Without these elements of character, mere book knowledge will do him no good. He

continued from page 78

His penchant for political theater was legendary. In 1991, during a mining protest, he once hopped the fence and "counted coup" on a giant earthmover with Black Hawk's war club. After the city of Ironwood, Michigan, was legally forced to allow a 1997 Ku Klux Klan rally, Bresette persuaded city officials to open the water mains after the rally and symbolically "cleanse" their streets of hate mongering.

Bresette was the principal architect of the Seventh Generation Amendment, an effort to create a constitutional amendment declaring clean air and water to be common property and a basic right for all. More than a decade after his death, the organizations he founded continue to function, and Native and non-Native environmentalists continue to push for the amendment. "He was like the north star," a close friend said after his passing. "He held up the sky over northern Wisconsin and the people followed him."[1]

1. Sandy Lyons, quoted in a remembrance posted to the Protect the Earth website, http://www.protecttheearth.org/Walter/aboutwalt8.htm.

Mother Earth Water Walk

Mother Earth Water Walk, Bad River, 2011. On June 12, 2011, Anishinaabe water bearers carrying water from the Pacific Ocean, Gulf of Mexico, Atlantic Ocean, and Hudson Bay converged on the Bad River Reservation, where the water was comingled and ceremoniously returned to Lake Superior.
Photo by Patty Loew

They arrived from the Four Directions, carrying saltwater from their homelands. On June 12, 2011, Water Women of the Midewiwin, the traditional spiritual society of the Anishinaabe, converged at Bad River for a ceremony in which saltwaters from the Atlantic and Pacific Oceans, Hudson Bay, and the Gulf of Mexico were mingled with the freshwater of Lake Superior. Josephine Mandamin, founder of the Mother Earth Water Walk, told the gathering that the purpose of the walk was to "raise consciousness about the importance of water." Carrying water in copper pots, core walkers set off from Olympia, Washington; Gulfport, Mississippi; Machias, Maine; and Churchill, Manitoba, and were met in Native and non-Native communities by other walkers who joined them along the way.

continued on page 81

will be the same lazy, shiftless, fickle-minded, intractable being that he was before."

In 1883, the Franciscan Sisters of Perpetual Adoration, a religious order with Bavarian roots, arrived in Odanah. With help from tribal members, who constructed a six-room log house, the nuns established St. Mary's School. The school received considerable financial support from the Bureau of Catholic Indian Missions and was also endorsed by tribal leaders, including the Catholic chief, Jean Baptiste Denomie. The Catholic school had a pronounced effect on its Protestant rivals, whose enrollment declined. Within a few years, the Presbyterian headmaster lost his government salary and was forced to close his school.

The corruption that existed elsewhere on the Ojibwe reservations was rampant at Bad River, where the Stearns Lumber Company held a monopoly on the timber contracts and a stranglehold on the tribal economy. The "Octopus," as an *Odanah Star* newspaper editorial called Stearns, owned three sawmills, the blacksmith shop, an icehouse, a barbershop, twenty-five miles of railroad track, and of course the "company store." Throughout the Allotment Period, Bad River tribal members complained that their Indian agent, Samuel Campbell, was conspiring with the Stearns company to cheat tribal members, arranging timber contracts for his Indian charges that were sometimes three times lower than the fair market value.

A federal audit that led to Campbell's eventual dismissal revealed that the Indian agent kept more than $30,000 of Indian timber money in a personal account at Northern National, a bank controlled by Stearns and other lumber companies. The Ashland account paid 2 percent interest, unlike accounts in which permanent Indian trust monies were held, which paid 5 percent. In 1906, a Chicago newspaper revealed that Campbell had made loans to Stearns from this account at little or no interest, enabling the lumber giant to buy the timber rights for more Indian allotments. The result of

In 1996, Ojibwe warriors (Ogichida) blockaded train tracks on the Bad River Reservation. The protest prevented a train from carrying sulfuric acid to the White Pine Copper Mine in Michigan's Upper Peninsula.
Courtesy of Great Lakes Intertribal Council

this "grafting," according to the *Chicago Record-Herald*, was "the protection and fostering of the interests of the banks and lumber companies [rather] than the interests of the Indians." By the end of allotment, the Bad River Band had lost more than 40 percent of its original land base.[24]

SOKAOGON (MOLE LAKE)

During the dispersal of the Ojibwe from Madeline Island, an advance party of Indians traveled southward to the area today bordered by Pelican, Metonga, and Pickerel Lakes. There they found a region with abundant rice near present-day Rhinelander. The Ojibwe who returned with them found not only rice but also ample game, waterfowl, and forests filled with maple for sugar and birch from which they made canoes and containers.

Under the leadership of Gichi-waabizheshi (The Great Marten), the Post Lake Band, as it became known, grew to about seven hundred members.

continued from page 80

They walked to warn about pollution from chemicals, agricultural runoff, carbon emissions, and leaking landfills, among other threats, and to demonstrate the need for pure water for future generations. Irene Peters, Water Walker from southern Ontario, said the event "will bring healing to Mother Earth and all the environment."[1] The destination of the walk was especially meaningful to the Bad River Ojibwe community, which in 2011 was very concerned about a proposed taconite mine near the headwaters of the Bad River and its effect on the tribe's wild rice beds.

The Water Walks began in 2003 when Anishinaabe women organized a walk around Lake Superior and continued for the next seven years with walks around all of the Great Lakes and the St. Lawrence River. Each walk attempted to highlight the overarching theme and draw attention to local water issues.

1. "2011 Mother Earth Water Walkers Converge at Bad River," *Mazina'igan*, Great Lakes Indian Fish and Wildlife Commission, Fall 2011, p. 1.

**Gichi-waabizheshi,
Mole Lake leader**

Courtesy of Fred Ackley
and Fran VanZile

Gichi-waabizheshi matured into a powerful war chief, and his band was recognized as the eastern vanguard of the Ojibwe, protecting the "eastern door" of the nation from enemy attacks. In 1806, the horrendous Battle of Mole Lake took place between the Sioux and the Ojibwe, the last large-scale conflict between the two nations over control of the rice beds. In 1999, Charles Ackley, the hereditary chief of the Sokaogon Ojibwe, recounted his grandmother's story about hearing the fierce sounds of hand-to-hand combat from a trench where the Ojibwe women and children lay hidden. "That battle killed more than 500 Indians—both Chippewa and Sioux." The casualties were buried together in a mass grave still tended by Sokaogon elders today.

After Gichi-waabizheshi's death, his son Migiizi (The Eagle) assumed leadership of the band. Migiizi's daughter, Madwejiwanokwe, married Willard Leroy Ackley, the first white settler to the area. For reasons that are unclear, Migiizi was prevented from attending the treaty council in 1854 and instead sent his speaker, Nigig, to observe the session. Although he was not authorized to negotiate any agreements, Nigig signed the treaty instrument. The next year, according to oral accounts, Migiizi met with the treaty commissioners and elicited a promise that twelve square miles of land in the Summit, Pelican, Metonga, and Pickerel Lakes area would be set aside as a homeland for the Sokaogon Ojibwe. It is said that two copies of the map were made, one for the chief and one for the government files. According to Sokaogon oral history, the boat carrying the agent sank in the Great Lakes, and the government's copy was lost. That fall, as the Sokaogon followed the deer herd east to the Peshtigo swamps, Bill Johnson, a white trader, grubstaked the hunters against future pelts. When the Sokaogon were unable to pay their debts, oral accounts say Johnson entered Migiizi's lodge and took the map as collateral. Johnson supposedly gave the plat in payment to another man named Straus, who committed suicide. The whereabouts of the map remain unknown.[25]

Lacking proof of their reservation agreement, the Sokaogon were left homeless. In the 1920s, government reports reduced the Post Lake Band to tragic footnotes about "starving and destitute" Indians roaming in Langlade and Forest Counties.

ST. CROIX

Along with the Sokaogon, the St. Croix Band represents the other "Lost Band" of Ojibwe. After the Ojibwe dispersal, extended families traveled southwest and established dozens of villages along the St. Croix and Mississippi Rivers. Others who became known as the Mississippi Bands continued farther west, settling Leech Lake and other communities in present-day Minnesota. Over the years,

A St. Croix delegation met with Wisconsin Governor Emmanuel Phillip on June 19, 1919. The St. Croix, who were left out of the 1854 treaty, remained landless until 1934.

WHi Image ID 95675

the inhabitants of the St. Croix River Valley intermarried with Ojibwe who had traveled farther west and, during times of peace, with Dakota Sioux, who had been pushed west after the Battle of Mole Lake. The Ojibwe moved freely between the various communities in a complex kinship network, which contributed to confusion about who the St. Croix were and to which lands they lay claim.

During the 1837 and 1842 treaties, the St. Croix had a distinct identity. The signature page of the first treaty identifies Chiefs Bizhiki (The Buffalo) and Gabemabi (The Wet Month), along with three warriors as being "from St Croix river." Five years later, the same chiefs, along with Ayaabens, are listed as signees on the second document. However, in the 1854 treaty only Ayaaben's signature appears, and he is listed with the Lac Courte Oreilles chiefs. In the eyes of the federal government, the St. Croix had ceased to exist.

Explanations about why the St. Croix were left out of the 1854 treaty and denied a reservation have been lost to time. Tribal historians speculate that perhaps Bizhiki acted deliberately, skeptical of any negotiations with federal officials who had not lived up to the

"Got Wheels?"

The Sixteenth Annual Northwoods-Mole Lake Jeep Jamboree, a guided off-road trail ride for Jeep owners and their families, was held in July 2011 at Mole Lake.

Photo by Tom Lindley, courtesy of the Wisconsin Off-Highway Vehicle Association

Got wheels? Pedals? Skis?

Over the years, the Sokaogon Chippewa Community has developed a trail system on the reservation to attract increasing numbers of hikers, bikers, off-road racers, and snowmobilers. In 2007 the Mole Lake Tribal Council granted access to the Wisconsin Off-Highway Vehicle Association for trail development, a move that brought hundreds of jeep and all-terrain-vehicle (ATV) owners to Mole Lake for the Great Northern Trail Ride and the North Woods Jeep Jamboree. Both events have become annual celebrations in which jeeps and ATVs navigate trails featuring old logging roads, mud holes, boulders, and steep climbs—"tow hooks mandatory."[1] Encouraged by its success with four-wheelers, in 2008 the tribe turned its attention to two-wheelers and hosted the First Annual Great Northern Bike Rally. Motorcyclists from around the country converged on Mole Lake to test their skills, enjoy live music,

continued on page 84

continued from page 83

and raise money for the American Red Cross. In winter, the tribe carves an oval track on the frozen lake behind the casino and sponsors races for ATVs, motorcycles, and vintage snowmobiles. The Mole Lake have worked to connect two major trails—the Sokaogon and Tombstone/Pickerel—to their downtown area and work with the city of Crandon and Forest County to boost tourism.

Nonmotorized tourism is also encouraged by the Sokaogon Chippewa. In addition to the tribe's annual Strawberry Moon Pow Wow in June, which is open to all, the Mole Lake offer guided canoe tours of Rice Lake and Swamp Creek, Wild Plant Tours, and historic tours of the Dinesen House Log Cabin and Chief Willard L. Ackley Homestead. "We have achieved so much in the last ten or eleven years," said tribal member Richard Ackley, "and I envision so much more." The Sokaogon hope to increase the number of visitors to Mole Lake, which will aid in "maintaining a sustainable tourism economy."

1. "Jeep Jamboree 2011 Guidebook," http://viewer. zmags.com/publication/067780ec#/067780ec/1.

promises of the past. Perhaps the St. Croix chief had expected to negotiate his reservation in talks with the Mississippian Bands. During the treaty talks a major split occurred within the Ojibwe Nation. Some Ojibwe living in Minnesota—the "Mississippi Tribe of Chippewa"—insisted on arbitrating an agreement separate from that negotiated by the six Wisconsin bands, two Michigan bands (Keweenah Bay and Lac Vieux Desert), and three eastern Minnesota bands (Bois Forte, Grand Portage, and Fond du Lac), known collectively henceforth as the Lake Superior Tribe of Chippewa.

It is possible that the St. Croix did not travel to La Pointe because of a crisis looming at home. Because of Zachary Taylor's removal order and the pressure to move west, many St. Croix were already living at Mille Lacs at the time of the 1854 treaty and "had common political interest and leadership."[26] They also had a common problem. Sometime around 1850, lumbermen had built a dam on the Rum River so that they could more easily float their logs down it in the spring. The dam, located at the mouth of a rice lake (now called Lake Onamia), threatened the resource "in such a manner that we shall have no rice crops, and of course starve to death," as Chief Nequenebe put it.[27] Tensions were so high that the Minnesota governor informed the commissioner of Indian Affairs that immediate attention was necessary "to prevent bloodshed between the Indians and lumberman [sic]."[28] Given promises broken in the 1837 and 1842 treaties, it is understandable why they may have decided to deal with the calamity developing at home rather than attend yet another treaty session. Whatever the reasons, the St. Croix, like the Sokaogon, became landless and remained that way until the 1930s.[29]

INDIAN REORGANIZATION

The sweeping social reforms of Franklin D. Roosevelt's administration included a major shift in Indian policy as well. A survey of Indian communities across the country, which became known as the Meriam Report (1928), had revealed extreme poverty, poor health, and cultural despair. When the Great Depression (1929–1933) descended upon the United States, the Ojibwe were no more affected than those in the general population. As Edward DeNomie, a Bad River tribal member, wryly observed: "It's always depression on an Indian reservation." But better times lay just ahead. In 1934, at the urging of BIA commissioner John Collier, Congress passed the Indian Reorganization Act (IRA), which effectively ended the assault on Ojibwe land and culture by halting allotment and dismantling the Indian boarding school system. The Ojibwe were given the opportunity to reconstitute their tribal governments and apply for community development monies through a $10 million revolving loan fund.

The Bureau of Indian Affairs also addressed the extreme hardship of the landless "lost bands." In 1936, the St. Croix Ojibwe adopted a constitution and petitioned for 1,750 acres of scattered land parcels in Burnett and Polk Counties. A year later, the Sokaogon Ojibwe followed suit and took possession of 1,680 wooded acres on the eastern shore of Rice Lake in Forest County. The newly created Ojibwe governments bore little resemblance to the traditional political structures of the past and instead reflected mainstream notions about democracy. The tribes were encouraged to adopt constitutions that resembled corporate charters with bylaws rather than statutes and a chairman rather than a chief of state. Still, reorganization offered the Ojibwe the opportunity to culturally reconstruct their communities and plan for the

Oldest Graduate

Doris Emery, at age eighty Lac Courte Oreilles Ojibwe Community College's oldest graduate
Photo by Patty Loew

In 2011, Doris Emery, age eighty, became the oldest graduate of Lac Courte Oreilles Ojibwa Community College, earning her associate of arts degree in Native American Studies—Language. Emery grew up speaking Ojibwemowin (Ojibwe language) but lost the ability to communicate in her Native tongue after she moved to Chicago at age twenty-two. She returned sixteen years later to the Sand Lake community on the St. Croix Reservation and found that "the old ones were still speaking the language, but the young ones were not," she recalled. Determined to help preserve Ojibwe language and culture, in 2007 Emery enrolled in classes at the St. Croix Outreach site and became an elder in residence. She "set a new bar of academic excellence" by earning straight As in college.[1]

1. "Happy to See Indian People Graduating," *News From Indian Country*, July 2011, http://indiancountrynews.net/index2.php?option=com_content&do_pdf=1&id=12002.

future, albeit under the watchful eye of the Bureau of Indian Affairs, whose ministrations sometimes proved suffocating.

The 1940s and 1950s brought dramatic changes to Ojibwe villages. World War II emptied Native communities of their able-bodied men. In World War I, even though they were not citizens and could not be drafted, Ojibwe men had volunteered for military service in astonishing numbers. Sixty men had enlisted from Lac Courte Oreilles alone. Their sons, who had been made citizens under the 1924 Indian Citizenship Act, also felt compelled to serve. Of the Ojibwe soldiers who fought in World War II—and some communities reached nearly total participation—three-quarters volunteered for service. For many Ojibwe, it was the first time they had been out of their homelands. The hunting and tracking skills they brought to the conflict were valued, as was their complex language. The Thirty-Second ("Red Arrow") Infantry Division, in which many Wisconsin men served in the South Pacific, made use of Ojibwe "code talkers" whose language was totally unknown to their Japanese adversaries.[30]

Like other Indian communities, who sent nearly twenty-five thousand fathers and sons overseas, the Ojibwe experienced the tragedy of war. The Lac du Flambeau Band lost three of its boys, including its most accomplished musician, Joe Sky. His cousin, Reva Chapman, remembered listening to his horn echo across the lake in the evenings: "As old as I am, I've never forgotten that music." Ojibwe women contributed to the war effort by knitting and sewing for the Red Cross, buying war bonds, and helping to boost food production beyond their needs. In 1942, they marketed hundreds of thousands of pounds of meat, fish, eggs, and vegetables. Although some Ojibwe women moved to urban areas intending to work in defense-related factories, most filled jobs vacated by white women who were awarded those higher-paying jobs.[31]

The postwar period saw a return to the assimilation efforts that predated John Collier's more liberal policies. A new policy known as "termination and relocation" emphasized preparing American Indians for city life. "Reformers" pressured the government to eliminate federal services to tribes. Although the Ojibwe escaped the fate of the Menominee, whose tribal status was terminated under this ill-fated policy, they were enticed to leave their reservations and relocate in major cities. Promises that they would receive job training, housing assistance, and social services evaporated, however, and more than one émigré found that "relocation services" amounted to nothing more than a one-way bus ticket to a large city.

Like other urban Indians, they found solidarity and comfort with other tribal Americans in big cities such as Chicago, Milwaukee, and St. Paul. Many found their voice in the "Red Power" movement that emerged in Native American urban arcas. In 1968, two Ojibwe brothers, Vernon and Clyde Bellecourt, cofounded the American Indian Movement (AIM) in Minneapolis. In 1971, Lac Courte Oreilles tribal members occupied the site of the Northern States Power Company dam near Hayward that had flooded their rice beds fifty years earlier. As a result of the AIM-supported takeover, the Lac Courte Oreilles received financial compensation and the right to operate the dam.

Three years later, on March 8, 1974, two Ojibwe brothers set in motion a series of events that would dramatically change Ojibwe history. Fred and Mike Tribble of Lac Courte Oreilles were arrested and charged with violating Wisconsin conservation laws. The two had been caught ice fishing on a lake, off their reservation but in territory on which the Ojibwe claimed treaty rights to hunt and fish. "When they said I was doing it illegally," Mike Tribble recounted, "I took the treaty out of my back pocket and I said, 'No, I'm doing this under treaty rights.'"

This was by no means a simple poaching incident. The arrests prompted a class action suit against the State of Wisconsin by the Lac Courte Oreilles, who accused state officials of systematically preventing the Ojibwe from exercising their rights to hunt, fish, and gather in the ceded territory as set down in the 1837, 1842, and 1854 treaties. Eventually the five other Ojibwe bands joined the suit. Initially, a federal judge ruled against the tribe; however, in January 1983, the US Seventh Circuit Court of Appeals reversed that decision. Later that same year, the US Supreme Court added some closure—at least temporarily—by declining to review the case.

The following year, when the Ojibwe began spearing fish in off-reservation lakes, they were met by angry protests. Thousands of anti-treaty demonstrators, organized by groups such as Stop Treaty Abuse (STA) and Protect American Rights and Resources (PARR), used political pressure, legal action, and civil disobedience to prevent tribal members from spearing walleye. By 1989, the confrontations had turned violent. On the water, tribal spearers faced rock throwing, boat swamping, and even gunshots. On land, their friends and relatives, who had come to the landings to support them, faced a torrent of racist abuse. Signs bearing such vitriolic messages as "Save a walleye, spear an Indian" and effigies of speared Indian heads led to Wisconsin being described in the media as the "Mississippi of the North."

The Ojibwe and their supporters borrowed heavily from civil rights workers who had earlier registered African American voters during the Freedom Summer of 1964. Several thousand "witnesses" from treaty support groups underwent training and learned nonviolent strategies. They traveled in caravans to northern destinations, identified themselves by wearing white armbands, and collected

In the late 1980s, thousands of non-Indian protesters converged on northern Wisconsin boat landings to protest the exercise of off-reservation treaty rights by the Ojibwe. Although many of the protesters argued on the basis of political and legal issues, racism was an unmistakable undercurrent in many of the protests.
Courtesy of News from Indian Country

In 1997, the Mole Lake Ojibwe successfully spearheaded statewide protests against a proposed sulfide mine in Crandon. The tribe feared the mine would pollute the environment and harm their wild rice beds. In 2003, Mole Lake and the Potawatomi purchased the mine site to prevent development of a mine.

Courtesy of *Potawatomi Traveling Times*

information for use in police reports, court proceedings, and civil rights investigations. Like the Freedom Riders, witnesses found local police support inconsistent. It was not until the Ojibwe won injunctive relief in federal court that the protests at the boat landings died down.

Between 1987 and 1991, federal court rulings defined and limited the scope of Ojibwe treaty rights and helped shape the manner in which the tribe exercised them. After Judge Barbara Crabb ruled in the Western District Federal Court that the tribe—not the state—had the right to regulate its off-reservation treaty activities, the Ojibwe created the Great Lakes Indian Fish and Wildlife Commission (GLIFWC) to oversee their harvests and provide biological expertise to the bands. Following state and tribal input, a 1989 decision established harvest levels and imposed safeguards to protect the fishery resource. A year later, Judge Crabb issued a decision that extended the Ojibwe deer-hunting season and set rules for trapping. However, the Ojibwe did not win on all legal points. In 1991, Judge Crabb ruled that the Ojibwe did not have the right to harvest timber commercially—a ruling state officials viewed as a major victory. That same year, she issued a summary judgment and allowed both sides the opportunity to appeal. When neither did, a contentious and expensive seventeen-year legal battle finally ended. In 1999, in *Minnesota et al. v. Mille Lacs Band of Chippewa Indians et al.*, a case involving the same Ojibwe treaties and the same treaty rights, the US Supreme Court ruled definitively to reaffirm the rights of the Lake Superior Ojibwe to hunt, fish, and gather on ceded lands in Minnesota, Michigan, and Wisconsin.[32]

The Mole Lake Ojibwe emphasized treaty rights in a prolonged battle to prevent several multinational corporations from opening a metallic sulfide mine adjacent to their reservation. The Sokaogon were fearful that the heavy metals used in the mining process and a drawdown of the water table would destroy the wild rice beds on Rice Lake, the state's largest inland wild rice-producing lake. In 1975, Exxon announced it had discovered a sixty-ton deposit of copper, zinc, and other metals and applied for permits to operate what became known as the Crandon Mine. The Sokaogon opposed it from the beginning, but after Exxon withdrew its permit application because of low mineral prices, the issue lay dormant.

In 1994, with copper and zinc prices up, Exxon reapplied for mining permits. The Potawatomi, concerned about their air quality, and the Menominee, fearful about treated effluent pumped into their Wolf River, joined the Sokaogon in trying to block the proposal, as did the Mohican Nation. Non-Indian environmental groups opposed to the mine embraced Ojibwe treaty rights as a legal strategy and used the rights in part to successfully push for passage of a mining moratorium bill, which ultimately stymied Exxon and its successors. In 2003, the Mole Lake Band and the Potawatomi bought the mine site for $16.5 million and vowed never to allow mining on the site.[33]

Apart from the treaty rights struggle, perhaps the most significant change that occurred in Ojibwe Country was the expansion of gaming. In 1987, Wisconsin voters approved creation of a state lottery, a class III gambling activity, in a statewide referendum that inadvertently presented opportunities for Indian tribes within the state. Federal law allows Indian nations to offer casino-type gambling on their reservations (and, in special circumstances, off the reservation) if the state in which they reside allows class III gaming. Therefore, beginning in the early 1990s, the Ojibwe opened casinos on all six of their reservations with varying degrees of success. St. Croix's three casinos, located across the border from the Twin Cities, have been very profitable. The casinos in more isolated Ojibwe communities, Red Cliff, Bad River, and Mole Lake, for example, have experienced more limited financial success. Overall, however, the Ojibwe have used the proceeds from their gaming concessions to dramatically improve the quality of life and diversify the economies on their reservations.

In 2002, the Bad River Band opened its new Gitche Gumee Convention Center, a facility accommodating more than four hundred conferees. A year later Bad

River used gaming dollars to purchase nearly 24,000 acres of its original reservation, a move that increased the tribal land base by nearly 20 percent. The Nature Conservancy, which had identified the Kakagon Sloughs as a prime estuary, negotiated the right to purchase 21,300 acres of land from lumber giant Plum Creek Timber Company for $4.5 million. It then transferred the rights to Bad River and sold the community an additional 2,400-acre parcel of forested wetland. Although it required years of austerity, tribal leaders considered the purchase a once-in-a-lifetime opportunity. In 2010, Bad River paid off the mortgage early, saving more than $2 million.[34]

The lean years that followed the land purchase worsened in 2006 when fire claimed the community's health clinic. However, in fall 2011 Bad River opened its doors to a new $5.2 million facility offering a full range of health services, including dental care. Like other Native communities, Bad River serves non-Indians as well as tribal members at its clinic. Signs of progress at Odanah are evident— from Bad River's contemporary tribal offices and renovated fish hatchery to its Moccasin Trail enterprise, featuring a supermarket, gas station, and post office. In 2005, the nation opened an impressive log structure containing the Nation's Housing Authority, and, with federal stimulus dollars, launched a multimillion-dollar "Green Project" to rehab more than forty homes with insulation, Energy Star appliances, and energy-rated windows. The Nation also used green architecture in its new six-thousand-square-foot Tribal Elder Center, which serves about three hundred seniors on the reservation. The exterior of the structure, which opened in 2009, was built with wood certified through the Forest Stewardship Council for sustainable harvesting, and the interior design features recycled materials.[35]

In 2011, Bad River's environmental vision was clouded by an announcement that a Florida-based company intended to open a taconite mine in the Penokee Hills near the headwaters of the Bad River. Tribal officials called it "an unprecedented threat" and expressed "grave concerns about potential contamination of both ground and surface waters."[36] They were particularly concerned about sulfates leaching into the watershed and mine waste dust containing mercury, arsenic, and other heavy metals contaminating their ancient wild rice beds. Manoomin (wild rice) is "extremely sensitive to water fluctuations and small amounts of contamination from sulfates produced by mine wastes."[37]

In fall 2011 Bad River learned that the EPA had approved its treatment as a state (TAS) application for water quality. The designation allowed the tribe to require that the flow and quality of upstream waters not harm its rice beds. Environmental groups including the Sierra Club, the Wisconsin League of Conservation Voters, Clean Wisconsin, Save the Water's Edge, and others were buoyed by the announcement. They too had mobilized against the proposed mine and criticized efforts by some Wisconsin legislators to weaken the state's mining laws. In summer 2011, Gogebic Taconite (GTAC) demanded new rules that would shrink the mining application review period from approximately four and a half years to three hundred days. As the issue heated up, the Sierra Club released data that showed GTAC's parent company, the Cline Group, had been cited nineteen times in three years for violating water quality standards at its Deer Run Mine in Illinois. Other taconite companies operating mines in Michigan and Minnesota had recorded dozens of violations and paid more than $1.3 million in fines. In spring 2012, after the Wisconsin Legislature failed to pass a new iron mining bill, Gogebic issued a statement saying, "We get the message" and announced it would leave the state.[38] In 2013, however, legislative leaders agreed to reconsider the mining issue.

Seventy miles south of Bad River, the Lac du Flambeau have invested their gaming dollars in health, education, and the environment. The Nation broke ground on the $5.7 million Peter Christiansen Health Center in May 2008, opening its doors to tribal and nontribal clients in fall 2009. The twenty-six-thousand-square foot facility houses a family practice, urgent care clinic, pharmacy, imaging center, and laboratory, among other areas, and provides a full range of family health and wellness services, including optometry, podiatry, and dental care. A circular design incorporating post-and-beam ceilings and murals depicting Lac du Flambeau's history acknowledges the role of culture in healing and healthy living.[39]

A clear sign of cultural health is the revitalization of language on the Lac du Flambeau Reservation. The Nation offers twice-weekly Ojibwemowin (Ojibwe language) classes at two sites on the reservation and provides books and tapes for home use. In fall 2011, the Nation began language immersion efforts in its Head Start program as a way to prepare four-year-olds for the language opportunities they will experience at the K–8 elementary school. The Niijii ("Friend") Woodland Indian Art Center received a federal grant to provide afterschool cultural activities, including a class that helps children create their own ceremonial outfits and powwow regalia. The goal is to have a majority of tribal residents speaking Ojibwemowin by 2020.

The cultural gains of the Lac du Flambeau in the twenty-first century have been tempered by concerns over the educational achievement of tribal students at the high school level. A 2007 study at Lakeland Union High School, for example, concluded that a "toxic educational culture" existed at the school and may in part explain why fewer than 50 percent of Native students graduate.[40] Many tribal residents say deep-seated resentment lingers over the treaty rights issue and spearfishing in particular. Predictions that spearing would ruin the northern

Wisconsin tourism economy, however, have failed to prove true. Personal income in Vilas and Oneida Counties, in which Lac du Flambeau is located and where spearing protests were especially intense, is growing at a much faster rate than that of the state as a whole.[41] In 2008 *Field and Stream* magazine ranked the Minocqua–Arbor Vitae–Woodruff area, adjacent to the reservation, as one of the top five places for anglers to live.[42]

With the Ojibwe band owning less than 65 percent of its reservation—the legacy of allotment—Native and non-Native residents of Lac du Flambeau share the same space and resources. Even as the Lac du Flambeau continue to spear fish off reservation in the ceded territory, the vast majority of fish harvested from the 250 lakes *on* the reservation are harvested by non-Indian anglers, who own homes and resorts on reservation lakes and whose fishing license fees until 1997 were paid to the state, not the tribe. In a clear assertion of sovereignty, the Lac du Flambeau negotiated an agreement with the state by which they were able to keep the revenue from fishing licenses sold on the reservation. In exchange, the largest spearing band agreed to set their spearing quotas in such a way as to ensure that anglers have a two and sometimes three-bag limit on off-reservation lakes speared by the Lac du Flambeau.[43] The tribal fish hatchery stocks fish in both reservation *and* off-reservation lakes, a conservation practice that benefits Indians and non-Indians alike.

In 2012, Lac du Flambeau was one of three Wisconsin tribes awarded settlement money from a lawsuit brought against the federal government for mismanagement of tribal trust funds. Under terms of the $1 billion *Nez Perce v. Salazar* decision, Lac du Flambeau received $5 million, Bad River received $3 million, and Lac Courte Oreilles received more than $8 million.[44]

The money could not have come at a better time for LCO, which like other Wisconsin tribes had seen a decline in casino revenues since the beginning of the downturn in the US economy. Instead of providing per capita payments to individual tribal members, the tribe's governing council informed members that it would use the award to pay off loans and conduct an assessment of its accounting practices in tribal programs, which had grown substantially over the past decade. With belt tightening and financial restructuring, LCO was able to avoid layoffs. In early 2013, LCO Secretary-Treasurer Mic Isham said the tribe's financial picture had improved, as had the government's overall efficiency.[45]

Perhaps the most visible sign of progress on the Lac Courte Oreilles Reservation is the expansion of the Lac Courte Oreilles Ojibwa Community College (LCOOCC). From its humble beginnings in 1982 with volunteer instructors in a makeshift classroom, LCOOCC has grown into a multisite tribal college offering sixteen associate degrees and seven certificates. There are LCOOCC satellite campuses in three other Ojibwe communities connected via uplinks and down-links and through a USDA-funded extension program. The tribal college is on the cutting edge of the green revolution, offering programs in renewable energy and green-building carpentry. Since its founding, the college has undergone eight phases of new construction. The most recent additions were the Cultural Resource Center in 2004 and a new library featuring a traditional lodgelike interior in 2007.[46]

The Lac Court Oreilles Band has also become a leader in environmental restoration efforts. Ironically, the tribe's greatest historical pain—the creation of the Chippewa Flowage and resulting loss of wild rice, sugar maple, and sacred sites—has become one of its most significant natural resources. In 2003 the tribe received "High Honors" and a $10,000 award from the Honoring Nations program for its Chippewa Flowage Joint Agency Management Plan. The award, sponsored annually by the Harvard Project on American Indian Economic Development, was used to develop a website to publicly share its story. The narrative's tone provides unique insights into the relationship the Lac Courte Oreilles have forged with the flowage and their non-Indian neighbors who now share the impoundment:

> While the Lac Courte Oreilles were unyielding in their demand that the Plan acknowledge tribal sovereignty, they were cognizant that the state of Wisconsin and the federal government had legitimate jurisdictional claims as well. The Tribe's willingness to acknowledge other governments' authority inspired a similar willingness on the part of those governments. Now, with the full support of the Wisconsin Department of Natural Resources and the US Forest Service, the Plan's preface alerts readers to the injustices suffered by the Lac Courte Oreilles while the Plan states that "all parties recognize the treaty rights of the Chippewa." Representatives of the state and federal governments to the Plan have become staunch defenders of the Tribe's sovereignty. In establishing the Plan, the Tribe appropriately recognized that its own sovereignty would not be compromised by its willingness to acknowledge other governments' sovereignty. By making the sovereign choice to work cooperatively with these other governments, the Tribe has been able to achieve goals that it could not have achieved alone.[47]

The decision to use the Honoring Nations award to communicate the tribe's story via the web was not surprising. The Lac Courte Oreilles rightfully could be called the epicenter of Native American journalism. In 1982, the tribe licensed WOJB radio and began broadcasting news, public affairs, music, and cultural programs even as it continued to publish a tribal newspaper, *The Lac Courte Oreilles*

Journal. Five years later, Native journalist Paul DeMain formed Indian Country Communications (ICC) and acquired the paper from the tribe, launching the for-profit national newspaper *News from Indian Country*.[48] Over the past thirty years other regional publications, magazines, and Ojibwe-specific newspapers have published from the Lac Courte Oreilles Reservation, including *The LCO Times*, *The LCO Sun*, *Ojibwe Akiing*, and *Ojibwe Times*. In 2010, DeMain debuted IndianCountryTV.com, a web-based Native news and information video channel.[49]

The story that dominated news coverage in the latter portion of the twentieth century and early years of the twenty-first century was the Crandon Mine. The controversy that so dramatically defined the Sokaogon Chippewa Community's recent history was partly tied to a little-known but critical environmental development known as treatment as a state status. In 1987, Congress amended the "cooperative federalism" framework of the federal Clean Water Act (CWA) to include tribal nations. It meant that tribes, like states, could regulate pollution limits within their borders, as long as their standards met or exceeded those of the federal government. It also meant that they could comment on—and perhaps even block—economic development that "threatens or has some direct effect on the political integrity, the economic security, or the health or welfare of the tribe."[50] As part of its anti-mine strategy, Sokaogon applied for and received TAS status from the Environmental Protection Agency.

Although the state of Wisconsin filed suit to block Sokaogon's TAS designation, in 2001 the US Court of Appeals for the Seventh Circuit unanimously ruled in favor of the Ojibwe band.[51] This ruling had broad implications for other Wisconsin tribes, which quickly filed applications for similar designations under not only the federal Clean Water Act but also the Clean Air Act. As of 2011, two of the Ojibwe bands had been granted TAS status for water and one had TAS status for air.[52] Additionally, the Ojibwe have pursued state, federal, and international "outstanding resource water" designations for certain lakes and rivers within the ceded territory, a legal maneuver they believe may provide an extra layer of environmental protection against mining and other operations that could adversely affect their resources.

In addition to their leadership role in the environment, the Sokaogon also have made gains economically. In 2004, Mole Lake opened its $4.8 million expanded and renovated casino; two years later it broke ground on a $6 million, seventy-five-room attached hotel. In 2007, the tribe opened a ten-thousand-square-foot Boys and Girls Club, featuring a regulation high school–sized basketball court, a computer room, and a game area for the more than two hundred children enrolled in the program. The Sokaogon also invested more than a quarter of a million dollars to restore a historic log cabin built by a pioneer remembered only as Old

Dutch Frank in the 1860s and later bought by Danish army offi cer Wilhelm Dinesen. In 2005, the Dinesen Log Cabin, as it became known, was added to the National Register of Historic Places. The age of the structure is only part of its appeal; Wilhelm Dinesen was the father of Karen Blixen, the prolific writer who published *Out of Africa* and other titles under the pen name Isak Dinesen.

Dinesen House, Sokaogon Chippewa Community. This historic cabin, constructed in the 1860s, was a stopping point along the military road between Fort Howard (Green Bay) and Fort Wilkins (Copper Harbor, Michigan). In 1873, it was acquired by the Danish adventurer Wilhelm Dinesen. Courtesy of Richard Ackley

Even as the Ojibwe bands develop their individual historic sites, a sense of the shared past remains. In 2010, an iconic pipe—historically significant to all the Ojibwe bands in the Great Lakes region—found its way home to the Red Cliff Band of Lake Superior Chippewa. Descendants of Benjamin Armstrong, the white interpreter and son-in-law of Chief Buffalo, returned to the Red Cliff community the pipe smoked by Buffalo and President Millard Fillmore when the chief journeyed to Washington, DC, in 1852. However, in a sense it never really left, according to Larry Balber, Red Cliff's historic preservation officer. "It stayed in the community. Armstrong was most trusted, and his family carried that through."[53] In 2011, Red Cliff held a welcome-home celebration for the four-foot-long pipe that has come to symbolize the tenacity of the Ojibwe people in establishing permanent homelands in Wisconsin.

Nowhere is the importance of culture more evident in Red Cliff than in the community's commitment to its youngest members. In 1998, Red Cliff opened a new early childhood center, which offers culturally appropriate preschool activities for fifty children ages three to five in three classrooms. Ginanda-gikendaamin (We Seek to Learn) is a unique three-year project, begun in 2010, that immerses infants and toddlers ages birth to three in Ojibwemowin, the Ojibwe language, and provides language learning opportunities for their parents. In 2013 Red Cliff extended the language immersion program to Head Start and in 2016 plans to expand it to grades K–2.[54]

The cultural integrity of the Red Cliff Ojibwe is inextricably tied to the environment and the community's commitment to a sustainable future. In 2002, tribal leaders invited landscape architects from the University of Wisconsin to participate in a "community planning and design initiative that would address the need for affordable housing while preserving their natural and cultural resources."[55] The result was a planning process and the Affordable Green Housing initiative adopted by several other Ojibwe bands as well. In 2009, Red Cliff built eight apartments for its elders, and by 2011 it had constructed forty-eight single-family homes with solar-assisted hot water and energy-efficient appliances. The

Affordable Green Housing approach has allowed the tribe to increase its housing stock by 30 percent and triple its assets. It's also provided much-needed employment on the reservation.

As one of the ten largest employers in Bayfield County, Red Cliff, through its tribal operations, programs, and economic activities, provides employment to more than three hundred people.[56] This figure includes fifty jobs created in 2011 with the opening of Red Cliff's $23.5 million Legendary Waters Resort and Casino. The seventy-eight-thousand-square-foot resort includes a conference center with entertainment and banquet facilities and a forty-eight-room hotel. The tribe continues to operate a successful campground and marina. Red Cliff's proximity to Bayfield, long an attractive tourist destination and the gateway to the Apostle Islands National Lakeshore, provides a unique opportunity for cultural and ecology-based tourism.

The opportunity to share those values came in August 2012, when Red Cliff made history by creating Frog Bay Tribal National Park, the first such park in the United States. Open to the public, the eighty-nine-acre preserve features a quarter-mile of sand beach and a diverse boreal forest of balsam fir, white cedar, spruce, yellow birch, white pine, and hemlock, among other species. The land, lost to the Red Cliff through allotment and recently reacquired through a federal grant, was "cherished by the tribe," according to Red Cliff Natural Resources Administrator Chad Abel.[57] "It's who we are," said Tribal Vice-Chair Marvin Defoe, who added that the park is a step "to making sure that the land is held in reverence."[58]

The St. Croix Chippewa Indians of Wisconsin have made great strides in ecological restoration and natural resource management. In 2004, the Environmental Protection Agency awarded St. Croix a $200,000 brownfields assessment grant to investigate numerous unlined dump sites in or adjacent to wetlands on tribal lands. There were fears that hazardous chemicals and other pollutants could leach into surface and groundwater, threatening the health of tribal members and compromising the tourism industry.[59] A year later the St. Croix Tribal Council approved a comprehensive brownfields rehabilitation ordinance and by 2010 had completed an inventory of sites in need of remediation, conducted staff training, and secured another EPA grant to begin cleanup efforts.[60] The encouraging developments in wetland protection were offset by sobering trends in wild rice production. Between 2007 and 2009, rice abundance in northwestern Wisconsin, especially in Burnett County, was "quite poor," with Upper Clam Lake posting crop failures all three years. Although scientists did not know for sure what caused so many stands to fail, they suspected that drought conditions, a relatively cool spring, and other localized environmental conditions may have been contributing factors.[61]

In 2010, there were more than 1,200 enrolled St. Croix members with most living in Big Sand Lake, Danbury, Round Lake, Maple Plain, Clam Lake, Gaslyn, Bashaw, and Balsam Lake. The administrative challenges facing the St. Croix Band of Ojibwe who must provide services to tribal members in noncontiguous communities fifty miles apart is considerable. However, the St. Croix have experienced more economic growth than perhaps any other Ojibwe band. From having no reservation in 1933, the St. Croix now hold nearly 4,700 acres primarily in Burnett and three other counties. They employ more than a thousand people at just one of their gaming facilities—the St. Croix Casino and Hotel in Turtle Lake—and have become the largest employer in Burnett County and the second-largest employer in Barron County.[62] In total, the tribe provides two thousand jobs to both Native and non-Native workers at its three gaming facilities and at its tribal center complex, which includes a family resources center, a youth center, a housing authority, a construction company, and various tribal departments. In 2001, the St. Croix opened a new health center with a full range of services including dental care and a pharmacy.

St. Croix was the first Indian nation in Wisconsin to venture into aquaculture. In 2001, the St. Croix developed the $20 million St. Croix Waters Fishery with a state-of-the-art recirculating aquaculture system. Thirteen miles of pipe wind through a 170,000-square-foot main building to more than 330 fish tanks containing yellow perch and hybrid striped bass. Plans are to grow the perch—a mainstay of Friday night fish fries—to one-third of a pound and then process the fish into one- to two-ounce fillets. The hybrid bass, a popular delicacy on the East Coast, will be grown to one and a half pounds, chilled, and shipped in the whole fish form. Like the other Ojibwe bands whose environmental vision influenced their economic enterprise, the St. Croix opted not to use a flow-through fish production system, which uses fresh water once and then discards it. Instead, they devised a recirculating system in which water is used, cleaned, and recycled. Because the St. Croix River, which carries an "outstanding resource waters" designation, will be used for wastewater, the process of securing permits from the EPA has been slow. In 2008, the St. Croix Band invited scientists from UW–Milwaukee's Great Lakes Water Institute to help address wastewater issues. When fully operational, the fishery will produce more than 1.5 million pounds of fish each year.[63]

The environmental, political, and legal successes of the six bands, along with the infusion of gaming dollars into depressed tribal communities, have given the Ojibwe a new sense of optimism. Housing and social programs have improved. Some communities are beginning to build economic infrastructures designed to last if and when their casinos close. All the Ojibwe bands have put a portion of their gaming profits into environmental programs, administered locally or through the Great Lakes Indian Fish and Wildlife Commission. Each band, for example, runs its own tribal fish hatchery and restocks not only lakes within its borders but also lakes throughout the ceded territory. Other programs include habitat enhancement, sea lamprey control, and shoreline improvement. Given the cultural importance of wild rice, it is not surprising that the Ojibwe annually reseed more than six tons of wild rice into dozens of existing rice beds and are working with state and federal officials to reestablish historical rice stands. Preservation of the "Food that Grows on Water" is of vital importance to the Ojibwe as they look seven generations into the future. In the solemn words of the tribe's Seventh Generation philosophy: "As those that walked before us provided for the well-being of today's people, so must we think of who will walk the Circle in many years to come."[64]

6 POTAWATOMI

Potawatomi oral tradition tells of three brothers: Ojibwe, the oldest, was the Faith Keeper; Odaawa, the middle brother, handled trade; Bodewadmi, the youngest, kept the Sacred Fires lit. Today, within this "family" of Ne shna bek (or Anishinaabe)—the ancient confederacy of Ojibwe, Odaawa, and Potawatomi—the Potawatomi still refer to themselves as the "Keepers of the Fire."[1]

When the Ne shna bek left their homes on the eastern seaboard between 500 and 1400 BP and moved back to the Great Lakes, the people divided their duties along traditional lines. The Ojibwe carried the sacred scrolls associated with the Midewiwin (traditional religious ceremonies), the Odaawa organized hunts and conducted trade, and the Potawatomi carried and tended the fires. Each responsibility was essential to the group's spiritual, cultural, and physical survival. The three "brothers" may not have had distinct tribal identities during the migration; however, within a century of their return to the Great Lakes region, they had evolved into separate (albeit closely aligned) nations.

Sometime prior to 1500 AD, the Potawatomi migrated again, this time to the shores of Lake Michigan. Over the next hundred years, they established more than a dozen villages between the present-day Michigan cities of Ludington and St. Joseph. Although much of their food continued to come from hunting, fishing, and gathering, they began to rely more heavily on farming and incorporated corn, beans, and squash into their diet.

The Potawatomi organized their village structure along patrilineal clans, although Potawatomi children were also closely linked to the families of their maternal grandfathers. This provided a wider kinship network and strengthened bonds between villages. Potawatomi always married outside their clans, often intermarrying with Ojibwe and Odaawa. These intermarriages reinforced the Three Fires alliance and offered an added measure of protection to

POTAWATOMI
2010 population: roughly 1,400 Forest County Potawatomi tribal members
1913 Land Purchase: 11,786 acres
1978: 14,439 acres (11,267 tribally owned)
1999: 12,280 acres (11,560 tribally owned)
2010: 12,000 acres

Potawatomi Reservation

1829

1833

Late nineteenth-century Potawatomi beaded moccasins

Wisconsin Historical Museum
1943.336,A

Potawatomi families and villages, who could depend on these kinship ties during times of military threat or stress.

The mode of transportation the Potawatomi brought with them from the north was useful for navigating the waters of their new home. Unlike their neighbors who relied on slower dugout canoes, the Potawatomi used lightweight canoes made of birch bark, which were faster in the water and easier to carry on land. The canoes served them well in warfare and trade—two activities that would dominate Potawatomi affairs during the next two centuries.[2]

By the early 1600s, the Potawatomi had heard rumors about the activities of pale-skinned newcomers with "Hairy Faces" to the east. The Ne shna bek recount that they were living on present-day Washington and Sugar Islands off the Door County Peninsula.[3] In 1634, upon learning of Jean Nicolet's impending diplomatic visit to the tribes of the western Great Lakes, the Potawatomi met him near present-day Green Bay. European trade goods acquired from other tribes were beginning to make their way into the Potawatomi economy. Tribal members were eager to trade directly for items such as metal knives, iron kettles, cloth, beads, and especially firearms. According to oral history, the price of a coveted gun was "beaver skins piled as high as a long-barreled musket."

No doubt the intense intertribal warfare that had erupted in the east convinced the Potawatomi of the usefulness of European firearms. Conflicts between the Five Nations Confederacy (Haudenosaunee) and their competitors over resources and trade agreements sent dozens of tribes fleeing west. By the 1650s, some of the refugees, including the Sauk, Meskwaki, Mascouten, Miami, and Potawatomi, had pushed their way into Ho-Chunk and Menominee Country and established a fortified village they called Mitchigami on the eastern shore of the Door Peninsula.

After the annihilation of the Huron by the Five Nations in the late 1640s, the Potawatomi took over the role of intermediary, brokering trade between the weakened French and the tribes of the Great Lakes. They filled their canoes with furs, lashed them together in flotillas, and fought their way past Haudenosaunee warriors to Montreal. The Five Nations responded by attempting to nip the trade threat at its source. Beginning in 1653, Haudenosaunee warriors, armed with Dutch- and English-made muskets, mounted three campaigns against Mitchigami. However, the Potawatomi and their allies, who were equipped primarily with bows and arrows, repelled each attack.

Top: Potawatomi at Skunk Hill (Power's Bluff) in Wood County, 1930. Skunk Hill is an important spot for gathering special medicines that grow in a unique "closed canopy" forest ecosystem.

WHi Image ID 3871

Right: Potawatomi at Skunk Hill, 2000. The Forest County Potawatomi have resisted the efforts of the Wood County Board to allow selective logging on Skunk Hill.

Courtesy of *Potawatomi Traveling Times*

In 1701, after the Haudenosaunee signed a peace treaty with the French, many of the refugee tribes returned to their homes in the east. Although the Potawatomi were swept into conflicts between the French and the Meskwaki Nation, the tribe enjoyed a few decades of relative prosperity. By this time, the Potawatomi had settled more than fifty villages between northwestern Ohio and northern Illinois and controlled an area of nearly 300 million acres. The extent of their influence made the Potawatomi important political and economic allies of the French. Decades of intermarriage between French traders and Potawatomi women bound the two nations in kinship as well.

The Potawatomi were staunch allies of France during the French and Indian War (1754–1763). Potawatomi warriors fought along three fronts: in the east, attacking English settlements from New York to Virginia; in the southeast, battling tribes allied with the English, including the Cherokee; and in French Canada, defending French outposts such as Quebec and Montreal. The Potawatomi were instrumental in several major battles, including one in 1755 in which they helped ambush and rout General Edward Braddock's force near present-day Pittsburgh.

The Potawatomi suffered tremendously with the defeat of the French. Years of British naval blockades had cut off the supply of trade items on which the Potawatomi had become dependent. The Potawatomi needed trapping equipment and ammunition in order to acquire pelts to trade. Unlike the French, the British declined to give gifts or extend liberal credit to their Indian trading partners. Even worse, they raised prices and restricted the supply of some essential items, such as gunpowder. The Potawatomi were not alone in their frustration.

In 1763, the Odaawa war chief Pontiac organized a pan-Indian revolt intended to drive out the British and restore the French. In May, allied warriors from tribes as far north as Lake Superior and as far south as the Gulf of Mexico attacked fourteen British forts. The Potawatomi led successful assaults on Fort St. Joseph and Fort Michilimackinac and participated in the siege of Fort Detroit. Although the rebellion fizzled, the British had learned a valuable lesson. They restored many of the French trading practices and even hired Frenchmen to conduct trade at some British forts. As a result, the Potawatomi reconciled with the British and once again enjoyed a free flow of trade items.[4]

The Potawatomi's decentralized political structure, which emphasized the autonomy of individual bands, was evident in tribal decisions during the American Revolution (1775–1783). Some bands remained neutral; others joined the war on the American side. Most Potawatomi, however, fought with the British. Like other tribes in the Ohio Valley, the Potawatomi grew increasingly concerned about white encroachment west of the Appalachian Mountains, which the British government appeared willing to stop. In order to secure Indian loyalties following Pontiac's Rebellion, the British had issued the Proclamation of 1763, which forbade white settlement west of the Appalachians. American colonists, however, ignored the edict and began trespassing into Indian Territory.

The Treaty of Paris (1783), in which Britain recognized American independence, made no mention of Britain's Native allies or their concerns about illegal white settlement. The American government viewed the tribes of the Ohio Valley as conquered enemies and made no attempt to control the flood of white settlers. Alarmed at the threat, the Potawatomi joined a pan-Indian alliance of more than a dozen tribes and two thousand warriors. In 1791, under the leadership of the Miami war chief Little Turtle, confederated warriors annihilated Arthur St. Clair's army along the Maumee River. The toll of six hundred soldiers killed (along with one hundred civilians, including fifty-six women) remains the single worst American military defeat by Indians.[5]

Four years later, however, the Potawatomi were on the losing end of the Battle of Fallen Timbers, which crushed the power of the Ohio tribes and opened the Northwest Territory to white settlement. Although the Potawatomi were pressured to sign the Treaty of Greenville (1795), they were not—as other Ohio Valley tribes were—forced to make land cessions. However, it was a portent of things to come. Between 1803 and 1805 the leaders of various Potawatomi bands signed treaties that ceded portions of Ohio, Indiana, and Illinois. In 1807, the Potawatomi were forced to cede the southeast portion of Lower Michigan.

Tenskwatawa (Tens-qua-ta-wa), or "the Shawnee Prophet," was the brother of Tecumseh and leader of a religious and political revival movement in the early nineteenth century. His pan-Indian followers included many Potawatomi who flocked to Prophetstown, in present-day Indiana, but in 1811 they were defeated by American troops under the command of William Henry Harrison at the Battle of Tippecanoe.
Painting by J. O. Lewis, 1925; WHi Image ID 26914

It is not surprising that a powerful messianic movement that emerged among the Shawnee found great favor among the Potawatomi. Tenskwatawa, a religious visionary who became known as "The Prophet," preached a return to traditional tribal values. He admonished his followers to reject white customs, religions, alcohol, and trade items that fostered dependency. His brother, Tecumseh, a Shawnee war chief, reinforced Tenskwatawa's spiritual doctrines and added his own: Indian land was owned in common; no tribe had the right to sell a birthright that belonged to all.

Beginning in 1806, followers of The Prophet began visiting Potawatomi communities, inviting them to attend a series of councils at The Prophet's village along the Auglaize River in western Ohio. Over the next year, support for the two Shawnee brothers grew among the Potawatomi—so much so that Main Poc, a noted Potawatomi war

Beaded garters once worn by Speaker Simon Kahquados, Forest County Potawatomi, late nineteenth century

Wisconsin Historical Museum 1943.332,A

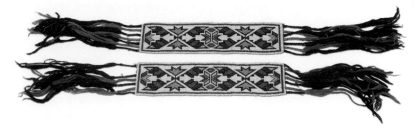

Speaker Simon Onanguisse Kahquados (1851–1930), a lineal descendant in a long line of Potawatomi chiefs. In honor of his request that he be buried on the Door Peninsula near his ancestors, his grave lies in Peninsula State Park near a totem pole erected in 1927 to honor the Potawatomi.

WHi Image ID 24374

chief, invited The Prophet to move his village into Potawatomi Country. Using Prophetstown—as the village became known—as a base, Tecumseh began visiting tribes throughout the Ohio Valley and Great Lakes region, encouraging them to join an alliance that would challenge the Americans and resist further surrenders of land by Native people.

By 1810, nearly three thousand Indians from more than a dozen tribes had flocked to Prophetstown. Young Potawatomi warriors, in particular, enthusiastically responded to Tecumseh's call. However, Tecumseh believed that he needed the support of the Cherokee, Chickasaw, Choctaw, and other southern tribes if he was to successfully confront the Americans. In August 1811, when Tecumseh was away recruiting in the southeast, seven hundred allied warriors—a majority of them Potawatomi—attacked William Henry Harrison's troops as he moved them into position near Prophetstown. Harrison repelled the Indian offensive and then counterattacked, burning Prophetstown and destroying Indian crops.

Lacking provisions for the winter, Prophetstown refugees stepped up raids against white settlements in hostilities that melded into the War of 1812. After the debacle at Prophetstown, Tecumseh reorganized his multitribal military alliance and offered help to the British. Together, they successfully attacked American-held forts in present-day Chicago, Detroit, Prairie du Chien, and Mackinac.

Not all Potawatomi, however, supported Tecumseh or the British. Some, like the bands near the cities of present-day Milwaukee and Peoria, leaned toward the Americans. However, in the confusion over loyalties, it was difficult to remain outside the fray. In retaliation for the assault on Fort Dearborn (Chicago), for example, the Illinois militia mistakenly attacked the village of Black Partridge, a Potawatomi chief who was friendly to the Americans. Ironically, on the day of the attack Black Partridge was away, attempting to rescue a relative of the

American Indian agent at Peoria. Eventually, nearly all the Potawatomi bands that fought did so on the side of the British.[6]

The last great challenge to American expansionism east of the Mississippi died with Tecumseh, who fell in October 1813 at the Battle of the Thames in Ontario. Following the battle, many Potawatomi slipped through American lines and returned to their villages. Their way of life was about to change dramatically. Over the next eight years, the Potawatomi were forced to cede portions of their homelands in four states. In a treaty signed in Chicago in 1821, however, federal negotiators pressured the Potawatomi into giving up nearly all of southern Michigan and a strip of land in and around the south end of Lake Michigan, including Chicago and Milwaukee. White expansion was so rapid, Chief Metea complained, "The plowshare is driven through our tents before we have time to carry out our goods and seek another habitation."[7] Treaty after treaty, parcel after parcel, the Potawatomi sold off their homelands. By 1829, the tribe had ceded about 70 percent of its original land base.

Poverty was an underlying factor in the decision to sell their lands. The Potawatomi had become increasingly dependent on European trade goods. As their homelands diminished, bands became isolated from each other. White farms and fences dotted the landscape. The Potawatomi had become accustomed to French credit, which allowed them to run up debts in the winter and pay them back with pelts in the spring. The shrinking land base, however, had made hunting less productive. The Potawatomi accumulated massive debts, which the Americans were only too happy to allow them to pay off in land.

The lack of central government placed the Potawatomi at a distinct disadvantage in treaty negotiations. Individual bands handled their own bargaining, sometimes selling land that did not rightfully belong to them. Indian agents sometimes appointed "chiefs" who did not have the authority to sign treaties or speak for tribal members. There were other divisions within the tribe. Years of intermarriage between Potawatomi women and European traders produced great numbers of mixed-blood Indians. Some of these "marginals," as one historian described them, represented an elite class of Potawatomi who used education and the favor of American officials to exploit tribal resources for personal gain. In a letter to President John Tyler, old chief Padegoshek complained that these "half-breeds," as he called them, "claim exemption from . . . your laws—professing to be *Indians*—and at other times claim the protection of them—because they are *whites*."[8]

In the late 1820s, a combination of greed and fear led western expansionists to push the Potawatomi from the last of their homelands. White lead miners had overrun the Fever River Valley in southwestern Wisconsin and northern Illinois,

Potawatomi family at Skunk Hill in Wood County, 1920. A ceremonial site, burial ground, and place to gather traditional medicines, Skunk Hill has remained culturally significant to the Potawatomi.

WHi Image ID 64640

trespassing on lands claimed by the Ho-Chunk, Potawatomi, and other Indians and brutalizing the rightful owners. In 1827, the Ho-Chunk war chief Red Bird ambushed a barge carrying mining supplies and raided several settlements near Prairie du Chien. The attacks left several white residents dead. Although the Potawatomi declined Red Bird's invitation to join the raids, this local uprising cast suspicion on the Potawatomi and provided justification—in the eyes of white miners—for the government to force the tribe to part with its lands in the lead district.[9]

On the national level, momentum was building for a plan to move all Indians living east of the Mississippi River to lands set aside for them in the west. After 1830, when President Andrew Jackson signed the Indian Removal Act, all treaties with the Potawatomi would include not only land cessions but also removal from their ancestral lands.

In the Treaty of Chicago in 1833, the Potawatomi signed away the last of their lands east of the Mississippi River. The negotiations reflected how isolated from each other and disparate the bands had become. Chief Simon Pokagon, who along with his band had converted to Christianity, fought removal and was allowed to remain in his village along the St. Joseph's River in Michigan. Another two thousand Potawatomi from southeastern Wisconsin and northern Illinois reluctantly agreed to move, but instead of heading west, they fled to northern Wisconsin and Canada. The bands from northeastern Wisconsin, however, were adamant about remaining in their homelands. After the treaty, they returned to their villages along Lake Michigan and lived unmolested until 1862, when the Sioux Uprising in Minnesota sparked panic among white settlers in Wisconsin toward all Indians. Potawatomi living in the Milwaukee area feared reprisals and forced removal west. Some Potawatomi families moved farther north or hid in the forests. Landless, they became known as the "Strolling Bands of Potawatomi."[10]

Potawatomi women
(from left) Eve Sahpenaiss,
Martha Philemon, and Sarah
Sahpenaiss, circa 1900
WHi Image ID 95709

Among the Potawatomi who made the trip west, the removals became known as the Trail of Death. The forced removal of Chief Manomin's (also known as Menominee) band in 1838, which claimed five or six lives each day, was particularly brutal. According to oral history, Potawatomi warriors were placed in chains and leg irons, crammed into wagons, and denied food and water until the end of each day's march. Any tribal member caught trying to slip food or water to them was severely punished. However, a small number of refugees under the leadership of Chief No-zha-kum managed to escape. No-zha-kum led them to Mexico, where they took refuge among the Kickapoo and participated in the Mexican siege of the Alamo in 1836.[11]

Along with the pressure to give up land, the Potawatomi also faced pressure to give up their traditional customs and religions. The Potawatomi had met French Jesuits as early as the 1600s and had accommodated this new religion. During the treaty period, however, they encountered Christian missionaries of many more denominations. Potawatomi treaties often stipulated the construction of mission schools and churches, which were viewed by federal negotiators as necessary to assimilate the Potawatomi.

Like other Ne shna bek, Potawatomi children were often sent to boarding schools, where school officials forbade them from speaking their language and discouraged them from practicing their customs or religious rituals. Masters of accommodation, the Potawatomi responded differently to these pressures. Many accepted Christianity. Others incorporated Christian doctrines into their own belief system. Some Potawatomi created spiritual sanctuaries with other Indians and secretly practiced their own rituals. George Amour grew up in one such hybrid settlement—the McCord Indian Village near the southern end of the Willow Flowage in present-day Oneida County. He described McCord as a place "where many disenchanted, disempowered people from the Midewiwin and Big Drum societies began to gather into a village setting." Made up mostly of Potawatomi and Ojibwe, but also home to a smattering of Menominee and Ho-Chunk, McCord was a refuge where "they could enjoy some economic stability and continue the practice and preservation of their religion, customs, and tradition."[12]

By the beginning of the twentieth century, the Potawatomi were scattered across seven states. The Strolling Bands in northeastern Wisconsin were especially isolated and impoverished. Because of their refusal to move west, they had been denied land and annuities. An inferior Indian boarding-school education had mainly prepared them to join the underclass. Potawatomi women became domestic servants for white families. Potawatomi men found work as day laborers or lumberjacks. Entire families sometimes hired themselves out as migrant workers, picking potatoes and berries for white farmers and canneries. A few eventually managed to save enough to buy back bits of their homeland and acquire homesteads.

In 1909, 457 Potawatomi were living near Laona in Forest County. Incredibly, despite the land loss and pressure to assimilate, these Strolling Bands of Potawatomi had never lost their political structure, their language, or their tribal identity. When a US Senate committee arrived to hear their grievances in the fall of 1909, few of the Potawatomi spoke English. In traditional fashion, they preferred to have

Agnes Menomin watches as her parents pick potatoes near Stone Lake, 1925. In the early twentieth century, itinerant farm work was an important source of income for the Potawatomi.
Courtesy of Milwaukee Public Museum; neg. 48652

their chief speak for them. Chief Kish-ki-kaam told the senators that his people wanted land in one piece. They were willing to have it allotted, but they wanted the land placed in trust "so that nobody can get it away from you." They had observed how the allotment process had worked with other tribes and had noted the massive land loss because of foreclosures. When asked if the Potawatomi were in agreement about having allotted land together, the chief attempted to steer the questioning back to the tribe's most pressing concern: "We want to know about the taxation," he told them.[13]

The chief's wish that the land be contiguous was not granted. The Potawatomi were allowed to buy only scattered parcels, most of it cutover and rocky. In 1913, these "Strolling Potawatomi" officially became the Forest County Potawatomi Community. The tribe bought its 11,444-acre reservation between Crandon and Waubeno in Forest County with money promised in the 1833 treaty. According to an agreement with the government, the land was allotted in 40- and 80-acre parcels and would be held in trust for twenty-five years, after which tribal members would be allowed to sell it.

Just before the trust period expired, however, Congress passed the Indian Reorganization Act (IRA) in 1934, which ended many of the federal government's onerous assimilation efforts. The IRA stopped the practice of allotment and phased out the federal boarding schools. It also allowed tribes to reconstitute their tribal governments. The Potawatomi were not permitted to reinstate their clan chiefs or traditional political structure, but instead were forced to adopt the mayor-council model of white government. Still, with the adoption of a tribal constitution in 1937, the Potawatomi at last possessed a refuge in their traditional homeland. The population began to grow steadily as other landless Potawatomi gravitated to the new tribal sanctuary.

The war years brought profound change to the Potawatomi, and to some, prosperity. Many Potawatomi men volunteered for military service and left Wisconsin for the first time. A few Potawatomi women migrated to Milwaukee and other large cities to take jobs in the defense industry—or, in many instances, to take the jobs vacated by white women who had gone to work in munitions and other factories.

The urban migration that began during World War II continued after the war, fostered by federal programs that reversed Roosevelt's efforts and once again sought to assimilate Native Americans. By means of the disastrous policy known as "termination," the government tried to free itself from its obligations to Indian people. It withdrew financial support from tribes, such as the Menominee, that enjoyed modest economic stability, stripping them of their official status as Indian tribes. Although the Potawatomi were too economically insolvent to be suitable targets for termination, tribal members did feel the effects of "relocation," a related policy.

Under relocation, the government intended to create incentives, such as job training, employment help, and housing assistance, so that Indians would move from their reservation to the cities, where they would find jobs and assimilate into white mainstream society. The reality for most Potawatomi, however, was a one-way bus ticket to Milwaukee or Chicago and directions to run-down housing.[14]

Nevertheless, the resilient Potawatomi accommodated these changes in their status and lifestyle. Many worked in the cities during the week and returned home to the reservation on the weekends. They formed pan-Indian relationships with other urban Indians and, in their own way, re-created—in contemporary fashion—the clan and family networks that had served them well in years past. During the turbulent 1960s, they raised their voices and demanded that government officials address the poverty, substandard housing, and educational inequities both on the reservation and in the cities.

The 1970s brought modest improvements when federal officials ended termination and reversed government Indian policy yet again. President Richard Nixon fostered a new era of self-determination in which the Potawatomi were encouraged to oversee many of their own programs and take over functions previously performed by the Bureau of Indian Affairs. This not only presented new political opportunities for the Potawatomi but promoted new economic opportunities as

Potawatomi Bingo Casino.
This 500,000-square-foot
gaming facility has sparked
growth and redevelopment
in Milwaukee's industrial
Menomonee Valley.
Courtesy of Potawatomi Bingo
Casino

well. In 1988, the federal government formally granted the Forest County Band of Potawatomi reservation status.

Of all the changes since the Forest County Potawatomi (FCP) acquired their reservation in 1913, gaming undoubtedly has been the most profound. In the late 1980s, the tribe signed a compact with the state of Wisconsin in which it established a casino just north of Carter and Potawatomi Bingo Casino (PBC) on its ancestral lands in the heart of Milwaukee's industrial Menomonee Valley. In the twenty years since PBC opened its doors as little more than a large pole barn, it has expanded twice into an elegant 500,000-square-foot facility with multiple gaming venues, three restaurants, and a state-of-the-art theater. It has allowed the Potawatomi to diversify their tribal economy, build an infrastructure, and spark urban renewal in a previously blighted area of the state's largest city. In 2010, PBC employed a diverse staff of roughly three thousand people, making it one of the largest minority-owned businesses in Wisconsin.[15] As a member of Menomonee Valley Partners, Inc. (MVP), it has helped promote redevelopment in the valley, link neighborhoods to valley businesses, and create a 70-acre community park.[16] Laura Bray, MVP's executive director, credited the Potawatomi with transforming the valley "once widely regarded as Wisconsin's worst eyesore" into a "nationally renowned model of sustainable redevelopment."[17] Payments to both the city of

Milwaukee and Milwaukee County have helped build and repair infrastructure and reduce the tax burden on non-Indians.

As the Potawatomi's main economic engine, the Milwaukee casino provides investment capital for the Potawatomi Business Development Corporation (PBDC), which was established by the tribal council in 2002 and began operations a year later. PBDC's first investment was in Four Fires LLC, a joint venture with three other Native American nations, including two California tribes, the Viejas Band of Kumeyaay Indians and San Manuel Band of Serrano Indians, and Oneida Nation of Wisconsin. Together the four nations built and operated a Marriott Residence Inn Hotel in Washington, DC, completed in 2004. PBDC also purchased ownership interests in a Denver-based commercial real estate company and a hotel development enterprise based in Sioux Falls, South Dakota.[18] The following year it added a manufacturing company that made prefabricated homes and a business that specialized in assisted-living centers for seniors. For the first time it was able to provide dividends to tribal members.[19] Over the next five years, PBDC added software development companies, additional manufacturing operations, and Advancia Corporation, a federal contractor specializing in aeronautics, defense management, and training. It entered into a business partnership with the St. Croix Ojibwe and purchased additional shares in Four Fires, "one of the most profitable inter-tribal investments in history."[20]

In 2009–2010, despite a deep downturn in the US economy, PBDC held its own, mostly because of its diversified portfolio and a 35 percent decrease in operating expenses. By the end of the first decade of the twenty-first century, the asset value of PBDC's portfolio had grown to $30 million. However, tribal leaders say the emphasis is not on how much money the Nation makes, but on sustainability and how well the community is able to provide for its children.[21] Some outside observers consider FCP's expanding economic infrastructure and path toward self-sufficiency a textbook example of what the National Indian Gaming Regulatory Act was intended to accomplish.[22]

Arguably one of the most significant investments the Forest County Potawatomi have made has produced dividends yet to be fully appreciated. For twenty years, the tribe, as part of its gaming compact with the state of Wisconsin, subsidized the Indian Community School (ICS) of Milwaukee. From its turbulent start in 1971 in an abandoned Coast Guard station occupied by American Indian Movement protestors, the school operated in fits and starts at various locations until it moved to the former campus of Concordia College in 1986. From 1990 until 2010, the Potawatomi provided payments to the school that rose to $28 million annually. The contributions allowed ICS to build a $350 million endowment, which was

Indian Community School at Bartlett Avenue. Following the 1971 American Indian Movement takeover of an abandoned Coast Guard station in Milwaukee, which became the site of the city's first Indian Community School, classes moved to Bartlett Avenue School. The site operated from 1980 until 1983, when a loss of federal funding forced its closure.

Courtesy of Drew LaBelle

used to construct a new 160,000-square-foot, earth-friendly K–8 school on a 177-acre campus in Franklin, Wisconsin. The school is open to all Native students and provides tuition-free education to more than 350 students from fifteen different tribes. With its focus on providing quality education within a cultural framework, the school, which opened its doors in 2006, hopes to develop the next generation of Native leaders.[23]

The tribe also has made significant contributions to non-Indians in Wisconsin through charitable gifts and the Potawatomi Foundation. In 1994, Potawatomi Bingo Casino devised Miracle on Canal Street, an annual fundraiser that by 2010 had provided nearly $10.5 million to local charities. Through the Potawatomi Foundation, created in 1999, the tribe has distributed more than $30 million to 275 nonprofit organizations.

In Forest County, the tribe's government and business enterprises, including the Carter Casino, hotel, and smoke shop and a new convenience store and gas station that opened in 2011, employ more workers than any other public or private entity. Its economic impact is also evident in vendor contracts, payments to local and county governments, and tourism dollars that ripple to neighboring non-Indian

Interior dome, Potawatomi Cultural Center. Dedicated in 2011, the Forest County Potawatomi Cultural Center, Library, and Museum features an impressive collection of historical documents, photographs, and audiovisual materials and an extensive book collection.

Photo by Christina Rencontre

communities. Some tribal enterprises, however, have fallen by the wayside. In 1992, the Potawatomi established a red deer herd in the hopes of exporting venison to European markets, but logistical issues and lack of a solid business plan stymied the effort. Over the years the FCP have gradually reduced the size of the herd but still use the meat for feasts and distribute it to elders.[24]

Potawatomi influence in northern Wisconsin, however, extends beyond jobs and money. The Potawatomi Health and Wellness Center, for example, is open not only to tribal members but also to non-Indians. Over the years the clinic has provided critical medical services to uninsured individuals of all races who do not qualify for state assistance.[25] This never-turn-anyone-away policy, according to tribal administrator Eugene Shawano, was an ethic passed down by two tribal healers, Ke wed nok (meaning "north wind") and Wa se gish gok (meaning "breaking daylight"). The clinic treats both members and nonmembers in emergency situations.[26] Other tribal services include a daycare center, senior programs including a center and home-delivered meals, and a housing office that provides financing help to tribal members for new and existing homes as well as rent-to-own opportunities.

The twenty-first century began with a flurry of new construction and grand openings. In January 2000, an assisted-living facility opened its doors on the reservation to elders and people unable to live on their own. In 2006, FCP unveiled a new $10 million tribal government building to house the eight hundred people employed by the tribe or some of its business enterprises. In 2011, the tribe opened a newly renovated cultural center, museum, and library featuring interactive maps and treaty exhibits, video displays, and a diorama that depicts its history and Ne shna bek alliance with the Ojibwe and Odaawa. Tribal members stay connected through a well-organized website and a newspaper, the *Potawatomi Traveling Times*.[27]

The tribe also has expanded its youth programs. The FCP Recreation Center features basketball and volleyball courts, a weight room, and a kitchen. In 2011, the Potawatomi were instrumental in bringing the US Indigenous Games to

Milwaukee. For the Potawatomi, it was an opportunity to "teach positive, healthy lifestyles" and contribute to a "positive community."[28] Twelve Potawatomi children ages thirteen to nineteen joined tribal members from other Wisconsin nations to form Team Wisconsin. They competed against eight hundred young athletes from tribal nations across the country and took part in cultural and spiritual activities organized by Wisconsin's eleven host tribes.

Collaborations with other tribes, such as the one that produced the Indigenous Games, have marked Potawatomi diplomacy since its earliest relations with other Indian nations. In contemporary times, the Potawatomi have been particularly effective in forming coalitions around environmental justice matters. No issue stands out more than the Crandon Mine struggle. In 1982, Exxon attempted to site a metallic sulfide mine near the Sokaogon Ojibwe, less than five miles northwest of the Potawatomi Reservation. Because of low mineral prices, Exxon temporarily scuttled the proposal. Twelve years later, when copper and zinc prices had increased, the company announced it would once again attempt to open the mine. Initially, Exxon wanted to dump treated effluent from the mine into a tributary of the Wolf River, a plan opposed by two other Indian nations, the Mohicans and the Menominee, located downstream from Crandon. The Potawatomi worked closely not only with the three other tribes, but also with non-Indian environmental groups who feared that sulfuric acid drainage might cause irreparable harm to the Wolf River watershed. Together, the coalition successfully sought a series of protective measures for the Wolf, including its federal designation as an Outstanding Water Resource. This meant that any wastewater entering the Wolf had to be absolutely pure, a standard Exxon could not meet.

In addition to collaborating on water quality issues, the Potawatomi carefully crafted another strategy to

Lillian Kelty

Lillian Kelty, Potawatomi elder. Like many Native people of her generation, Lillian Kelty attended an Indian boarding school and, following World War II, moved away from her community during the government's relocation program. After living many years in Chicago, she—like many relocated Indians—returned to the reservation.
Photo by Christina Rencontre

Lillian Kelty was born in a Potawatomi sugar bush camp nearly a century ago. In 1916, her mother was pregnant with her when Lillian's grandmother asked for help making maple sugar at their camp near Arpin, Wisconsin. "I call myself a sugar baby," Kelty said. At age ninety-seven, Kelty is the oldest member of the Forest County Potawatomi tribe. She's seen dramatic changes in her lifetime. As a child, she experienced the terror of having the tribal police come to take her away to an Indian boarding school in Lac du Flambeau. She was forbidden to speak her Native tongue. "They wanted us to lose our language," she said. "They tried to change us. Take our Indian away from us."

Kelty, a full-blooded Potawatomi, married twice. After her first husband died, she met and married her second husband, an Ojibwe

continued on page 116

continued from page 115

from Lac du Flambeau. They moved to Chicago and had five children. Eventually she returned to Wisconsin Rapids, where her tribe bought her a house. She takes great satisfaction in her grandchildren and great-grandchildren, who are encouraged to learn about their culture. "Now they've got schools for that," Kelty said about Lac du Flambeau, where one of her sons lives. "Chippewas are teaching their children how to talk Chippewa."[1]

During her years in Chicago, Kelty had a number of jobs. She worked at the Spiegel Catalog Company and for two shoe factories, Florsheim and BP Shoes. She also repaired binoculars, clocks, and radios. In her younger days she traveled frequently between Chicago, northern Wisconsin, and Kansas, where one of her sons and the family of her mother, a Prairie Band Potawatomi member, live. She didn't like the winters in Kansas, however, and after living there a year returned to Wisconsin, where her other children reside. When asked about the secret to her good health and longevity, Kelty replied, "Never smoked in my life."[2]

1. The Potawatomi and Ojibwe (Chippewa) languages are very similar. The two tribes are also known as Anishinaabe and are culturally and historically connected.

2. Interview with Lillian Kelty by Christina Rencontre, Crandon, Wisconsin, October 20, 2011.

protect their community. In 1993, concerned about possible air pollution from the mine, the tribe asked the US Environmental Protection Agency to declare the air quality on the reservation class I, a designation intended to create another hurdle in the mine-permitting process. The Potawatomi also began exploring another federal opportunity treatment as a state (TAS) status, a management process for monitoring air and water quality that, if granted, allows tribes the right to comment on any pollution permits issued by the state to business entities whose emissions might degrade the tribe's air or water quality.[29] "It's important for us to do this," Potawatomi elder Billy Daniels Jr. said in a 1999 interview, "so we can breathe. Today it's hard to breathe."[30] For FCP tribal chair Harold "Gus" Frank, TAS was about the state and federal governments recognizing the Potawatomi as a sovereign. "We're not against industry per se. We understand that industry is a vital part of the American way of life," he said. "But there's a way to make sure that they meet certain standards to insure that we have the quality of life that we like to have also."[31]

The obstacles the Potawatomi and their allies erected along the permit path eventually led to a state mining moratorium law in 1998.[32] By that time, Exxon had already given up and sold its interest to the first of three other multinational mining companies that would try, and fail, to gain the necessary permits. In 2003, the Potawatomi and Sokaogon Ojibwe purchased the 5,770-acre mine site from the mine's last owner, Nicolet Minerals Inc., for $16.5 million.[33] "We have lost so many resources, so many wild places, in just a few generations," Frank said in a news release. "This purchase protects the Wolf River, the wetlands, and the groundwater of Northern Wisconsin."[34]

The saga of the Potawatomi's efforts to protect air quality dragged on for years after the Crandon Mine issue was resolved. Although Wisconsin reluctantly agreed to the Potawatomi's class 1 air quality designation in 1999, the state of Michigan did not and filed suit. In 2009, the US Court of Appeals for the Seventh Circuit ruled in favor of the Potawatomi, thus ending a fifteen-year battle. A year later, the EPA gave final approval to FCP's class 1 air quality designation.

In 2011, the Potawatomi began an ambitious reforestation project, hand-planting more than five thousand trees in the southeastern portion of the reservation. When the tribe secured its reservation in 1913, the first-growth timber was gone. Based on cultural and historical research, the Potawatomi focused on four species: red oak, white pine, white birch, and aspen.[35] The long-term goal was to regenerate the forest for wildlife habit, cultural use, and cover for tribal hunters. Along with reforestation, the tribe also began work on its first comprehensive biological diversity inventory to provide baseline information for future monitoring and conservation efforts. The Potawatomi have also become a national leader in energy conservation. In 2011, the tribe became the first Indian nation to meet 100 percent of its electricity needs through wind-generated renewable energy (see "Green Power" sidebar).

Along with a substantial commitment to environmental sustainability, the Potawatomi have invested heavily in programs that sustain the language and culture of their people. Annual language camps in the summer and storytelling sessions in the winter bring Potawatomi speakers from Canada and other communities together to share history and tradition. Culture camps provide opportunities to play traditional games and for Potawatomi children to learn from their elders. Without a school on the reservation, the tribe offers language classes for both children and adults at the FCP cultural center, library, and museum. By 2013, a group of elders that have been working with

Green Power

In 2011 the Potawatomi became the first Indian nation in the country to meet 100 percent of its electricity needs through renewable energy. It entered the Environmental Protection Agency (EPA)'s "Green Power Partnership" by buying renewable energy credits—sufficient to supply power to all of its operations in Forest County and at its casino in Milwaukee. The annual purchase of 55 million kilowatt-hours of wind-generated renewable energy reduced the tribe's carbon emissions by 20 percent. "As a people, the Potawatomi have been taught to protect the resources Mother Earth provides," said Potawatomi chairman Gus Frank. "Ensuring that our facilities are powered by clean, renewable resources is another way we can reduce our own impact and decrease the amount of harmful emissions that are released into our air and water from burning coal."[1]

Following an energy audit in 2008, the Potawatomi adopted dramatic energy-conservation measures. These included converting to a four-day workweek by most government employees, switching to compact fluorescent lights and LEDs from incandescent bulbs, installing motion-activated light sensors, modifying cooling and heating systems, and upgrading exterior lighting at the tribe's gaming facility in Milwaukee. This upgrade improved energy efficiency in the facility's parking lot by more than 70 percent. These green initiatives landed the tribe on the EPA's list of top twenty local government green power purchasers.

1. "Forest County Invests in Sustainability," *Potawatomi Traveling Times*, February 15, 2011, 4.

linguists hope to have the first Potawatomi dictionary completed, a gift to succeeding generations.

In their inimitable approach to challenge, the Potawatomi are using modern technology to preserve their language and culture, from electronic translators to animated software programs. In October 2010, the tribe announced plans to install broadband internet on all reservation lands in Forest County, an initiative intended to expand educational options to reservation families. The initiative will also allow non-Indians living near the reservation to purchase broadband internet service not previously available. The tribe left open the possibility that it may extend its service to greater Forest County and other areas of northern Wisconsin.[36] Not surprisingly, the Potawatomi are handling this themselves, through One Prospect Technologies, a Crandon-based company acquired in 2006.

Throughout the latter part of the twentieth century and first decade of the twenty-first century, the Potawatomi charted a course toward self-sufficiency. Using gaming proceeds, the tribe diversified its economy and invested in its physical and cultural landscape. In its external relations it has not forgotten the ancient obligations that bind it to other members of the Ne shna bek family, the Ojibwe and Odaawa. However, in some ways, the "Bodewadmi" have expanded their family to include their non-Indian neighbors. Through job creation, charitable giving, and responsible energy policies, the "Keepers of the Fire" hope to be a positive influence in the creation of a sustainable future for all.

7 ONEIDA

When the Oneida first encountered Europeans, they occupied an area of at least six million acres in present-day New York state. They were part of the Haudenosaunee, or "People of the Longhouse," meaning the Five Nations Confederacy, which also included the Seneca, Cayuga, Onondaga, and Mohawks. Later, when the Tuscarora joined in the 1720s, they became the Six Nations Confederacy. Europeans sometimes referred to them as the Great Iroquois League or the Iroquois Confederacy. However, *Iroquois* is not a Haudenosaunee word. Rather, it derives from the French corruption of a derogatory Huron word meaning "black snakes."[1]

The Oneida refer to themselves as the *On^yote:aka*, meaning "People of the Standing Stone." According to oral accounts, the name derives from the practice of the Oneida people to move their villages every ten to fifteen years. At each new location, a large, upright stone appeared. Oral tradition tells of a time prior to the formation of the confederacy when the Haudenosaunee fought each other in an endless cycle of violence. Hiawatha, the Great Peacemaker, visited their villages and delivered the Great Law of Peace: "Together you are like the five fingers of a warrior's hand," he told them. "United you are powerful; divided you are weak."[2]

Although some western historians speculated that the Haudenosaunee formed their league as late as the sixteenth century, in response to the European threat, Oneida oral history is clear that the Five Nations Confederacy was founded long before European contact. From its formation until the late eighteenth century, the league was the most powerful political system in North America.

Fifty councilors or chiefs chosen by the clan mothers made up the Grand Council, which was composed of an unequal number of representatives from each tribe: fourteen Onondaga, ten Cayuga, nine

ONEIDA

2010 population: 16,567
1838 Treaty: 65,430 acres
1978: 2,581 acres
(2,108 tribally owned)
1999: 6,340 acres
(5,846 tribally owned)
2010: 65,400 acres
(23,122 tribally owned)

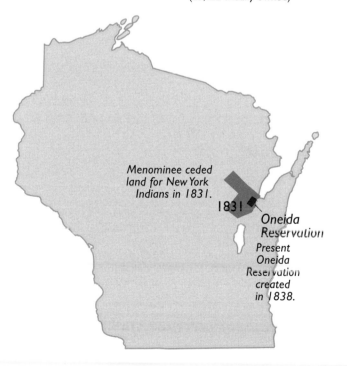

Menominee ceded land for New York Indians in 1831.

1831

Oneida Reservation

Present Oneida Reservation created in 1838.

Oneida, nine Mohawk, and eight Seneca. A complex voting system prevented one nation from exerting more political power than the others. The chiefs, selected on the basis of their political and spiritual strengths, guided the five nations during times of peace. When the Haudenosaunee faced outside threats, war chiefs took charge. The league was a confederacy in the truest sense. Each tribe was free to pursue its own national interests, which it did from time to time.[3]

By the seventeenth century, the Oneida lived in large villages—at least two communities, but possibly as many as nine—in the eastern United States, mostly in modern-day New York and Pennsylvania. There were also Oneida living among other Haudenosaunee, especially the Tuscarora, with whom they were especially close.

The first documented Oneida encounter with Europeans was not a positive one. In 1615, Samuel de Champlain, who had established Quebec six years earlier, participated in raids with the Huron against the Haudenosaunee. Most likely it was an Oneida village that Champlain and his allies attacked. During a three-hour battle, Champlain's men set fire to the village and killed a number of its defenders. Fifteen members of Champlain's party were wounded, including Champlain, who took arrows in the leg and knee. The next recorded encounter came in late fall of 1634 when a Dutch physician visited the Oneida. Dutch traders had sent Harmen Meyndersten van den Bogaert to investigate reports that the French had been trying to initiate trade among the Oneida. He described the Oneida village in this way:

> This castle [village] is also located on a very high hill and was surrounded by two rows of palisades, 767 steps in circumference, in which there are 66 houses; but built much better and higher than all the others. There were many wooden gables on the houses, which were painted with all sorts of animals. They sleep here mostly on raised platforms, more than any other Indians. . . . I saw houses with 60, 70 and more dried salmon."[4]

What van den Bogaert described was a typical Haudenosaunee village with dozens of longhouses surrounded by a defensive palisade. The palisade consisted of two or three rows of posts set in the ground—a formidable barrier that encircled the entire village. The longhouses, which varied in length between forty and two hundred feet, were built of long saplings about two to three inches in diameter. Workers thrust each sapling into the ground and then bent it forward, making a hoop that they secured in the ground opposite to form two outer walls and an arched roof. They created vertical end walls by lashing more saplings to the

Oneida and other members of the Six Nations Confederacy refer to themselves as Haudenosaunee, or "People Building the Longhouse." The longhouse, occupied by members of the same clan, traditionally featured two doors, no windows, sleeping and storage spaces, and common fire pits.

Courtesy of the Wisconsin Department of Tourism

roof, leaving doorways at each end. Once they had constructed the frame, they fastened sheets of elm bark, resembling large shingles or slates, to the structure.

The floor plan provided compartments for individual families and fireplaces in the central aisle running the length of the longhouse. Sleeping platforms adjoined the house walls with storage at either end of the house. The entire dwelling represented an extended family, or matrilineage, whose clan symbol—a wolf, bear, or turtle, for example—appeared above the door. A man marrying an Oneida woman moved into his wife's longhouse, and their children became members of her clan.

The Oneida were principally agricultural people, raising corn, beans, and squash using "slash and burn" agricultural methods. This involved burning off the ground cover, planting crops, and rotating the fields to another area when the land lost its fertility. The women made decisions about the land, worked the fields, and gathered roots, berries, and nuts. The men supplemented the diets of the community with game and fish. The Oneida also "deer farmed" by burning underbrush, and sometimes the forest trees themselves, to create the necessary deer browse.[5] When the Oneida depleted the firewood or exhausted their garden soil, they moved. They also relocated their villages for defensive purposes and to eradicate disease brought by Europeans.

Strong spiritual beliefs, expressed in the traditional teachings of the longhouse, united Oneida communities. Other religions, including Gaiwiio, a postcontact vision introduced by the Seneca prophet Handsome Lake, reinforced their cultural and spiritual bonds with other Haudenosaunee. The arrival of European diseases, however, would greatly test these belief systems. Within a few decades of encounter, perhaps as many as eighteen hundred of the four thousand Oneida had died from smallpox, influenza, measles, and other diseases for which they had no immunity.

Like other Haudenosaunee communities, the Oneida participated fully in the fur trade, aligning themselves economically with the Dutch and later the British against the French and their economic allies. Their French partners included principally the Algonquian nations but also the Huron, a tribe related linguistically to the Oneida but not a member of the league. Attempts by both the Huron and the Haudenosaunee to monopolize trade erupted in the Beavers Wars (1624–1697), which sent dozens of tribes fleeing westward.

By 1649, with flintlock rifles acquired from the Dutch, the Haudenosaunee had asserted their military might and extended their economic and political influence to nearly all of their neighbors. These included many Indian nations beyond the St. Lawrence River to the north, southward to present-day South Carolina, and westward as far as the Mississippi River. Tribes who wished to participate in the Haudenosaunee trade network were allowed to "come in under the wing" of one of the original Five Nations.

The Haudenosaunee then turned their attention to other tribes, including the Anishinaabe—Ojibwe, Potawatomi, and Odaawa—who had moved to fill the intermediary position vacated by the Huron. When the Anishinaabe attempted to send flotillas of furs by canoe up the St. Lawrence to Quebec, they met fierce resistance from Haudenosaunee warriors. The league often dispatched—not always successfully—large war parties into the Great Lakes to cut off trade at its source. In 1655, for example, an allied force of Ojibwe, Odaawa, and Nipissing defeated a large war party of Oneida and Mohawks on the eastern shores of Lake Superior.

The Five Nations were skilled in the art of economic diplomacy. After the Dutch departed, the Haudenosaunee quickly incorporated British trade items into their network, supplanting French items that were often more expensive and less well-made. In this way they weakened the French economically. At the same time they used British fears about French influence among the Algonquian tribes to manipulate Great Britain diplomatically. For example, the Haudenosaunee persuaded the British to coax their Indian allies, such as the Cherokee, Choctaw, Chickasaw, and Creek Confederacies, into becoming allies, convincing them that it would diminish French political power in the Southeast.

Occasionally divisions arose within the Haudenosaunee, especially after Christianity was introduced. The Haudenosaunee practice of adopting large numbers of enemy tribal members into the Nation after a military defeat promoted factionalism, because many of these subdued Indians had converted to Catholicism. In 1667, the Jesuits persuaded a few Christian Oneida families to settle near their mission at La Prairie in the St. Lawrence Valley. The soil was not suitable for corn, however, so the families moved from La Prairie to a new village, Caughnawaga. This group, initially made up of Oneida but later dominated by Mohawk Christian families, became a major French ally. For the next hundred years, the Caughnawaga danced a precarious dance, fighting with the French against the English, but withdrawing when Haudenosaunee allies joined the British in fighting against the French.[6]

Other Christian missionaries arrived in Oneida territory, including Samuel Kirkland, a member of the Missionary Society of Scotland. Kirkland worked among the Oneida for forty years, preaching a gospel of farming, prohibition, and religious-based education. His goal was to instill in the Oneida the skills that would let them succeed in what was becoming a white, European-dominated society.

The years of the American Revolution were pivotal for the Oneida and the other members of the confederacy. In 1775, concerned about the disunity that was erupting between England and the American colonies, the Haudenosaunee sent a delegation to Albany to meet with representatives appointed by the Continental Congress. American officials did not ask for the confederacy's help, but rather asked it to maintain its neutrality, promising, as Britain had done, to continue to trade with the league.

Oneida lace makers, circa 1900. The Oneida are a matrilineal community, meaning clan membership is determined by the mother's lineage.

Courtesy of the Oneida Nation Museum

By this time, however, pro-American and pro-British factions had developed within the league, which had now expanded, with the addition of the Tuscarora, to become the Six Nations Confederacy. Joseph Brant, an influential Mohawk leader educated in Britain, was very pro-British, as was his sister, Mary, who was the common-law wife of William Johnson, the British Indian agent. Brant persuaded the Mohawk, Seneca, and Cayuga to secretly support the British. Individual Oneida, such as Honyere Doxtator, however, aligned themselves with the Americans. Doxtator collected a number of Oneida warriors and offered his services to a company of white militiamen. Other Oneida and Tuscarora served as scouts, runners, and intelligence gatherers for the Americans.

In 1777, the league officially ruptured. At Brant's urging, the Mohawk, Seneca, and Cayuga agreed to join the offensive against the Americans. The Oneida and smaller numbers of Tuscarora and Mohawk accepted a war belt to help the Americans. Their contribution was considerable. The Oneida helped break the siege of Fort Stanwix and distinguished themselves at the Battle of Oriskany in 1777. Doxtator's wife, Dolly Cobus (also known as Polly Cooper), fought alongside the men at Oriskany, where she loaded her husband's musket for him after he was wounded and fired her own weapon against the enemy.[7]

During the winter of 1777, at Valley Forge, the Oneida supplied George Washington's troops with six hundred bushels of corn and other provisions. Dolly Cobus cooked for Washington and his staff at Valley Forge and taught soldiers how to prepare the corn but declined payment for her services. As a thank-you, the Continental Congress appropriated funds to buy a black shawl that Cobus had admired—a gift that has been passed down from generation to generation and is still owned by members of the Oneida Nation.[8]

Despite their loyalty during the American Revolution, after the war the Oneida faced hostility from their white neighbors and the skullduggery of unscrupulous developers, including the Ogden Land Company, which claimed to hold preemptive rights to much of the Haudenosaunee land. In 1785 and again in 1788, New York officials forced the Oneida into a series of fraudulent leases that transferred more than 5.5 million acres of Oneida land to the state. These illegal New York treaties directly violated terms of the Treaty of Fort Stanwix (1784), which confirmed Oneida ownership of their lands. Subsequent treaties negotiated with the state after 1790 and adoption of the Trade and Intercourse Act, which held that only the federal government had the right to negotiate Indian treaties, were invalid. The words of Good Peter, an Oneida chief, articulated the depth of Oneida despair over the loss of their land: "The voice of birds from every quarter cried out you have lost your country—you have lost your country! You have acted unwisely—and done wrong."[9] It was during this anxious and chaotic time that a powerful and perplexing agent of change emerged.

Eleazer Williams was born into a mixed-blood Mohawk family at Caughnawaga about 1787. Baptized Catholic but educated by Congregationalists, Williams accepted a position offered by the Episcopal Church as missionary to the Haudenosaunee. In 1816, Williams arrived to begin his ministry and within a few years began laying plans for an ecclesiastical "Grand Iroquois Empire" somewhere west of Lake Michigan. With money from the Ogden Land Company and encouragement from the US War Department, New York state officials, and the Foreign Missionary Society, Williams began exploring a land purchase from the Menominee and Ho-Chunk Nations.

In 1821, Williams accompanied a delegation of Oneida and other New York Indians to Green Bay and asked for an eighteen-mile-long, four-mile-wide strip of land along the Fox River north of Lake Winnebago. Under pressure from the United States government, the Menominee and Ho-Chunk agreed. The following year, Williams returned with a larger delegation and attempted to extend the land purchase to 8 million acres. The Ho-Chunk refused and withdrew from the council.[10] The Menominee, who later complained that they misunderstood the

Eleazar Williams, an Episcopal missionary of Mohawk descent, accompanied a delegation to Green Bay in 1821 and returned the following year with a larger contingent of Oneida, who settled along the Fox River.
Sketch by George Catlin; WHi Image ID 3021

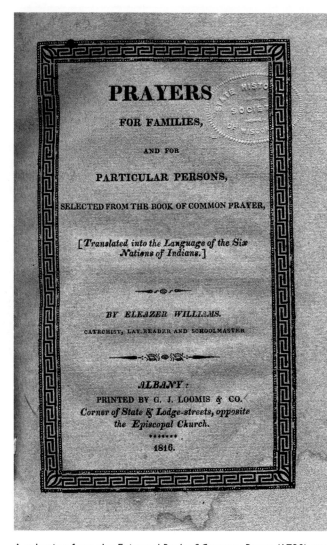

IONTERENNAIENTHAGWA
ORHONKENE.

¶ *NE agwa hentewatierente ne Orhonkene, no-nen agwegon heniagot-ketsgwen ne tsiagononsa, hen-ionterennaien—tenhonwanonweraton ne Rawenniio tsi skennon tha-hakorhenne. Tsie iatha gati henie-riwagaratate, nok ne tsini-iakon ne ganonskon hen-ieterontake, agwa a-iagothahonsateke, nok, a-iawen-hens, tokenske-onwe Rawennijoke nongati nagoni-konra na-iotieraton, tsinigariwes a-iagoterennaien-take.*

TEWATERENNAIEN.

Tahonwaroniaienton ne Niioh Ron-waniha, nok oni ne Niioh Ronwaienha, nok oni ne Niioh Ronikonratokenton.

Tagwaienha ne garonhiake tesiteron ; a-iesasennatokentiste ; a-onwe ne Sa-wenniiotsera ; Tsini-sanikonroten etho ni-iawenn nonwentsiake, tsiniio ne ga-ronhiake; Tagwanataranon ne kenwente niatewenniserake iagionnhekon ; nok sasanikonrhen tsinikon gwanikonraksa-ton ; tsiniio nii tshiongwanikonrhens

A selection from the *Episcopal Book of Common Prayer* (1790), translated into the Oneida language by Eleazer Williams

From *Prayers for Families and for Particular Persons: Selected from the Book of Common Prayer, translated into the Language of the Six Nations of Indians* by Eleazer Williams; Wisconsin Historical Society Rare Books Collection

terms of the treaty, maintained that they agreed only to allow the New York Indians to share the land as joint occupants.

In 1823, about one hundred Oneidas and an equal number of Mohicans who had sought refuge with the Oneida in New York some years earlier arrived in Wisconsin and settled along the Fox River. The following year, scores of families joined them and both groups created a permanent settlement at Duck Creek. However, the migrations did not have universal support within the Oneida community. In a letter to President James Monroe, Oneida chiefs representing those who intended to stay in New York complained that Williams was "scheming" with land speculators and was a "tool" of the Ogden Land Company. They disputed his claim of $10,026.43 for "services" and argued that he was not authorized to remove the New York Indians.[11]

As pressures continued in the east, however, Oneida continued to emigrate to the area west of Lake Michigan. "With the loss of land there was most certainly a loss of the natural environment needed to support the Oneida people both culturally and economically," said twenty-first-century Oneida historian Carol Cornelius. The Oneida who remained in New York knew the implications of heavy logging by white settlers: "The trees provided the natural environment for plants, animals, fish, and medicines which Oneida people utilized on a daily basis." Many Oneida believed that the only chance for survival was in the west.[12]

By 1838, more than 650 members of the tribe were living at Duck Creek, planting corn, potatoes, and turnips on about four hundred cleared acres. The successive waves of émigrés reflected different religions and different political philosophies. The early arrivals were primarily Episcopalians belonging to the First Christian Party, as they described themselves. The next group tended to be Methodists who belonged to the so-called Orchard Party, later known as the Second Christian Party. Later arrivals were "pagan," or traditional people.

The Menominee had never accepted the treaty terms that brought the New York Indians to their homeland, and, in 1831, they negotiated a treaty with the United States that reduced the Oneida land holdings to 500,000 acres. No Oneida were present at the treaty session. In the Treaty of February 3, 1838, the First Christian and Orchard Parties negotiated their own agreement with the United States that officially established the reservation boundaries and awarded unequal sums of money to each party. Using a formula that assumed each individual needed 100 acres for subsistence, the treaty set aside a total of 65,400 acres for the Oneida to be held in common. Oneida who migrated from New York to Wisconsin after 1838, however, were not recognized as being entitled to share in the ownership of the reservation. These Oneida, known as the "Homeless Band," remained landless until 1891.

"New York Indians," most likely Oneida and Mohican, being sworn into Civil War service in 1861

WHi Image ID 1909

A heavy influx of white immigrants into the Green Bay area in the 1840s and 1850s placed new pressures on the tribe. The American Civil War years (1861–1865) brought prolonged droughts, early frosts, and periodic outbreaks of smallpox. One hundred thirty-five Oneida men—about 10 percent of the total Oneida population of thirteen hundred—volunteered for duty with the Union Army. They paid a terrible price: one out of four volunteers was killed.

Shortly after the war, the Oneida began talk of another removal farther west or allotting the reservation as a means of providing property for the landless Oneida who had arrived from New York and Canada after the 1838 treaty. Thirty-year-old Cornelius Hill, a Bear Clan chief who in 1903 would be ordained an Episcopal priest, led a successful fight against removal. However, the community became deeply divided on allotment, which began in 1891, four years after Congress passed the General Allotment Act.

The results, as elsewhere in Indian Country, were nightmarish. Unfamiliar as they were with white people's concept of taxation, many Oneida lost their lands by failing to pay their taxes. Others fell victim to the unscrupulous practices of various land companies. By the 1930s, less than 5 percent of the original reservation remained in the hands of Oneida tribal members.[13]

In 1934, the Indian Reorganization Act (IRA) officially ended allotment and allowed the Oneida to reorganize their tribal government. Under provisions of the act, however, US officials pressured the tribe into writing a constitution and adopting a white form of government at the expense of the tribe's traditional clan council of chiefs.[14] The US government bought back nearly 1,300 acres and placed it in trust for the Oneida Nation. The IRA also ended other policies of forced assimilation, such as government boarding schools.

The educational experience for Oneida children had been a mixed one. Although the Episcopal and Methodist churches operated schools on the reservation, many Oneida children were sent to faraway government schools, including Carlisle in Pennsylvania and Hampton in Virginia. Both the church schools and the government schools emphasized the use of English and discouraged the expression of Oneida culture. "When I went to school, they used to punish us if we spoke Indian," a seventy-two-year-old Oneida woman remembered. Many parents,

Oneida Civil War veterans outside Parish Hall on the Oneida Reservation, circa 1907
WHi Image ID 35050

Girls in the Oneida Indian School laundry room. Indian schools typically offered a half-day of academics and a half-day of industrial training.
Courtesy of Milwaukee Public Museum; neg. A-621-4C

wishing to protect their children from the harsh treatment they had endured, encouraged their children to adopt white ways. "They [my parents] were shamed into not teaching history," said another. "My mother and father both spoke Oneida, but [not so much] in front of us kids."[15] The result was a decline in the usage of the Oneida language skills and a forcing underground of traditional Oneida cultural practices. It also led to a scattering of the Oneida people. Although some tribal members found jobs in the white communities that now surrounded them, many of the best-educated Oneida moved off the reservation and never returned.

During World War I, 150 Oneida men were among twelve thousand Indians who volunteered for active duty, even though many were not citizens. In World War II, more than 70 percent of Oneida men enlisted and more than two hundred were killed. Because of the complexity of their language, Oneida men were used as "code-talkers" by the US Army's Thirty-second Infantry Division, which fought in New Guinea and the Philippines. Oneida women supported the war effort by buying war bonds and moving to urban areas to take jobs in defense-related industries. A few even enlisted in the military.[16]

After the war, Oneida continued to migrate to urban areas, particularly Milwaukee, and experienced what other relocated Indians experienced: substandard housing, marginal jobs, and cultural disconnection. Under the leadership of several Oneida, however, the pan-Indian community constructed a kinship network

Oneida boys pick berries during a school outing.
Courtesy of Milwaukee Public Museum; neg. A-621-1

that amounted to a home away from home—a kind of urban reservation—that provided a patchwork of social services under the auspices of various church and government organizations. The Oneida, perhaps better equipped to deal with urban life because of the proximity of their reservation to Green Bay, took leadership roles in the pan-Indian and Red Power organizations that emerged in Milwaukee during the late 1960s and early 1970s.

The 1980s were a momentous decade for the Oneida. As one of the first Indian tribes to sign a gaming compact with the state of Wisconsin, the Oneida became a textbook example of how to use casino dollars to successfully create an infrastructure. Oneida's award-winning ten-thousand-acre farm, eighty acres of which is certified organic through the Organic Crop Improvement Association, is a window into the Nation's "Seventh Generation" approach to sustainable development. A Seventh Generation philosophy requires that decision makers today consider the impact of their actions on generations 240 years in the future. Oneida Nation Farms and Apple Orchard is part of Tsyunhehkwa (meaning "life sustenance"), a program that includes an agricultural component and a cannery operation. The Oneida raise grass-fed beef and bison and free-range chickens, which they sell to both tribal members and the public. For a small fee, they also allow both tribal and non-tribal members to use their cannery facilities.[17]

Six of the organic acres are planted in white corn, one of the culturally significant "Three Sisters" food crops. Traditional ceremonies mark the cycle of the white corn—a tobacco offering when the corn is planted; a Green Corn Ceremony when the corn ripens; and, since 1993, an annual Community Harvest and Husking Bee, where the Oneida and their friends hand gather the corn and create more than two hundred braids of sixty-five ears each and hang them to dry. The rest is stored in the Nation's solar greenhouse.

Tsyunhehkwa Herbs and Organics. The Oneida Nation operates Tsyunhehkwa, meaning "Life Sustenance," a multifaceted integrated food system offering organic produce, herbs, and botanicals as well as a community cannery and retail store.
Photo by Reynaldo Morales

Jeff Metoxen, Tsyunhehkwa manager, coordinates the annual Harvest and Husking Bee. The community festival brings tribal members together to snap, husk, braid, and dry white corn, one of the "Three Sisters" sacred food items in the Oneida tradition.
Photo by Reynaldo Morales

The Oneida sell some of the corn raw or dehydrated and process the rest into soup, bread, and flour, which is available at the tribe's retail store.[18] The Oneida practice rotational planting and contribute to research and outreach efforts through associations with agricultural groups, universities, technical colleges and other tribal colleges, including the College of Menominee Nation, and community-based workshops for the public. In 2005, Harvard's "Honoring Nations" program singled out Oneida Nation for its highest award, identifying Oneida Nation Farms as an example of "excellence in tribal governance."[19]

Oneida's commitment to sustainable agriculture is consistent with its environmental leadership. The greenhouse is just one aspect of its Seventh Generation approach to land tenure and community building. The Nation received a grant to explore the use of solar panels to augment the radiant heat generated by the greenhouse and solar-energy batteries to power the electric fence that contains the farm animals. In 2011, a team of Oneida Nation High School students earned the top prize in a national renewable energy competition. The team's winning project turned cooking grease into usable biodiesel fuel, a "real world challenge" designed to "help promote tribal self-sufficiency."[20]

In 2011, the Oneida Nation moved forward with a $23 million biomass-to-energy project that could convert upward of one-third of the Nation's waste to diesel fuel. The gasification project, which received a conditional use permit from the city of Green Bay where the plant would be located, could potentially power as many as four thousand homes and substantially reduce the amount of trash diverted to landfills.[21] The Oneida Nation originally intended to build the facility in the village of Hobart but changed locations after residents there objected to the Nation's plan to place the land in trust and demanded that the Oneida waive their right to sovereign immunity with regard to the project.[22]

This issue points to ongoing tension between the Nation and the village of Hobart—tension that exists to some degree between most of the Indian nations in Wisconsin and municipalities located partially or wholly within their reservations. As the nations attempt to buy back reservation land lost through the allotment process and return the land to nontaxable trust status, townships and villages see their property tax base diminished and the tax burden on individuals increased. With the exception of Hobart, the Oneida Nation has negotiated service fee agreements with its other municipal neighbors, and, despite the problems inherent with competing and overlapping jurisdictions, generally has a good working relationship with them. However, until the village of Hobart acknowledges the sovereignty of the Oneida Nation, something it has so far refused to do, the Nation says it will not negotiate with this particular neighbor.[23]

The increasing political and economic clout of the Oneida is evident in the Nation's distinction of being one of Brown County's largest employers. About three thousand people work for the Oneida Nation, more than 40 percent of them non-Indians.[24] Today the Oneida Nation owns a convention center, including a casino, Radisson hotel, and multiple restaurants. It also owns interests in three other hotels. In 2008, it bought a thirty-six-hole championship golf course. Other holdings include convenience stores and travel centers in Green Bay, DePere, Pulaski, and Oneida; smoke shops; an environmental engineering corporation; the farm and orchard; a family fitness center; and a bank.[25]

In addition to its commercial interests, the tribe operates a public museum and library and provides health services, housing, utility services, an arts program, and more than a hundred other programs to its members. One of its most stunning successes is the Oneida Tribal School. The school, built in the shape of a turtle—symbolic of the Haudenosaunee creation story—offers about four hundred kindergartners through eighth-graders a culture-based curriculum.

Aerial view of Oneida Tribal School. The school's shape is a reminder of the Oneida creation story, in which the earth is created on Turtle's back.
Courtesy of George W. Brown Jr. exhibit, Ojibwe Museum and Cultural Center, Great Lakes Intertribal Council

Titletown Oneidas

In 1895, laundry deliveryman Fred Hulbert, who had played football at Wayland Academy in Beaver Dam, moved to Green Bay and put together a football team made up primarily of the sons of Irish railroad workers. The team struggled its first two seasons but then picked up Tom Skenandore, an Oneida who had played football for the Carlisle Indian School. Having been coached by the legendary "Pop" Warner, Skenandore was such a renowned athlete that Hulbert offered him twenty dollars a game to play for Green Bay's town team.

The Oneida Gate at Lambeau Field in Green Bay. The Oneida Nation, whose association with the Green Bay Packers goes back to the city's earliest professional football teams, is a longtime sponsor of the team.
Photo by Reynaldo Morales

It turned out to be a wise investment. In 1897, Skenandore led the team to a championship, the first of many to follow. Because he was paid, you could say that Skenandore was the first professional athlete to play football in Titletown. Shortly afterward, two more Oneida Indians—Carlisle teammates Jonas Metoxen and Martin Wheelock—joined the team, which won another championship in 1904. Wheelock

continued on page 134

continued from page 133

had so much talent that as a "free agent" he inspired a bidding war between Green Bay and Marinette, which offered him twenty-five dollars a game and a furnished apartment! The early success of Hulbert's town teams generated enthusiasm for football and paved the way for Curly Lambeau's Acme Packing Company team that would eventually become the Green Bay Packers of the National Football League. Today the Oneida maintain a close relationship with the Packers, as evidenced by the Oneida Nation Gate at Lambeau Field and a monument, *The Pride*, that honors the history of these early Indian football players.[1]

1. Denis Gullickson and Roberta Webster, audio interviews by Reynaldo Morales, Oneida, Wisconsin, June 8, 2011. See also *Before They Were the Packers: Green Bay's Town Team Days* by Denis Gullickson and Carl Hanson (Black Earth, WI: Trails Publishing, 2004), 11–28.

Its stated mission is to "illustrate and reflect the world as it is, as it has been, and as it can be in the natural presence of Mother Earth and all living and non-living inhabitants." The Oneida Nation also offers early childhood, Head Start, high school, and higher education opportunities to its tribal members. Moreover, the financial stability of the Oneida Nation has permitted it to repurchase 22,000 acres, or roughly one-third, of its original reservation. By 2020, the Oneida hope to own 51 percent of their original 65,000-acre reservation.[26]

Hopes that the US government would reverse the two-hundred-year-old wrongs committed upon the tribe faded in 2005. In an earlier decision, the US Supreme Court ruled that state officials had acted illegally in dispossessing the Oneida of 270,000 acres of land in New York and ordered them to pay damages. However, a subsequent suit, involving the Oneida of New York, has clouded that decision. The case involved the city of Sherrill, New York, which attempted to impose taxes on land parcels purchased by the New York Oneida, who, invoking sovereignty, refused to pay them. In 2005, the Supreme Court ruled that the New York Oneida could not reestablish sovereignty on homelands they had purchased on the open market because the passage of time had "precluded the tribe from rekindling embers of sovereignty that long ago grew cold." It was "impractical," according to the court, since large portions of their "ancient lands" were now in the hands of "innumerable innocent purchasers." The court suggested that the Oneida return the land to nontaxable status by other means—petitioning the Bureau of Indian Affairs to place the land in trust.[27] In 2010, however, a US Appellate Court blocked an attempt by Sherrill to foreclose on the lands in question, citing the Oneida's "sovereign immunity." In November 2012, attorneys for two New York counties asked the US Supreme Court to review the case.

The relationship of the three branches of Oneida—New York, Wisconsin, and the Thames in Canada—adds another complex layer to resolution of the land claims issue. The three nations sometimes find themselves on the same side in legal battles and sometimes as opponents. Culturally, however, the bonds that connect the Oneida have remained strong, as evidenced by longhouse activities and cooperative education and language programs. In Wisconsin a political, economic, and cultural renaissance continues in the Oneida Nation, propelled by a growing income stream and rooted in traditional Haudenosaunee values.

8 STOCKBRIDGE-MUNSEE COMMUNITY (MOHICAN)

STOCKBRIDGE-MUNSEE COMMUNITY (MOHICAN)

2010 population: 1,565
1856 Treaty: 44,000 acres
1978: 15,320 acres
(3,450 tribally owned)
1999: 16,200 acres
(16,044 tribally owned)
2010: 22,139 acres

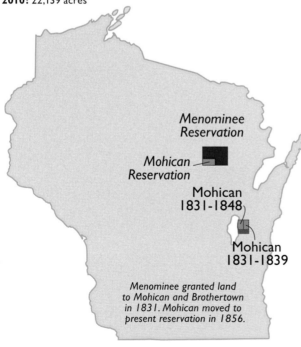

Menominee Reservation

Mohican Reservation

Mohican 1831–1848

Mohican 1831–1839

Menominee granted land to Mohican and Brothertown in 1831. Mohican moved to present reservation in 1856.

Muh-he-con-neok, the name the Mohican give themselves, translates to "People of the Waters That Are Never Still," a reference to the Hudson River—not their original homeland, according to oral tradition, but similar to the land they had left.[1] According to Mohican oral history written down by the tribe's historian, Hendrick Aupaumut, in the early 1700s, "A great people traveled from north and west. They crossed waters where the land almost touched"—a reference that does not necessarily equate to Asiatic origins.[2] Some of the people, known as the Lenni Lenape, situated their villages along a river later known as the Delaware. Eventually, they would be referred to as the Munsee Delaware. Others traveled north to the Hudson. At the time of European contact in the early seventeenth century, the Mohican occupied the Hudson River Valley north to Lake Champlain; east into Massachusetts, Vermont, and western Connecticut; and west to Schoharie Creek near present-day Albany, New York. The Dutch apparently thought *Muh-he-con-neok* was too difficult to pronounce and called them *Mahican*, the word for "wolf" in the Mohican language and one of the tribe's three principal clans. The Mohican spoke an Algonquian dialect and are linguistically related to most of the Great Lakes tribes, among whom they would settle in the nineteenth century.

The Mohican occupied as many as forty villages in New York, each fortified by a palisade that enclosed and protected about two hundred inhabitants. Tribal members lived in wigwams—circular structures made of bent saplings and elm bark—or longhouses, which sheltered several families of the same clan. As often as necessary, the Mohican moved their villages in order to locate near fresh garden soil. The Mohican were gardeners who practiced polyculture, intercropping corn, beans, and squash together with sunflowers. Women did the gardening; men provided fish—primarily herring, shad, trout, and shellfish—and game. Mohican towns were headed by sachems selected on the basis of heredity and matrilineal descent and advised by a council of clan leaders.[3] The principal clans were designated the Bear, Wolf, and Turtle. The sachems met regularly in the main village of Shodac, east of Albany, to discuss civil matters. In times of war, the sachems passed leadership to a war chief chosen on the basis of his proven ability. During military crises, his authority was absolute.[4]

James Fennimore Cooper's misidentification of the tribe in *The Last of the Mohicans* has confused many people. Cooper was actually writing about the Mohegan, a tribe that inhabited present-day eastern Connecticut. His character Uncas, for example, was a real figure in Mohegan history. Indeed, the two tribes may have been one people before contact, but they had distinct identities by 1609 when the English explorer Henry Hudson encountered the Mohican. An account of that meeting published in the early twentieth century, in which the Mohican supposedly presented Hudson with a "covenant chain shining with beaver's grease," is viewed with skepticism by contemporary tribal historians. They agree that covenant chains came considerably later, although they acknowledge that the beaver trade commercially linked the two cultures until the 1670s.[5]

OBSERVATIONS

ON THE

LANGUAGE

OF THE

MUHHEKANEEW INDIANS;

IN WHICH

THE EXTENT OF THAT LANGUAGE IN NORTH-AMERICA IS SHEWN; ITS GENIUS IS GRAMMATICALLY TRACED; SOME OF ITS PECULIARITIES, AND SOME INSTANCES OF ANALOGY BETWEEN THAT AND THE HEBREW ARE POINTED OUT.

COMMUNICATED TO THE

Connecticut Society of Arts and Sciences,

AND PUBLISHED AT THE REQUEST OF THE SOCIETY.

By JONATHAN EDWARDS, D. D.

PASTOR OF A CHURCH IN NEW-HAVEN, AND MEMBER OF THE CONNECTICUT SOCIETY OF ARTS AND SCIENCES.

NEW-HAVEN, PRINTED BY JOSIAH MEIGS, 1788; LONDON REPRINTED BY W. JUSTINS, SHOEMAKER-ROW, BLACKFRIARS.

M,DCC,LXXXIX.

The title page from an early account of the language spoken by the ancestors of today's Stockbridge Indians. The author, Jonathan Edwards, grew up in the Indian community of Stockbridge, Massachusetts, where his father was a missionary and where he became fluent in Mohican and other Algonquian languages.

From *Observations on the Language of the Muhhekaneew Indians* by Jonathan Edwards; Wisconsin Historical Society Library Rare Books Collection

The Mohican, who could marshal about a thousand warriors out of their total population of eight thousand at the time of contact, became a formidable ally of the Dutch. The Dutch practice of taking Native slaves had alienated many of the coastal tribes, but the Mohican, who lived far enough inland that they had not had that experience, were eager to trade. After Hudson returned to Holland aboard his fur-laden ship, the word spread that the Mohican were willing and friendly traders. The next few years saw a tremendous influx of Dutch settlers into Mohican territory.

Like the tribes of the Great Lakes, the Mohican quickly adapted to the fur trade and incorporated European trade items into their economies: guns, ammunition, copper kettles, knives, axes, scissors, and liquor, particularly rum. Because of their strategic location and their proximity to Dutch trading centers, the Mohican exerted great influence over the trade in wampum, the purple and white whelk shells that served as the principal monetary exchange in North America until British and American silver replaced it in the eighteenth century.

Initially, European trade brought prosperity to the Mohican. In time, however, it fostered economic dependence and fed hostilities between the Mohican and their nearest neighbors, particularly the Mohawk. The flashpoint in relations between the Mohican and the Mohawk came in 1624, with the construction of Fort Orange by the Dutch. Trade intensified because of the new fort, and the two Indian nations quickly exhausted the supply of fur-bearing animals in their countries. When the Dutch approached the Mohican and asked them to facilitate trade with other Algonquian tribes to the north, the Mohawk attacked the Mohican. Fighting quickly spread to allies of the two nations, and although the Mohawk and the Mohican arranged a truce in 1628, the conflict—known as the Beaver Wars—continued sporadically between the Haudenosaunee and the Algonquian until nearly the end of the seventeenth century. The Haudenosaunee prevailed. As part of the peace agreement, the Mohican were forced to pay the Mohawk a quantity of wampum each year and to serve as mercenaries in Haudenosaunee raids against tribes to the south.[6]

Even more than war, European diseases took a deadly toll on the tribe's population, which dwindled to less than a thousand. The conflicts with the Mohawk and white encroachment pushed the Mohican from their homeland. By 1724, the Mohican were reduced to two villages along the Housatonic River in Massachusetts.

By then—ravaged by warfare and disease, their ancestral lands reduced, their power threatened on all sides—the Mohican were vulnerable to the messages of missionaries who arrived in their communities. Many became Christians. They were particularly interested in the British god because, as one Mohican sachem put it, "We see that he doth better to the English than other gods do to others."[7] In 1734, the Mohican agreed to host a Calvinist mission in a village they called the Great Meadow, known to the Europeans as Stockbridge. Within a few years, several hundred Pequots, Wappingers, and other converted Indians settled there. Although the Mohican formed the core of the community, to white settlers they and the other Christianized Indians began to lose their distinct tribal identities and became known simply as the Stockbridge Indians.

During this time, the Mohican began intensively to reconstruct their culture. The tribe found itself surrounded by fences and boundary lines. Unable to pick up and move when their garden soil was exhausted, as had been their tradition, the Mohican borrowed farming methods from their white neighbors. Some worked as farmhands and lumberjacks. Others moved into skilled trade positions. Mohican men frequently began hiring themselves out as mercenaries, providing military support to the British against the French. Mohican women moved through the countryside, selling handmade baskets, wooden bowls, brooms, and moccasins.[8]

Mohican culture absorbed white culture. Most tribal members replaced wigwams with frame houses and buckskin with cloth. Heavily influenced by Christian missionaries, Mohican families shifted from a matrilineal to a patrilineal focus. They worshiped in churches and sent their children to school. They were also drawn into the imperial conflicts of white colonists.

Unlike their allies, the Shawnee and Delaware, who were trying to drive the British out of the Ohio Valley, most Mohican supported the British during the French and Indian War (1754–1763) and Pontiac's Rebellion (1763). The Mohican suffered great risks during these conflicts, and the threat of massacre was never far off. When Indian families fled their settlements in fear, whites moved in and took over their homes and farms. After the Mohican returned, the white squatters refused to leave. At the request of the tribe's sachem, Daniel Nimham traveled to England to seek redress from King George III, and British officials promised to help return the lost land to the Mohican. But the coming of the American Revolution delayed any action.

Woven Stockbridge-Munsee bag
Wisconsin Historical Museum 1954.1678

The Mohican entered the war on the side of the Americans. They fought in the siege of Boston and at Bunker Hill. Mohican served as scouts at Saratoga and in numerous other battles. In 1778, Nimham himself was killed at the Battle of Kingsbridge. The tribe's losses during the war were devastating. Half its fighting men were killed, and of those who did return, many found that white intruders had moved onto their lands and into their homes. Mohican loyalty to the United States was largely repaid with hostility and theft.[9]

The bleak future that loomed for their Stockbridge settlements forced the Mohican to look for a new home. When the Oneida, who had also fought on the side of the Americans, invited them to live in their Nation, the Mohican accepted. In the mid-1780s, the Mohican packed up and resettled in "New Stockbridge" near Oneida Lake in upstate New York—the first migration that the "Many Trails People" would endure. In 1802, after the Mohican extended an invitation to a band of Christianized Delaware Indians living in New Jersey, the Delaware moved north to join them.

In 1818, two groups of Mohican led by John Metoxin and Joseph Quinney left New York, traveling overland and sometimes by water to the White River area in present-day Indiana to live among their friends and relatives, the Munsee Delaware. The two groups traveled separately and took different routes—a trip that lasted many months. Metoxin's sixty or seventy followers wintered in Piqua, Ohio, but by the time they arrived in Indiana, the Delaware had been forced to sell their holdings and were preparing for removal farther west to lands in southwestern Missouri. In 1821, Eleazer Williams, an Episcopal missionary, secured a portion of Menominee and Ho-Chunk land for the New York Indians. The Mohican of Stockbridge, the Munsee, and the Brothertown decided to accompany him far to the west, to the upper Great Lakes region.

Between 1822 and 1829, groups of Mohican arrived in what is today east-central Wisconsin. The first émigrés settled at Grand Cackalin (known today as Kaukauna) on the Fox River. Controversy over the land sale, however, led to new treaty negotiations, and in 1834 the Mohican and

Austin Quinney (Ikutauam), an elected chief of the Stockbridge band, helped negotiate a series of treaties intended to secure land for the band and its members. In this painting, Quinney wears a presidential peace medal; the wolf at his side represents his clan animal.

Portrait by Amos Hamlin, 1849; Wisconsin Historical Museum 1942.478

Brothertown Indians moved again to new lands along the eastern shore of Lake Winnebago.

Meanwhile, momentum was building in Washington to remove all the Native peoples living east of the Mississippi River to territory west of the Mississippi. Passage of the Indian Removal Act in 1830 created great uncertainty among the Mohican. "Fearing the inevitable," some Mohican and a group of Munsee Delaware from Canada asked to move to Indian Territory in 1839. To accommodate them, the tribe's chief sachem, Austin Quinney, negotiated a land cession whereby half of the Mohican's best land—23,040 acres—was sold to the government in order to finance the removal of the Mohican who wanted to move west. About 70 of the 217 Mohican, along with 100 of the 132 Munsee Delaware, attempted the long, arduous trip. Many died along the way. Some arrived in Oklahoma and were absorbed by other tribes. Others eventually returned to Wisconsin.[10]

The Mohican's hardship continued through the next decade. In 1843, Congress extended citizenship to the Mohican, a move that split the tribe into two factions. Some Mohican accepted citizenship and sold their lands to white developers—or lost their property when they failed to pay their taxes. Others, including John W. Quinney, who was elected grand sachem in 1852, resisted apportionment and refused to cooperate with those who coveted Mohican land. Under Quinney's leadership, the Mohican withstood numerous efforts to remove the tribe and alienate the Mohican people from their land. In 1856, the Mohican negotiated the last of their treaties, which resulted in another move, this time to the townships of Bartelme and Red Springs in Shawano County, which had previously formed part of the Menominee Reservation.[11]

John Quinney, Stockbridge Indian and sachem during the Mohican Nation's migration west to Wisconsin in the 1820s
Portrait by Amos Hamlin, 1849; Wisconsin Historical Museum 1942.227

Other Quinneys rose to prominence in the tribe. John Quinney's sister, Electa, became the first female public schoolteacher in what would become Wisconsin in 1848. Born in 1802, Electa Quinney was educated in mission schools in Connecticut and New York. She taught school in New York for six years before her family, along with her tribe, left for Wisconsin. In 1827, the tribe constructed a church and a log schoolhouse modeled after white schools in New York and New

England. It was a free school, open to anyone of any denomination. A year later, Electa took over the classroom, and the tribe paid her salary. In a letter to friends back east, she expressed her optimism: "The people have much improved since leaving New York."[12]

The years following allotment (1887–1934) were extremely difficult for the Mohican. Timber companies clear-cut the tribes' lush pine forests, leaving a denuded landscape susceptible to erosion and forest fires. To survive, some Mohican moved to the Menominee Reservation while others returned to their homelands in New York. In 1871, Congress reduced the two-township reservation to just half a township, "the culmination of fraud and deception on the part of government representatives in collusion with whites interested in timber on the Stockbridge's land."[13]

The intended transition from lumbering to agriculture did not occur to the extent the government had hoped. Much of the land was not suitable for farming; the soil was thin and sandy, and the growing season was too short. The inability to make a living on the land created considerable hardship, made worse by the Great Depression and a widespread drought during the early 1930s. Edwin Cuish, whose parents had a small farm, remembered a big dust storm "that came all the way from Oklahoma," darkening the sky at midday and smothering their crops. Feed for the family's livestock was so scarce "they had to cut leaves off the trees in order to feed the cows."[14] Priscilla Church and her husband, George, decided to move to Milwaukee to find work. She remembered that her husband told her to pack lightly because it would be like "vacation" since they'd be gone only a short time. "Longest vacation I ever had," Priscilla recalled. They lived in Milwaukee for twenty-three years.

Those who stayed on the reservation faced tremendous pressure. In 1937, Eureka and Elmer Davids, who had eight children, lost their farm to foreclosure. In a letter, Eureka pleaded with the bank. "We are American Indians, as you know, natives of this land. We have tried to make a home like our white friends. It looks as if we have failed when we apply for help to save our home."[15] Seventy years later their daughter, Dorothy, recalled the heartlessness of the action. "When Pa went to the bank to pay the interest on the mortgage, the banker and his lawyer said, 'We don't want your money, Elmer. We want your land,' and they took it."[16]

By 1934, only 16,000 acres of the original 40,000-acre Mohican reservation remained in tribal hands. In addition to the land deprivation, the Mohican also experienced the loss of their most precious resource: their children. Mohican, like other Indian nations, were forced to send their children to boarding schools, where white educators discouraged the use of traditional language and cultural

Mohican blacksmith shop near Stockbridge, circa 1913

WHi Image ID 38527

expression. "They tried to erase us," explained Dorothy Davids, who attended the Lutheran Mission School in Red Springs. "They tried to make us into something else." Davids described herself as one of the luckier children. Every Friday afternoon, her grandfather, whose farm on the reservation was adjacent to the school, came to the mission to pick her up and take her home for the weekend. She was among the fortunate ones: other children stayed at the mission for the entire school year, returning home only in the summers, if at all. Some Mohican children attended schools in Gresham and Tomah, but a few were sent as far away as Flandreau, South Dakota, and Carlisle, Pennsylvania.[17]

The experiences of Mohican children at the mission school were mixed. Bernice Miller Pigeon recalled her years there, during the 1920s, as happy ones. She met lifelong friends, including a young Mohican girl from Oshkosh who became her best friend. "Rachel lived in the city. I never would have met her if it wasn't for the school." Like Davids, Pigeon was able to return to her family each weekend. Often she would invite schoolmates who lived far away to spend Saturdays and

Sundays with her on her family's farm. As one of ten children she was no stranger to hard work and did not mind the chores to which she and the other children were assigned at school. "My job was to bake. I worked in the bakery one hour every day after classes." She and two other girls baked thirteen loaves of bread each day.[18]

Davids described the school as "not bad" but a place where punishment could be harsh: "I do remember getting thrashed with a cat-o'-nine-tails for some infraction and then walking over to my grandpa's house, sobbing," Davids said. "He marched me back to the school, up the stairs, down the hall, into an office. . . . I don't know what he said to the matron, but I never got thrashed again." Still, she conceded, "They did teach us to read and write." Davids, who became the first American Indian woman to graduate from the University of Wisconsin–Stevens Point and who later earned a master's degree at the University of Wisconsin–Milwaukee, believes the fundamental skills Indian children learned in boarding schools proved useful. "A lot of leadership emerged from that basis. It doesn't mean they made leaders out of us, but by getting some skills, later we were able to stand up and criticize some of the government's policies."[19]

Federal Indian policy, with its emphasis on eliminating tribal culture and alienating Native people from their land, offered much to criticize. However, that changed in 1934 with passage of the Indian Reorganization Act (IRA). The IRA signaled a new shift in the government's approach toward its Native population, away from the assimilationist policies of the past and toward a recognition that Native culture could be a source of strength and opportunity. Federal policy makers began closing Indian boarding schools and buying back tribal land lost through the allotment process. Under the IRA, the government returned 15,000 acres of land to the Mohican, which allowed them to rebuild their community. In 1938, the Mohican approved a constitution and elected a new tribal council with Harry Chicks as its president.[20] Strong leaders like Arvid Miller, who cofounded the National Congress of American Indians and the Great Lakes Inter-Tribal Council, followed and served as council president for twenty-six years.[21]

Mohican men, like other Indian men in Wisconsin, enlisted or were drafted into the military during World War II. They served in integrated units, which made their progress difficult to track. However, at least ninety tribal members served honorably. Some, including Aught Coyhis, were highly decorated. Coyhis, an army medic, was awarded four Bronze Stars for his service at Omaha Beach, one of the infamous Allied landing zones on D-day. Mohican women such as Ernestine (Quinney) Murphy, Sarah Chicks, and Alvira Burmeister served in support, reserve, or nursing units, as did non-Indian women like Dorothy Murphy, whose husband, Roger a Mohican tribal member—also served During the war, Ernestine Quinney, who enlisted in the US Marine Corps, met her future husband, Virgil Murphy, who served in the US Air Force.

On the home front, countless other Mohican supported the war effort by working in the defense industry. Bernice Miller and Leona Bowman, for example, moved to Sturgeon Bay during the war and built ships for the US Navy. Like other Indian people, many Mohican gravitated to the cities after the war as part of the government's relocation program.

By 1966, fewer than half the Mohican listed on the tribal rolls resided on the reservation. Patricia "Dolly" Miller, for example, moved to Chicago and supported the founding of the American Indian Center. In 1971, after members of the American Indian Movement (AIM) occupied an abandoned coast guard station on Milwaukee's shoreline, Miller became secretary of the Indian Community School that was established there. In Chicago, while working for the American Indian Center, Dorothy Davids saw the tragic effects of relocation: "Native people losing their jobs, being evicted, and having a hard time adjusting to urban life . . ." She remembered being called to a run-down apartment where a woman with a three-week-old baby was in the throes of a breakdown. Davids, who helped the woman commit herself to a hospital, was concerned about leaving the infant with the woman's husband, who had been drinking. "There was a young Navajo woman, newly married, who was washing dishes at the center, helping out, and I remember saying how worried I was about that baby. And, she said: 'I'll take it.' And you know, she took care of that baby for oh, maybe three weeks, until its mother was out of the hospital." For Davids, the Indian Center was an important link for Native people. "It was a second home, a lifeline."[22]

The quiet work of urban Indian centers, such as the one in Chicago, was overshadowed by the more boisterous and sometimes confrontational activities of AIM, which gained national prominence in the 1960s and 1970s. Armed confrontations and takeovers, such as those at Wounded Knee in South Dakota and the Alexian Brothers Novitiate in Gresham (both in 1973), focused national attention on historic injustices and on the problems facing contemporary Native people, such as political corruption, miserable health care, and poverty. "For me, AIM was part of the cutting edge," Davids explained. "But they made the people standing behind them look more reasonable. Without AIM, a lot of the changes wouldn't have occurred." AIM was useful in other ways to activists like Davids who were working within the system. "Lord, all we had to say was, 'I guess we'll just have to call in AIM,' and we usually got what we wanted. It was an exciting time."[23]

The arrival of gaming in the late 1980s ushered in exciting economic times for the Mohican. In 1992, the nation opened the North Star Casino and Bingo Hall in Bowler, Wisconsin. Seventeen years later, the Mohican replaced that gaming facility with a $100 million complex featuring three hundred thousand square feet of gaming, entertainment, and conference space and a ninety-seven-room hotel, improved in 2011 with the addition of a salon and spa. The resort also features a year-round RV campground and the Little Star Convenience Store with smoke shop and gas station. Resort guests and the public are able to enjoy the tribally owned Pine Hills eighteen-hole golf course. In 2006, the Mohican opened an LP gas company that serves three hundred customers. By 2010, the Mohican Nation had become Shawano County's largest employer, providing jobs to nearly nine hundred people, half of them non-Indian.[24] The Mohican are proud that even during the worst of the recession in 2008–2011, they did not lay off any workers. "It took smoking and gambling for Indians to get on their feet," Bernice Miller Pigeon observed wryly. "I'm looking forward to when gaming stops. Maybe we'll have other industries to keep us going."[25]

The dramatic success of the Mohican Nation's economic enterprises has had a ripple effect on community life. In 1995, the tribe opened the Mohican Family Center with space for cooking and sewing classes; a fitness center; and a full-sized gymnasium for basketball, volleyball, and powwows. Five years later, the tribe replaced its aging clinic with the new thirty-thousand-square-foot Stockbridge-Munsee Health and Wellness Center, offering a full range of health, dental, and behavioral services. The tribe also operates the Ella Besaw Center, an eight-bed community-based residence facility to support elders and people with disabilities who cannot live independently. Stockbridge-Munsee Housing has escalated new home construction, including the Moshuebee Apartments for Elders. In 2009, the tribe received a $2 million federal grant to build a six-unit elderly and disabled apartment complex near Moshuebee.[26] The two facilities are located near the elderly center, which provides on-site and home-delivered meals, respite care, and social activities.

Future plans include construction of a cultural center and a new administration building using green building techniques for maximum energy efficiency. In 2011, the Mohican unveiled a new state-of-the-art wastewater treatment facility intended to "grow businesses and protect our environment."[27]

The Mohican are active land stewards. In 2000, in cooperation with the US Geological Survey, the Mohican Environmental Department installed monitoring wells to sample and test water for nitrates. There were concerns that decades of dairy farming, improper manure management, and the use of nitrate fertilizer

The "Many Trails" symbol found on Mohican Nation Stockbridge-Munsee signs reflects the multiple movements of the Nation. The tribe moved from present-day New York and Massachusetts to Wisconsin, first to a site near present-day Kaukauna, then to the eastern shore of Lake Winnebago to the west side, finally acquiring a permanent home in the present-day towns of Bartelme and Red Springs in Shawano County.

Photo by Reynaldo Morales

by corn growers may have contaminated some of the groundwater on the reservation. The study was intended to ensure that any new construction would take place in areas with potable drinking water. The Mohican are particularly committed to managing their 19,000-acre forest in a sustainable way. They earn approximately $500,000 a year in stumpage income from the 800,000 board feet harvested each year.[28] In 2003, the US Fish and Wildlife Service awarded the Mohican $250,000 to develop an integrated fish and wildlife management plan. Some of the funds were used to hire a biologist who coordinates habitat restoration and wildlife sustainability projects with the tribe's conservation and forestry departments. In 2011, the Nation's Environmental Department adopted an

The Stockbridge Bible

In 1745 an emissary for England's Prince of Wales presented a two-volume Bible to the Stockbridge Indians. It was a symbol of their successful conversion to Christianity. Forty years later, when the tribe moved to live near the Oneida in upstate New York, they constructed an oak chest to protect it during the journey. The chest and its contents moved again with the Stockbridge in 1820 when the community made its way west to Wisconsin. It remained with them through various moves in Wisconsin and was known to be in the home of Sote Quinney as late as the 1920s. When Quinney passed away, the pastor of the Presbyterian Church ordered the Bible moved to the church basement and ten years later sold it to Mabel Choate of Massachusetts, who wanted to create a museum celebrating the life of the missionary who had converted the Stockbridge. Although tribal members objected to the sale, it was too late.

The Stockbridge were uncertain about where the Bible resided until 1951, when Jim and Grace Davids visited the Mission House Museum in Stockbridge, Massachusetts, and saw the Stockbridge Bible on display. As news spread that the cultural artifact had been located, tribal members began traveling to the museum to see their Bible. In 1975, a group including nine students visited, and later the young people urged tribal elders to seek return of the Bible, which they did initially through personal pleas and later

continued on page 148

continued from page 147

through attorneys. However, museum officials refused to budge. For fifteen years the Mohican pressed their case until finally, in 1990, a Massachusetts court approved its transfer. The Bible now resides in the Arvid E. Miller Memorial Library/Museum in Bowler.[1]

1. Karen Coody Cooper, *Spirited Encounters: American Indians Protest Museum Policies and Practices* (Lanham, Maryland: AltaMira Press, 2008), pp. 82–83.

aggressive pesticide policy that restricts the use of pesticides applied from commercial planes, boats, or land vehicles and on all applications applied to greater than a half-acre of private lawn or garden.

And as the Mohican look to the future, they continue to piece together their past. The tribe has restored a number of historic stone cottages built by the Works Progress Administration during the 1930s and 1940s. One of the most energetic bodies of the Nation is the Mohican Historical Committee, which supports the impressive Arvid E. Miller Memorial Library/Museum. The research library's collection includes books, manuscripts, letters, maps, microfilm, and audiovisual materials. The museum, which is open to the public, has a collection of pre- and post-contact cultural artifacts, including the two-volume Stockbridge Bible dating to the eighteenth century.[29]

Though the tribe is by no means wealthy in the twenty-first century, the Mohican have experienced economic growth unprecedented in three hundred years. Tribal members have returned to the reservation for jobs and opportunities. A sense of optimism is reflected in the cultural renaissance that is under way in the Mohican Nation. Youth drums, powwows, and artistic expression are beginning to flourish. The past has left an indelible imprint on the tribe, evident in an emblem found on banners, jewelry, T-shirts, and tribal letterhead—the "Many Trails" symbol. It reminds tribal members of the traumatic removals and difficult paths that marked Mohican history, but it also encourages them about the possibilities in the journey that lies ahead.

9 BROTHERTOWN INDIAN NATION

Despite its lack of federal recognition, the formal name of the Brothertown Indian Nation speaks to the tribe's own sense of identity as a *nation*. Until 1839, the United States recognized the sovereignty of and maintained a government-to-government relationship with the Brothertown. Although the United States today views the Brothertown in a considerably different light, the Brothertown continue to have a functioning government as they struggle to reassert their sovereign rights and reclaim federal acknowledgment as an Indian nation. Unlike the other Indian nations described in this book, the Brothertown Indian Nation is the only federally unrecognized Native tribe in Wisconsin, a distinction that presents unique challenges to its community.

The Eeyamquittoowauconnuck or Brothertown is an Indian nation with distinctly Christian roots, an amalgamated tribe descended from various Algonquian-speaking peoples of southern New England. Its ancestors include the Pequot, Mohegan, Narragansett, Niantic, Montauk, and Tunxis, whose numbers were decimated by European diseases, drought, famine, and war.[1] Two large-scale conflicts, the Pequot War (1637) and King Philip's War (1675–76), in particular, factored heavily in the history of the peoples who would become the Brothertown.

The arrival of the first American colonists at Plymouth in 1620 created tremendous political instability among the Indian nations along the eastern seaboard. Shifting loyalties over the next decade resulted in the Pequot, their allies, and the Dutch pitted against the Mohegan, the Narragansett, and the English, who ultimately prevailed. Many Pequot were killed. Those who survived were enslaved, were placed under control of the Mohegans, or found refuge with other tribes. Within fifty years, alliances had shifted again. This time an even larger war

BROTHERTOWN
2010 population: 3,000+
1838 Treaty: 23,000 acres
1839: Tribal status terminated
1999: Landless
2010: Largest concentration around Fond du Lac

Brothertown
1831–1839

Menominee granted land to Mohican and Brothertown in 1831.

Students and teacher at a school in Brothertown, Wisconsin, date unknown
WHi Image ID 95434

Samson Occom, religious leader of the Brothertown Indians during the migration west to Wisconsin in the 1820s
WHi Image ID 59460

broke out between the English and their allies, including the Mohegans and Pequots, and the Wampanoag, led by Metacom or "King Philip" and Narragansett. As had occurred following the Pequot War, surviving Natives who had opposed the colonists were sold into slavery or absorbed into other tribes.

By the eighteenth century, many Native people were weary of war, and their tribal identities had blurred because of these conflicts. In the 1740s, during a religious movement known as the "Great Awakening," missionaries converted disillusioned and disenfranchised Native people and gathered them into seven "Praying Towns."[2] These communities included Charlestown in Rhode Island; Groton, Stonington, Farmington, Niantic, and Mohegan in Connecticut; and Montauk in New York.[3] A number of these Native communities sent their young men and women to Eleazer Wheelock's Indian Charity School in Lebanon, Connecticut. While there, they imagined a new life for their people—in a community where they could practice their faith and "live amicably."[4] Two of the students, Samson Occom and Joseph Johnson, suggested that the Praying Towns unite to form a utopian community based on the values of peace and brotherhood. In 1773 delegates from the seven towns met in Mohegan to discuss the concept and selected Johnson to visit the Oneida Nation to ask if the Oneida would share some land.[5] The Oneida agreed to give these Christian refugees a ten-mile-wide strip of land near present-day Utica in upstate New York.

In spring 1775, Johnson led an advance party to Oneida. The group was made up of young men, most of them from Farmington, who would clear trees, plant crops, and construct houses to make the transition easier for the main party, which had yet to arrive. However, these Christian Indian immigrants found themselves swept up in the events of the American Revolution. The Six Nations Confederacy, of which Oneida was a member, initially had tried to stay neutral. Eventually, although most of the confederates sided with the British, the Oneida threw in their lot with the Americans. The advance party paid the price. The English and their allies overran the territory where the Oneida and the would-be Brothertown were living and by 1777 had forced them from their homes. These Christian émigrés sought refuge with the Stockbridge Indians in Massachusetts, where they remained until the war's end. After the war, the advance party, sans Johnson, who had died in the summer of 1777, returned to Oneida, where they resumed preparations.

In 1784, led by an "old and ailing" Occom, the main party arrived in Oneida and a year later officially adopted a name. "But now we proceeded to form into a Body Politick—we Named our Town by the name of Brotherton, in Indian Eey-amquittoowauconnuck."[6] The Brothertown selected trusted elders to serve as "Peacemakers" who would settle disputes and provide leadership.

Like the Mohicans and the Oneida, the Brothertown prospered in New York until unscrupulous land speculators, such as the Ogden Land Company, orchestrated a series of fraudulent treaties and illegal land leases. In 1821, after the state of New York purloined half their lands and distributed them to white settlers for the town of Paris, Brothertown representatives joined a delegation of Mohican and Oneida who traveled to present-day Wisconsin hoping to buy land where the tribes could reside free of white encroachment.[7] In 1821, representatives of the three tribes signed a treaty with the Menominee and Ho-Chunk in which they believed they had purchased 860,000 acres. The following year the New York Indians and the two Wisconsin nations signed a treaty for 8.72 million acres. Under terms of the agreement, the Brothertown received more than 150,000 acres along the Fox River near present-day Kaukauna.[8]

The Menominee and Ho-Chunk, however, maintained that they had agreed only to allow the Brothertown and the other two New York tribes to *live* on the land, not own it. They protested "so profusely that the United States Senate refused to ratify either treaty."[9] Meanwhile, New York officials stepped up their demands that the federal government permanently remove the Brothertown, Mohicans, and Oneida—pressure that had a ripple effect on the Menominee. In 1831 federal negotiators coerced the Menominee into a treaty that ceded a portion of their lands for "the benefit of the New York Indians."[10] When the ink was dry, the Menominee had lost three million acres and the Brothertown had a twenty-three-thousand-acre reservation along the east side of Lake Winnebago in Calumet County.

Between 1831 and 1836, ships carrying five groups of Brothertown docked in the Port of Green Bay. Tribal members built a church near Jericho and hoped to carry out their Christian vision without fear of removal. However, their optimism lasted just a few years. Attracted by the rich soil, white farmers poured into Michigan Territory, and, just as had happened in New York, the Brothertown were perceived to be in the way. Once more, the federal government devised plans to move the Brothertown, pressuring them to exchange their fertile lands in Wisconsin for marginal lands in Kansas.[11] Thomas Commuck, one of the original émigrés in 1831, wrote that the Brothertown faced an "overwhelming tide of fate, which seems destined in a few short years, to sweep the Red Man from the face of existence."[12]

To the Brothertown, the safe port in these uncertain political seas appeared to be citizenship. They knew that if their land was held in common, subject to the vagaries of Congress, which had recently passed the Indian Removal Act, they could face an endless future of relocations. In 1834, they asked that the federal government privatize their communally held reservation and grant individual title to their members. Three years later, in 1837, the tribe filed a similar petition and requested US citizenship. On March 3, 1839, Congress allotted the Brothertown lands and conferred citizenship on 387 new landowners, making the Brothertown the first American Indians to become US citizens.[13]

> [T]he said Brothertown Indians, and each and every of them, shall then be deemed to be, and from that time forth are hereby declared to be citizens of the United States . . . and their rights as a tribe or nation, and their power of making or executing their own laws, usages, or customs, as such tribe, shall cease and determine: Provided, however, That nothing in this act shall be so construed as to deprive them of the right to any annuity now due to them from the State of New York or the United States, but they shall be entitled to receive any such annuity in the same manner as though this act had not been passed.[14]

The immediate effects of the decision were positive. The congressional act itself explicitly protected their treaty rights related to annuity payments, and, unlike other Wisconsin tribes in the mid-eighteenth century, the Brothertown were never targeted for removal by a US president.[15] However, the long-term consequences of the 1839 act were disastrous. From the perspective of US policy makers, it meant that "Federal acknowledgment of the historical Brothertown Indian tribe ended"[16]—that the Brothertown were no longer a sovereign government and no longer entitled to the rights negotiated by treaty. From the Brothertown perspective, it meant that they were members of *two* sovereign governments, and their relationship with the United States, including matters related to rights and treaties, remained intact. They "did not seek relief of the right to self-govern or to be dissolved as an Indian Tribe."[17]

Allotment took its inevitable toll, and the Brothertown quickly lost their lands to foreclosures and tax sales. Within a few decades, many members were living with friends and relatives on the Oneida and Mohican Reservations and, if they were lucky, providing day labor in neighboring white communities. Yet, despite their uncertain political status, the Brothertown maintained their cohesiveness. The council continued to meet and function as a government, tribal members maintained their social network, and headmen continued to provide leadership. The tribe petitioned Congress over land issues and joined a lawsuit with other New York tribes over treaty matters.

In 1878, when the United States decided to sell unallotted Brothertown lands to non-Indians, it approached the Brothertown for permission, an act the tribe later offered as evidence that the United States still recognized it as a distinct political entity. The land sale required approval from the tribe—yet more evidence that the Brothertown still had a functioning government. After tribal members voted in favor of the sale, Congress appointed five trustees from the community to sell the land.[18] In the 1920s, the Brothertown joined the Oneida and the Mohicans in a lawsuit involving land in New York state. The legal battle was unsuccessful, but it demonstrated that although the United States may have determined that the Brothertown had ceased to exist as a tribe, the Brothertown clearly believed otherwise.

In 1950, four years after Congress established the Indian Claims Commission to address the wrongs committed against Native nations, the Brothertown filed suit, seeking reparation for lands lost in Wisconsin because of the reworking

A logging operation at Brothertown, Wisconsin, circa 1925
Courtesy of Robert Elyard; WHi Image ID 95354

of the 1822 treaty with the Menominee and Ho-Chunk. After fourteen years of litigation, the Brothertown won their battle and received a portion of the $1.3 million award. Robert Fowler, an attorney and Brothertown member, assembled a tribal roll so that the payment could be dispersed on a per capita basis.[19] The suit, the award, and the tribal roll became pieces of evidence the Brothertown would use to document their federal acknowledgment petition.

The Brothertown were not the only Indian nation to have been terminated. Large tribes like the Menominee in Wisconsin and the Klamath in Oregon and more than a hundred smaller tribes, mostly in California, were set adrift during the 1950s. The next two decades saw considerable confusion in which the Bureau of Indian Affairs (BIA) did not consistently equate termination with a lack of acknowledgment and loss of rights. For example, the mother of Kathleen Brown-Pérez, a legal scholar who has been active in the struggle for Brothertown recognition, received a BIA scholarship to attend college. Then, in the late 1970s, she and others received a letter from the BIA informing them that they "may not be eligible for Indian money to go to school."[20] The persistence of terminated nations in demanding federal acknowledgment led the BIA in 1978 to establish a procedure by which terminated tribes could regain federal recognition. The Brothertown immediately began preparing their case and in 1980 notified the BIA that the Nation intended to seek federal acknowledgment.[21]

The federal acknowledgment process is rigorous and requires that the petitioning tribe meet seven criteria:

a) The petitioner has been identified as an American Indian entity on a substantially continuous basis since 1900.

b) A predominant portion of the petitioning group comprises a distinct community and has existed as a community from historical times until the present.

c) The petitioner has maintained political influence or authority over its members as an autonomous entity from historical times until the present.

d) A copy of the group's present governing document including its membership criteria. In the absence of a written document, the petitioner must provide a statement describing in full its membership criteria and current governing procedures.

e) The petitioner's membership consists of individuals who descend from a historical Indian tribe or from historian [sic] Indian tribes which combined and functioned as a single autonomous political entity.

f) The membership of the petitioning group is composed principally of persons who are not members of any acknowledged North American Indian tribe.

g) Neither the petitioner nor its members are the subject of congressional legislation that has expressly terminated or forbidden the Federal relationship.[22]

Each criterion demands "exceptional anthropological, historical, and genealogical research and presentation of evidence"—far beyond the means of most of the 350 groups that have sought recognition, according to the National Congress of American Indians.[23] During an oversight hearing by a House committee, petitioning tribes described the process as "impossible" and "egregiously unreasonable."[24] The committee's ranking Democrat complained that since the BIA adopted the procedures, "Only 16 applications have been approved and they were approved after a tribe has often had to wait up to 20 years for a decision."[25]

The Brothertown's 1980 petition was classified by the Office of Federal Acknowledgment (OFA) as "undocumented/unable to process." In 1995, the Brothertown filed a documented petition under the name "Brothertown Indians of Wisconsin." Five years later, the tribe formed a recognition committee to compile a supplemental document, revised and updated to include oral histories, photographs, correspondence, diaries, journals, and newspaper articles. After learning that the OFA would finally review its case in 2008, under the name "Brothertown Indian Nation," the tribe submitted ten banker's boxes of documents, appendices, and evidence to support its petition.[26] However, OFA investigators were unconvinced. They determined that the Brothertown met only two of the seven criteria (d and f) and, with proper documentation, could most likely meet a third (e). In August 2009, the BIA issued a preliminary finding in which it rejected the Brothertown petition. The tribe received two six-month extensions to respond and offer more evidence, which it did in August 2010. Kathleen Brown-Pérez, the Brothertown attorney who chaired her tribe's federal recognition committee during this critical period, reacted to the BIA's preliminary finding:

> They say that we did not have governance, that we did not have a natural Indian community, that outside scholars did not recognize us as a living, breathing tribe. . . . We had treaties with the US government. Our history is very, very, very documented.[27]

HOME COMING JULY 1. 1917
QUINNEY WIS.

Although terminated as an Indian nation in 1839, the Brothertown have maintained a continual presence in Wisconsin through activities such as an annual homecoming. This photo, from 1917, is evidence of the Brothertown's efforts to maintain a sense of community.

Courtesy of David Hankwitz; WHi Image ID 95356

Brothertown history is documented not only by written accounts but also by oral history, which the OFA will not accept as evidence. This is a bias many petitioners criticize as "disrespectful" of Native cultures, which are rooted in oral tradition.[28] The process has taught the Brothertown to look within for affirmation of their Indianness. As Brothertown tribal chair Richard Schadewald observed, "The most significant thing for us the last ten years has been the awareness that we do not need to look to Washington or anybody else for our identity."[29] Their sense of community is solidified at annual picnics and homecoming celebrations and through tribal newsletters, social media, and the Brothertown Indian Nation website. As they did in the earliest days of their nation, tribal members today still elect four "Peacemakers."[30]

With no access to federal funds, the tribe has had to rely on its own ingenuity to generate revenue. Its members have sold crafts and operated bingo games to pay rent on tribal offices and provide money for scholarships. As Brown-Pérez put it, "The tribe has had to nickel-and-dime our way into survival." Yet some members believe that the daunting task of operating a government with donations and fundraisers has brought the Brothertown closer together and reminded them that "we have to stick together because no one else is going to help us."[31]

In October 2010, the Brothertown did receive help from the Oneida Nation of Wisconsin, which purchased the "Brothertown Papers" from a private nontribal collector and is sharing them with the Brothertown. Ironically, and perhaps fittingly, as Darren Kroenke, a former Brothertown Indian Nation tribal council member who spoke at the repatriation ceremony, pointed out, the gift comes in the "Seventh Generation"—236 years after Joseph Johnson first traveled to the Oneida and asked for land for his band of Christian Indians. Kroenke reminded the audience that Johnson's visit resulted in "the formal adoption of the 'Seven Towns of New England Indians' as 'Younger Brothers,'" by the Oneida, "formalizing a relationship that was proscribed by the Peace Maker in the Great Law of Peace:"

The Great White Roots of the Tree of Peace

Roots have spread out from the Tree of Great Peace: one to the north, one to the east, one to the south and one to the west. These are the Great White Roots and their nature is Peace and Strength. If any man or any nation outside of the Five Nations shall obey the laws of the Great Peace (Gayanerekowa) and shall make this known to the statesmen of the League, they may trace back the roots to the Tree. If their minds are clean and if they are obedient and promise to obey the wishes of the Council of the League, they shall be welcomed to take shelter beneath the Tree of the Long Leaves.

For Kroenke, with this gift the Oneida, as "Elder Brothers," renewed their commitment to their "Younger Brothers," the Brothertown, and honored the relationship between the two nations.[32]

The Brothertown maintain a cultural presence in the Fond du Lac area by participating in events such as Celebrate CommUNITY at the County Expo Center. In 2012, the Gordon Williams Gii Tass'se Brothertown Drummers led the opening flag ceremony.
Courtesy of *The Reporter*, Fond du Lac, Wisconsin

Brothertown Archaeology Project

The laborious task of documenting the continuing existence of an Indian nation as "a distinct community . . . from historical times until the present" is a key determination in federal acknowledgment. Logic holds that if a "distinct community" lived in an area, its members would most likely have died and been buried there as well. As a graduate student, archaeologist Dr. Craig Cipolla, University of Leicester, researched cemeteries and gravestones in New York (2008) and Wisconsin (2009) in a project that may help the Brothertown in their recognition efforts. Some of Cipolla's collaborative scholarship focuses on settlement patterns and the relationship between Brothertown landscapes and community formation.[1]

Cipolla has used ground-penetrating radar to survey Union Cemetery in Calumet County, a burial ground renamed to honor veterans of the Civil War. The cemetery was sometimes referred to in obituaries as "Brothertown Cemetery." As historical artifacts, the gravestones in Union Cemetery may provide solid evidence that the Brothertown maintained a continuous presence in Wisconsin.

1. "The Place of Space in Brothertown Ethnogenesis," paper delivered to Contemporary and Historical Archaeology in Theory Conference, Boston University, Boston, MA, November 2011, as summarized on Craig Cipolla's website, http://web.mac.com/craigcipolla/Craig_N_Cipolla/Research.html.

The Brothertown Papers date to the mid-eighteenth century, but more importantly, they chronicle seventy-five years of the tribe's distinct and continual presence since its arrival in Wisconsin. The Brothertown hope the archive will help them in the federal recognition process.[33] If the OFA's final decision is to deny the Brothertown federal recognition, tribal officials say they'll seek an act of Congress to restore their sovereign-to-sovereign relationship with the United States. "We've been through a lot, and there is no government that is going to tell us that we have to stop existing," Brown-Pérez observed.

"We're not going anywhere."[34]

10 URBAN INDIANS

Another important Native community, though it may lack tribal sovereignty and a geographic homeland, maintains a significant presence in Wisconsin. Since earliest remembered times, Native people have always inhabited the places that became Milwaukee, Green Bay, Madison, and other familiar cities. Today, however, urban Indians represent more than two-thirds of all Native people in the state.[1]

By far, the largest concentration of urban Indians is in Milwaukee, where the "mother" of Milwaukee was a Menominee Indian married in 1820 to Solomon Juneau, the French Canadian who cofounded the city. Josette Vieau Juneau gave birth to the couple's seventeen children and helped run the family's trading post, stockade, and home.[2] Potawatomi, Menominee, Ojibwe, and Ho-Chunk peoples were a regular presence in Milwaukee until the early nineteenth century when Indian removals sent many of their nations west. It would be a hundred years before they began returning to the city.

World War II saw the biggest influx of Native people to Milwaukee. Although some urban Indians found high-paying work in the US defense industry, many more filled lower-paying jobs vacated by whites who found such work.[3] In the 1950s, the migration intensified because of the federal government's termination and relocation policies, and by 1960, nearly 1,800 Native Americans were living in Milwaukee.[4] Today, although the US Census lists 6,634 Indians living in Milwaukee County, the population is most likely underreported. Most social service providers agree that the number of Native people in the Milwaukee metropolitan area is at least 10,000 and could be as high as 13,000. The underreporting is a consistent challenge for the US Census Bureau because of irregular housing, questions about confidentiality, and the mobility of

Solomon Juneau's fur trading post in what is now Milwaukee, 1833. Juneau's Menominee wife, Josette Vieau Juneau, sometimes called the "Mother of Milwaukee," took care of the couple's seventeen children and ran the post in her husband's absence.
WHi Image ID 4714

159

Twentieth-century urban Indians organized sports teams as a way to build community in cities. Frank Bear (Oneida), cofounder of United Indians, coached the Milwaukee Bravettes, an all-Indian women's baseball team funded by the Women's Guild of Milwaukee. Pictured from left to right: (first row, kneeling) Marge Jackson, Ellen Danforth, Estelle Webster, Marlene Silas, and Lydia Parker; (second row, kneeling) Karen [last name unknown] and Opal Skenandore; (third row) Alberta House-Metoxen, [first name unknown] Elm, unidentified, and Erma Wheelock.

Courtesy of Opal Skenadore

Native American families who migrate to and from their reservation for employment and other opportunities.[5]

The second-largest concentration of urban Indians is in Brown County, where the estimated 6,696 population includes the Oneida Indian Reservation.[6] Nearly 2,000 Native Americans reside in Dane County, which includes Madison, the state capital, and an additional 3,000 live in five counties with midsize cities (Eau Claire, La Crosse, Janesville, Beloit, Racine, and Kenosha). Although city Indians are more likely than their reservation counterparts to earn higher incomes, compared to white urbanites they are also more likely to be unemployed, live in poverty, and reside in substandard housing. They are also less likely to have college degrees and face more obstacles in accessing health care.[7] The most difficult challenge, however, especially in the decades immediately following World War II, has been cultural isolation. In 1957, Bernadine Vigue and her family moved from the Menominee Reservation to Gary, Indiana, where "you could live right next door to somebody and not even know who he or she was." She recalled, "My mother felt really isolated because on the reservation, even though there is poverty, there is still a lot of community."[8]

Oneida Indians who moved to Milwaukee connected with each other and other tribal peoples through Consolidated Tribes of American Indians, founded by one of their own, Alpheus Smith, in 1937. Consolidated Tribes sponsored social events and held dances to promote fellowship and help preserve Native culture. In the 1950s, it fielded sports teams, including a lacrosse team. Frank Bear, an Oneida who would later establish the pan-Indian social organization United Indians of Milwaukee, coached the Milwaukee Bravettes, an all-Indian female baseball team.[9] Sports, powwows, and other activities helped strengthen pan-Indian kinship networks in urban areas and create what one historian described as "concrete reservations."[10]

Reservations—even those socially constructed in the city—"act as force fields pulling Indians together," wrote Gail Guthrie Valaskakis, a Lac du Flambeau Ojibwe. Whether they live in the same neighborhood or are flung out across town, Indians "living the borders of blood and belonging" somehow find each other.[11]

Many urban Indian youth found themselves at the Ace Boxing Club, run by Del Porter (Ojibwe), a middleweight state Golden Gloves champion who founded the nonprofit club in 1960. "I noticed kids were hanging out, getting in trouble," Porter said in a 2002 interview. "Nowhere to go. Nothing to do." Until his death in 2008, Porter provided free training and conditioning to thousands of Milwaukee's at-risk youngsters, telling them to get off the streets and into the ring. "He took us to tournaments all over the country and paid out of his own pocket," said Angel Villarreal, a three-time state Golden Gloves champion under the legendary boxing coach. Porter worked four jobs to keep the boxing club open.[12] Native-run organizations and businesses, like the Ace Boxing Club and Indian bars, provided a home away from home for many relocated urban Indians. However, some Native people made frequent trips back to their home communities. Many Oneida, for example, traveled to and from the reservation on weekends to visit family members and attend community events. As Opal Skenandore, an Oneida who was raised in Milwaukee, recalled, "Others stayed away [from the reservation] and returned only when necessary, and others lost touch and never returned."[13]

The American Indian Movement (AIM), which began as an urban movement in the late 1960s, played a significant role in mobilizing urban Indians around socioeconomic issues and reconnecting them to reservation communities. Most Americans knew of AIM only through media accounts of the organization's more sensational activities—the occupation of Alcatraz in 1968, the Trail of Broken Treaties in 1972, and Wounded Knee in 1973.[14] However, AIM's takeover of an abandoned coast guard station on Milwaukee's lakeshore and its role in the establishment of the Indian Community School of Milwaukee (ICS) may be its most enduring legacy.

In 1970, three Oneida mothers, dissatisfied with the education their children were receiving in Milwaukee's public schools, began to teach their children themselves in the basement of a local church. Their intent was to "restore American Indian dignity" and promote "pride in Indian youth through cultural education."[15] They recruited a Menominee education major at the University of Wisconsin–Milwaukee, Dorothy LePage, to do her student teaching at the facility and become its first director.[16] The women also recruited other Native and non-Native college students as volunteer teachers and assistants. By the spring of 1971, the school had twenty-six students and a critical shortage of space. In late summer, the space problem was solved when about twenty members of the Milwaukee chapter of AIM took over the abandoned coast guard station on Lake Michigan near downtown Milwaukee and claimed it for use as an Indian center. The expected push back from federal, state, and local officials never materialized, and

About 350 urban Indian children attend school at the Indian Community School of Milwaukee, which moved to a sprawling 177-acre campus in 2006. The award-winning design by architect Antoine Predock features natural materials, organic interior spaces, and an exterior that follows the topography of the landscape.

Courtesy of Timothy Hursley

in September classes quietly began with forty students, a number that grew to seventy by the end of November.

The school was funded by donations and small grants and was operated by volunteers. None of the teachers or staff received a salary. In 1972, the financial picture somewhat stabilized when the school received money through the Title IV program of the Indian Education Act, which allowed it to operate—"albeit on a shoestring budget"—for the next six years.[17] A complicated series of transactions resulted in a new home for the school. In 1978, the US General Services Administration declared the former coast guard station "surplus" and transferred ownership to Milwaukee County, stipulating that the county find a suitable site for the school. The city of Milwaukee then deeded the former Bartlett Avenue School to the county, which in turn gave a parcel of land to Milwaukee Public Schools. Two years later ICS opened in the former Bartlett Avenue School with 120 students. It continued to operate until 1982, when disaster struck.

The 1982–83 federal budget devastated programs for all Native Americans, but it particularly crippled the ones that supported urban Indians. The Reagan administration reduced Indian housing funds by 96 percent, urban Indian health care by 50 percent, and economic development and jobs expenditures by 45 percent. Some programs, including legal services to Indians, were completely eliminated.[18] Indian education also suffered. For the first time in ten years, the Indian Community School of Milwaukee received no Title IV funds and was forced to close.[19]

A group of Native women organized a new school board, sold the Bartlett School building to a developer, and in 1987 used the proceeds to buy an 11.5-acre campus that had been vacated by Concordia College and that included classrooms, dormitories, a library, and a gymnasium. The buildings needed major rehabilitation, so the women renovated them, one at a time. A sixteen-unit dormitory was remodeled into elderly housing. Another reopened as a dormitory for Native college students. A daycare center for Indian children was established, and other Native community groups moved in as well. The rent generated from these occupancies helped, but the school continued to struggle. Still, ICS had established itself as the heart of the American Indian community in Milwaukee.

Then in 1988 the passage of the National Indian Gaming Regulatory Act provided a unique opportunity. The women signed an agreement with the Forest County Potawatomi (FCP) to place the 11.5 acres in trust, a move that angered some neighbors concerned about FCP's interest in erecting a casino on the property. Eventually the ICS board purchased a two-acre parcel in the Menomonee Valley, on which Potawatomi Bingo Casino would be built. In 1990, the BIA placed both tracts of land in trust, and the tribe leased the 11.5-acre parcel back to the school. Under a revenue-sharing agreement that ended in 2010, the school received annual payments from the Potawatomi that grew to $28 million a year and allowed the ICS to create a $350 million endowment. A stable funding source enabled school officials to pay better wages and benefits to their teachers and begin planning for a new, permanent home for the school.

In 2006, with an enrollment of about 350 students, the Indian Community School of Milwaukee opened the doors to a new 165,000-square-foot facility that the *Milwaukee Journal Sentinel* called an "earth-friendly *tour de force*" set into 177 acres of rolling hills and woodlands in the Milwaukee suburb of Franklin.[20] Organic interior spaces flow to the exterior, where earthen berms frame prairie and woodlands and boardwalks direct the visitor to wetlands. As stated in the founders' mission statement, "Traditional values, culture, language, heritage, and spirituality" inform the core K–8 curriculum.[21]

Until 2010, urban youth in Milwaukee could attend a Native-centric high school, Spotted Eagle, that also emphasized education within a cultural framework. Concerned about academic failure and dropout rates among Native students, in 1994, a group of parents and professionals created the school as an alternative to high schools within the Milwaukee public school system. Spotted Eagle offered a school-to-work program in which students received academic credit for working in supervised fields including automotive, child care, landscaping, and customer service.[22] Community service was a hallmark of the school's pedagogical approach. Each student performed one hundred hours of service in hospitals, schools, parks, or other institutions. Students also served on conflict-resolution committees, an opportunity for decision making that most did not find in their regular high schools. The goal was to "enable success by infusing American Indian art, literature, and values into the curriculum and imparting the curriculum in a relaxed, caring, and democratic environment."[23]

Located in one of the more dilapidated buildings on the old Concordia campus, Spotted Eagle closed in June 2010. However, five months later, the Potawatomi received approval from the Milwaukee City Council to begin a five-year, $29 million urban renewal project at the site. In early 2011, they began renovating Pritzlaff Hall, which will become the new home for Spotted Eagle High School and other tribal services, and Wundar Hall, which will become a tribal business incubator.[24]

Like schools, faith communities have been an important part of urban Indian life. The Congregation of the Great Spirit, established in 1989, ministers to Catholic Indians in Milwaukee. Sunday Mass begins with drumming and smudging—the ceremonial burning of sage, sweet grass, cedar, and tobacco. "This is like home," one parishioner said. "It's a place to gather and pray that also honors Indian traditions."[25] Through its Siggenauk Center, the congregation operates food and clothing banks, conducts social justice meetings, and offers craft classes. At the Lutheran Church of the Great Spirit, located on Milwaukee's southeast side, parishioners also smudge and, in keeping with many Native traditions, pray to the Four Directions. Church members worship in ways that reflect the heritage of its members.[26] United Methodist Church (UMC) has a Native American ministry on Milwaukee's south side. In 2011, however, budget cuts forced it to curtail its entire outreach effort, which included Ojibwe language classes and group counseling for addiction. "We're just keeping the doors open," said Pastor Rob Odum, who called the decision "ironic" in light of UMC's planned "Act of Repentance to Indigenous Peoples" at its 2012 conference.[27]

Schools and churches, although critical, are not the only glue that holds urban Indians together. Both the Oneida Nation and the Ho-Chunk Nation have branch offices on Milwaukee's south side. These offices provide social services and are intended to help tribal members stay culturally connected. The Menominee Community Center of Chicago, established in 1994 and funded by the tribe since 1996, sponsors powwows and traditional feasts and provides meals for homeless tribal members. The center, which serves about five hundred Menominee in the Chicago area, also organizes trips back to the reservation for important cultural events. In 2003, Harvard University's Honoring Nations program recognized this "unique partnership" between a tribal government and an urban Indian center and awarded it "high honors."[28]

Health and wellness centers also play a vital role in urban Indian life, providing not only clinic services but also counseling and behavioral programs and referrals. Disturbing statistics on urban Indian health provide evidence that a desperate need exists for these clinics. A 2009 report indicated that three health disparities stood out among the Milwaukee Indian population: chronic liver disease and cirrhosis at a rate four times higher than in the general population, and deaths from diabetes and alcohol-related injuries three times higher than in the population as a whole.[29] Obesity and recreational smoking rates were also higher than those reported by non-Indians.[30] Access to health care remains an obstacle for many urban Indians in Milwaukee. More than 34 percent of Native people reported they were unable to see a doctor because of cost issues. Nearly 28 percent had no health insurance—double the number of people without health coverage in the general population—and 22 percent lived in poverty. The vast majority of Indians in its service area were under age forty-five (79 percent). One in four clinic visitors did not have a high school diploma.

The statistics were similar to those for the other urban Indian clinic in Wisconsin, the United AmerIndian Health Center Inc. in Green Bay (serving Brown and Door Counties). Like the Milwaukee health center, the clientele skewed younger (77 percent under forty-five years old), had similar high school dropout rates (23 percent), and had similar poverty rates (19 percent). After cancer and heart disease, unintentional injury and diabetes were the leading causes of death, with unintentional injury rates twice and diabetes rates four times that of the general population.[31] As with the Milwaukee facility, clients had similar tobacco use patterns and obesity rates and were more likely to be uninsured. The Green Bay facility closed in 2008 when IHS announced it would not renew its $276,000 contract.[32] Indian Health Service officials say the United AmerIndian Health Center did not see enough patients and did not meet IHS criteria. The clinic's proximity to the highly regarded Oneida Community Health Center may have reduced the number of patients who used the facility.[33]

The vulnerability of urban Indians to the vagaries of federal funding is obvious. There is no sovereign Indian nation to lobby on their behalf or provide much-needed services. Until the early 1990s, for example, the urban Indian business community in Milwaukee was small and pretty much on its own. In 1991, a handful of Indian entrepreneurs and businesspeople from various tribes formed the American

Ada Deer (Menominee, at left), former Assistant Secretary of the Interior, Bureau of Indian Affairs, and longtime friends Georgiana Ignace (Menominee) and her husband, Dr. Gerald Ignace (Couer d'Alene), who in 1974 founded the Milwaukee Indian Health Center. The Ignaces devoted their lives to urban Indian health issues, particularly in Milwaukee. In 1999, the center was renamed the Gerald L. Ignace Indian Health Center.

Courtesy of Siobhan Marks

Indian Chamber of Commerce of Wisconsin (AICCW). The chamber promotes Native American economic development by providing financial products and services, business management counseling, networking, and advocacy. Through donations from corporate sponsors and fundraisers, it has distributed more than $242,000 in scholarships to 129 American Indian college students. Although it is located in Milwaukee, it supports Indian-owned small businesses and entrepreneurs throughout the state. "By being in Milwaukee, we're closer to state and federal government and the corporations that provide opportunities to our members," executive director Craig Anderson explained. "It's hard to maintain that contact and visibility if you're way up north."[34]

From its first eleven years when it operated largely with volunteers, AICCW has evolved to become a national model for American Indian economic development. In 2004, the chamber established the American Indian Construction and Trade Association (AICTA) to assist Indian-owned companies, two-thirds of which are in the construction industry. Although the Wisconsin Department of Transportation's Disadvantaged Business Enterprise program (DBE) provides opportunities to American Indian and other minority-owned businesses in order to ensure a level playing field in contract awards,[35] in 2006 there were only nine American Indian DBEs in the entire state.[36] AICTA worked with its members to create business profiles that are sent to prime contractors and assisted Indian businesses in becoming DBE certified. By 2011, the list of certified Indian-owned DBEs in Wisconsin had grown to seventy-five. Chamber members receive notifications about upcoming government products and bid deadlines while prime contractors can search an online directory listing more than 125 Native-owned businesses. AICTA represents its members on industry boards and committees and lobbies on state and federal policies that affect American Indians in the construction and trade industries.

Perhaps the most significant achievement of the AICCW was the creation of the First American Capital Corporation (FACC) in 2002, which manages a revolving loan program. In 2007, FACC became the only American Indian Small Business Administration microlender in the country. FACC mentors provide technical assistance and "gap" funding to Native entrepreneurs on and off reservations to help them grow their businesses. "Bankers want the sure thing. They don't want to deal with tribal courts and that sort of thing," FACC president Jeff Bowman explained. "So there were a whole bunch of people being ignored because of unique circumstances."[37]

The impediments to Indian enterprise *are* unique. On the reservation, tribal governments have sovereign immunity—meaning, as with all governments, they cannot be sued. Disputes can end up in tribal rather than in county courts. Confusing laws and competing jurisdictions in Indian Country may scare away non-Indian investors and potential business partners. Off the reservation, as Bowman put it, "Indians have intellectual capital, but often no monetary capital."[38] Because Indian land is held in trust by the federal government, Native people or even their tribal governments, in most cases, do not technically own their land and thus cannot use it as collateral.[39] "Some of our customers are a guy with a truck and a set of tools. We're helping 'the little guy,'" Bowman said. With seed money from the Wisconsin Department of Commerce and grants and loans from a number of federal agencies, FACC has provided $2.5 million in business loans to Native plumbers, electricians, manufacturers, and other small-business owners and helped create and retain 250 jobs. Through its activities, the chamber estimates that it has generated another 350 jobs. Together, the three entities—the chamber, AICTA, and FACC—provide a full range of financial services to Native entrepreneurs and small-business people to strengthen American Indian communities and economies. "We've created millions of dollars of opportunities to American Indian businesses that they didn't have access to before," according to Anderson.

Skyscrapers frame Oneida dancers Ken Metoxen (left) and Kirby Metoxen (right) at Indian Summer Festival in Milwaukee, the largest celebration of its kind in the country.

Courtesy of Barb Jakopac

One of the oldest and most active Indian organizations in Wisconsin is United Indians of Milwaukee (UIM), which formed as a nonprofit organization in the early 1960s "to continue the traditional ways of the Great Lakes tribes in an urban setting."[40] Members of eleven different tribes met in various churches until 1969, when they drafted a constitution and adopted bylaws. That same year they leased an old firehouse in the Walker's Point area of the city's south side and organized cultural and social activities. Over the years UIM has offered weekly drumming and craft sessions, community meetings, seasonal ceremonies, and traditional feasts. It has participated in a number of community events, including the annual Holiday Folk Fair, and provided cooks for Indian Summer Festival, held on Milwaukee's lakefront each September. In 2011, it held its thirty-second annual powwow at State Fair Park in West Allis, and it sponsors smaller powwows throughout the year. Over its fifty-year history, the organization has worked to increase public awareness of Native American history and culture. In 1992, a year commemorating the five-hundredth anniversary of European encounter, for example, United Indians of

Milwaukee opened its doors on Columbus Day—a "day of mourning"—to feed the city's poor.[41]

In Green Bay, the United AmerIndian Center (UAC), which opened in 1976, offered an array of services ranging from transportation and employment counseling to health screening and housing. At one time, the center operated the largest homeless shelter in the state as well as four other shelters. "They had nothing," lamented Shirley Hill, the center's first director. "Oneida tribal services ended at the reservation boundaries, so if you weren't Oneida, you were out of luck." As an Oneida community health official, she witnessed the suffering that went on, especially among the homeless, in particular veterans and people who were mentally and physically disabled. "They slept in doorways, under bridges, and in the parks," she recalled.[42] The center provided stages of support, from shelters and self-help programs to jobs and permanent homes, including residence for low-income tenants in an eighteen-unit apartment complex located above the center. For many homeless people in Green Bay, the UAC became their home address so that they could receive mail.[43]

Although many of its services, including transportation, were available to anyone, some were Native focused, like the Head Start and TRAIL programs for Indian youth.[44] The center also provided cultural grounding for Green Bay's urban Indians. It had a drum circle, arts and crafts classes, and harvest classes. Elders held their monthly meetings there, as did the Alcoholics Anonymous chapter. The Ho-Chunk Nation scheduled quarterly meetings there for the three hundred tribal members who live in the Green Bay area. The Menominee Nation also scheduled public hearings there from time to time.

By 2003, the center was "doing it all."[45] With a modest $800,000 annual budget, a few paid staff positions, UW–Green Bay college interns, and a lot of volunteers, UAC was a hub of social services and cultural activities as well as a clinic offering health screenings, counseling, and referrals to thousands of Indians and other low-income urbanites. After 2005, the center experienced a series of misfortunes. Always dependent on IHS grants, the center lost its funding from the Indian health agency. IHS awarded $276,000 to the Native American Services Center, which opened its clinic across the street from the AmerIndian Center.[46] UAC mortgaged its property in an effort to continue to provide services, but it could not continue. "The bank foreclosed," said David Webster, who served as UAC's director from 2003 to 2005.[47] "They lost it all." In 2008, the Native American Services Center also went defunct.

The demise of the United AmerIndian Center was a significant loss for Green Bay's urban Indians. The cultural void it left, however, was partially filled by the transformation of the American Indian Studies (AIS) program at UW–Green

Bay and the establishment of a degree in First Nations Studies. In 2005, AIS changed its name to the Center for First Nations Studies (FNS), and two years later it won approval from the UW Board of Regents for its new major: an interdisciplinary degree that emphasizes the oral traditions of Native communities, especially those of the Great Lakes nations.[48] Today the energized department offers cultural programs open to the community; sponsors the annual American Indian Studies Summer Institute;[49] and connects its students to Native communities through language classes on the Oneida Reservation and through internships with Native organizations, businesses, and tribal governments. FNS supports four elder oral-traditional scholars in residence who reflect its mission to provide students with a holistic worldview and promote a non-Western approach to teaching

Milwaukee's Indian Summer Festival celebrated its twenty-fifth anniversary in 2011. Conceived of by Milwaukee police officer Butch Roberts (Oneida) and first organized by volunteers, the three-day festival has attracted more than 1.3 million visitors.
Photo by Donald S. Abrams, courtesy of the Wisconsin Department of Tourism

Ingrid Washinawatok: Flying Eagle Woman

Menominee activist Ingrid Washinawatok (1957–1999) spent her life advocating for the human rights of indigenous people. Along with two others, in 1999 she was kidnapped and killed in Colombia while attempting to organize a community school.

Courtesy of Mary Annette Pember

Her life ended the way she had lived it—defending indigenous rights.

Ingrid Washinawatok, a member of the Menominee Nation, was an internationally known human rights advocate murdered by left-wing guerrillas in Colombia in 1999. An urban Indian born and raised in Chicago during Menominee termination, Washinawatok was an active member of the American Indian Movement (AIM) and mobilized communities against racism. "Why is everything starting in 1492?" she asked during a speech in 1992, the five-hundred-year anniversary of Columbus's voyage. "Where is MY history?"

Washinawatok moved to New York to direct a Native foundation, Fund for the Four Directions, and cofounded the Indigenous Women's Network. She was a delegate to the United Nations Commission on Human Rights and chaired its Committee on the International

continued on page 171

and learning.[50] UW–Green Bay, like many other campuses in the University of Wisconsin system, sponsors an annual powwow that provides an opportunity for Indian and non-Indian students to socialize with Native community members and learn about Native food, music, and cultural expression.

Milwaukee, "the City of Festivals," sponsors Indian Summer Festival, the largest annual Native festival of its kind in the country.[51] Each September, contemporary and traditional Native musicians and artists, environmentalists, schoolchildren, Native sports enthusiasts, vendors, and the public come together for three days of celebration. The festival begins with an education day for schoolchildren, where students learn about Wisconsin Indian history and tour a re-creation of a traditional village erected by one of the Indian nations of Wisconsin. Cultural representatives explain indigenous plants and medicines; demonstrate traditional skills like tanning, finger weaving, and beading; and tell stories. Organizers see it as a way to "negate ignorance, stereotyping, prejudice, and racism."[52] Over the next two days, more than a thousand dancers in full regalia perform in exhibition and contest dances at the festival's powwow. Indigenous artists from around the world create and exhibit their work, and food vendors sell fry bread, buffalo sandwiches, corn soup, and other Native cuisine. Contemporary Native rock, hip-hop, country, and other artists perform hourly on multiple stages, while in another venue athletes demonstrate traditional sports like lacrosse.

The festival was the brainchild of Butch Roberts, a Milwaukee police detective and member of the Oneida Nation who worked during other ethnic festivals on the city's Summerfest grounds as part of his job. As Roberts explained, "People need to know that we've always been part of America. We need to reinforce that and let people know about our contributions."[53] With a $5,000 grant from the Oneida Nation, a modest cash

loan, and volunteers—most them off-duty police officers—the first festival, in 1987, attracted twenty-three
thousand visitors. "What a beautiful way to present
our cultures," Roberts recalled, "to share your food and
music with people from all over the country."[54]

"I was so hungry for Native culture," said Alice
Loew, an Ojibwe artist who in 1987 was asked to create the first Eagle Staff used in the festival's grand
entry.[55] "I was like a blank page, an empty book,"
she explained. She had grown up as an urban Indian
whose father had been "bruised" by Indian boarding
schools and tried to protect his children by not passing down the language or culture. For Loew, Indian
Summer Festival was a "coming-out celebration," a
source of pride and affirmation.[56] Her nephew Jim
Denomie, who directed marketing for the first festival,
said his most vivid memory came after a performance
by Joanne Shenandoah, a contemporary Oneida singer
from New York. "I was in the backstage area and saw a
grown man sitting on the stage steps crying," Denomie
recalled. "For a lot of urban Indians, it was the first
time they'd seen Native culture portrayed in a positive
light."[57]

Roberts credits the Warrens, the Denomies, and
other urban Indian families he recruited with creating
a memorable festival. Over the years attendance has
more than doubled.[58] "One of the best things we ever
did," Denomie said, was *not* to launch Indian Summer
Festival in 1986 as planned. "We weren't ready. We
didn't know how to run a festival, so in 1986 we worked
other festivals to learn how to put on our own." Roberts remembered that some of the movers and shakers
behind Milwaukee Summerfest, including executive
director Elizabeth "Bo" Black, were not convinced that
the city's Native community could succeed in pulling
off an event of such magnitude. "But when she [Black]
saw eight thousand schoolkids on the grounds the first
day, he said, "she was like Dorothy in Munchkinland."

continued from page 170

Decade of the World's Indigenous People. A
year before she died, New York City recognized
her as its American Indian Woman of the Year.

In 1999, between right-wing paramilitary
units, left-wing guerrillas, and drug lords,
Colombia was an extremely dangerous place.
More than six hundred people had been killed
in the area over the previous two years. Yet
when the U'wa Indians there asked Washinawatok to help them organize a community school
to protect their language and strengthen their
culture, she didn't hesitate. In March 1999, she
and two other human rights activists, Lahe'ene
Gay and Terence Freitas, were kidnapped and
executed.

At her funeral in New York City, more than
a thousand visitors paid their respects to her
husband, her fourteen-year-old son, and her
Menominee family. At an honoring feast in Keshena in 2005, she was remembered as a "true
Menominee warrior," someone who reached
out to the young people of her tribe, advocated
for Native people on a national level, and fought
injustice on an international platform.[1]

1. Numerous sources were used for this article, including Washinawatok's 1992 speech in
New York City. Listen to the Pacifica audio
stream at the Democracy Now website, www
.democracynow.org/1999/3/8/u_s_activists
_killed_in_colombia. Also see "Washinawatok Honored during Sturgeon Celebration,"
Menominee Nation News, April 25, 2005, p. 1;
"About Ingrid Washinawatok," National Council
of Churches, www.ncccusa.org/news/99news61a
.html; "In Memoriam: Ingrid Washinawatok,"
Native Americas Journal, www.thepeoplespaths
.net/News99/0399/NAJ990331Memoriam
.htm; and "Colombia Rebels Say Own Fighters
Killed 3," *New York Times*, March 11, 1999, www
.nytimes.com/1999/03/11/world/colombia
-rebels-say-own-fighters-killed-3.html.

He described Black as a "staunch supporter" of Indian Summer Festival from that point forward and an ally in its fund-raising efforts.[59]

In 2011, Indian Summer Festival celebrated its twenty-fifth anniversary. Still operating with a volunteer board and the equivalent of more than twenty-two hundred volunteers over the three-day event, it continues to support 120 American Indian small businesses. Over the years, nearly 1.3 million visitors from around the world have experienced the festival. The growth of this event mirrors the increasing visibility of urban Indians in Milwaukee, who embrace both a traditional and contemporary identity. Their struggle for recognition testifies to the power of pan-Indian collaboration and their unique approach to overcoming decades of cultural isolation.

BEYOND

As Indian nations in Wisconsin look to the next decade of the twenty-first century, they do so from communities that are generally stronger economically, politically, and culturally than they were in 2000. It is not accurate to say that gaming has brought prosperity to a new generation of Native people. Indian nations lagged so far behind most other communities in Wisconsin that it is fair to say only that some tribes are finally catching up. However, most Indian nations in the state are nowhere near the goal of self-sufficiency that proponents of the National Indian Gaming Regulatory Act envisioned. For the Brothertown, federal recognition must come before any serious conversations about self-sufficiency can take place.

Tribes that perceive themselves economically to be the "have-nots" continue to press for off-reservation casinos, efforts that will undoubtedly meet resistance from Native nations with existing gaming operations in the area. The global recession that began in 2007 helped shape a landscape that is both favorable and unfavorable to more casinos. Communities hit hard by declining tax revenues and joblessness, especially in the southern part of the state, have courted tribes in the hope of securing casinos. Others are weary of gaming and worry that in tough economic times, out of desperation the people who can least afford to gamble, sometimes will.

Yet the signs of economic progress from gaming are everywhere, from new health clinics and assisted-living facilities to early childhood development centers, schools, and better housing. Nations that did without the infrastructure most mainstream communities take for granted—banks, grocery stores, gas stations—finally have the basic necessities of everyday life. So there is reason to be hopeful about the future of the Indian nations of Wisconsin.

Corn husk doll
Wisconsin Historical Museum 1996.118.91

173

That optimism is shared by thousands of urban Indians who are returning home to their reservations—part of a trend that Native journalist Tim Giago described as the "biggest story in Indian Country."[1] Many older tribal citizens who left for cities during the relocation era of the 1950s believe they can find a better way of life on the reservation, where elders are held in high esteem and the cost of living is relatively low. Returning tribal member Mike Wiggins lived in Milwaukee for twelve years, earning good money as a cement finisher. "My job was in the city," he said, "but my heart was at the reservation." When an employment opportunity opened up at the Bad River Casino, he returned home to take it, and fifteen years later he rose to become tribal chair.[2]

This "ruralization" of urban Indians has not been without its challenges. City Indians weary of the drugs and crime of urban America—hoping to "get away from it all"—have sometimes brought it all back with them. Nearly all the Native communities in the state have seen a sharp rise in drug activity. Law enforcement efforts have been hampered by the size and remoteness of some of the reservations, where fewer than ten tribal police officers patrol one hundred square miles. In 2002, one Indian nation was so infiltrated by a Milwaukee gang, the Latin Kings, and cocaine trafficking that it declared a state of emergency. In 2007, the eleven federally recognized tribes banded together and, with various state and federal law enforcement agencies, formed the Native American Drug and Gang Initiative to stem the flow of illegal drugs and gang activity.

Another significant trend is under way in Wisconsin's Indian Country. Tribes are not only adding population to their reservation communities; they're also adding land, or, more precisely, reacquiring land that once was theirs and attempting to place it in trust, a development that has created some resentment among neighboring non-Indians. These land-into-trust challenges will likely become more frequent as tribes that lost land through the allotment process or termination attempt to buy back land within their reservation boundaries. Indian trust lands, which are not taxable, represent a loss of revenue to municipalities and county governments. The town of Hobart, for example, has attempted to block the Oneida Nation from returning tribally purchased lands to trust status. Although Oneida voluntarily makes up for the tax loss through service agreements with other neighboring municipalities, Hobart so far has refused such an agreement. In Menominee, attempts to buy back Legend Lake parcels have met with restrictive covenants and potential lawsuits. On every reservation affected by allotment or termination, Indian nations have been asked—as they have since European contact—to accommodate non-Indians who live near or within their borders.

At the close of the twentieth century, the infusion of gaming dollars into Native communities ravaged by years of poverty and neglect began to express itself in better housing, more jobs, and expanded tribal government programs and services. The twenty-first century began promisingly enough, but in the latter part of the first decade, as it did across America, economic growth fizzled. Nearly every Indian nation saw its casino profits dip and its tribal economies struggle. Some tribes tightened their belts, cut employee hours, suspended 401(k) contributions, or took other cost-saving measures; few laid off workers.

The revitalization that began in an era of reasserted treaty rights and self-determination continues to express itself in art and culture. Reservation pow-wows, such as the Honor the Earth celebration at Lac Courte Oreilles and Strawberry Moon Pow Wow at Mole Lake, continue to grow in popularity, as does Brothertown's Homecoming each fall at the Fond du Lac Fairgrounds. However, there is universal concern over the loss of Native languages. A 2007 *National Geographic* report predicting that half the world's seven thousand languages would die out by the year 2100 resonated deeply with elders and culture keepers of every Indian nation in Wisconsin.[3] With the passing of each Native-language speaker, a sense of desperation sets in. The language has already gone dormant in two communities, the Stockbridge-Munsee Community, and the Brothertown. Every tribe in Wisconsin has prioritized language preservation. Red Cliff began early childhood language immersion classes; the Ho-Chunk established speaker-apprentice programs; the Menominee and Potawatomi sponsor summer language camps.

Although the state of Wisconsin and the eleven federally recognized tribal governments have created successful partnerships in many areas, including health, social services, and natural resource enhancement, an underlying tension still exists, as evidenced by the jurisdictional disputes that frequently surface. Of all the disagreements over environmental issues, none bears watching more than mining, especially during times of economic downturn when voters feel they must choose between creating jobs and protecting the environment.

The Mining Moratorium Law passed by the Wisconsin legislature in 1997 and the purchase of the Crandon Mine by the Sokaogon Ojibwe and Forest County Potawatomi in 2003 were viewed by many Native Americans as temporary victories. The late Hilary "Sparky" Waukau, a Menominee elder who devoted much of his life to opposing the mine, warned that Native people could never let down their guard. "As long as those valuable metals are in the ground, we as human beings can never rest," he said, "because the beast of greed and exploitation will be over our heads and over generations who inhabit this part of the country to the end of eternity."[4]

The deep anxiety Native people have about threats to their environment cannot be overstated. Damage to their natural landscape means damage to their cultural and spiritual landscapes because both are inextricably tied to the land. If resources are fouled by pollution, Native communities cannot pack up and move. They are bound to their ancestral place. Already, those places are transforming because of climate change—lake ice is melting sooner, clan animals are disappearing, and invasive species are crowding out native plants and medicines.

Some tribes, including Bad River, Mole Lake, and the Potawatomi, have used legal strategies, such as treatment as a state (TAS) status, to establish their own air and water quality standards. Other Indian nations undoubtedly will seek TAS status as well. This designation, awarded by the EPA, brings tribes into the decision-making process about industrial permits and allows them to protect their air and water resources. Some Native communities have sought federal "Outstanding Water Resource" status for rivers and streams that flow through their reservations, such as the Wolf and Bad Rivers and Potato Creek. This designation sets a higher level for discharge and makes it difficult for industry to use such a river to dump treated effluent. In 2009, the Forest County Potawatomi became only the fifth tribe in the United States to acquire a class 1 air quality designation for their reservation. However, it came at a substantial cost—fighting fourteen years of lawsuits filed by the states of Wisconsin and Michigan.

Local conflicts have already merged into a broader strategy advocated by an increasing number of tribes and tribal citizens—the Seventh Generation Amendment, a proposed constitutional amendment that states:

> The right of citizens of the United States to use and enjoy air, water, wildlife, and other renewable resources determined by the Congress to be common property shall not be impaired, nor shall such use impair their availability for the use of future generation.

The amendment speaks to the obligation Native communities believe they have as land stewards, to the plants and animals, to their non-Indian neighbors, and, as First Peoples—Ho-Chunk, Menominee, Ojibwe, Potawatomi, Oneida, Stockbridge-Munsee Community, and Brothertown—to themselves.

NOTES

CHAPTER 1

1. Anthropologist Paul Radin details the Red Horn story in "Winnebago Hero Cycles: A Study in Aboriginal Literature," in "Indiana University Publications in Anthropology and Linguistics," supplement to *International Journal of American Linguistics* 14, no. 3 (Baltimore: Waverly Press, 1948), 115–36.

2. Robert J. Salzer, "Chapter 4: Wisconsin Rock Art," *The Wisconsin Archeologist*, edited by Robert A. Birmingham, Carol I. Mason, and James B. Stoltman, 78, no. 1/2 (January–December 1997), 48–77.

3. Frances Densmore, *Chippewa Customs* (Minneapolis: Ross & Haines, 1929; repr., St. Paul: Minnesota Historical Society Press, 1979), 88–97.

4. For more on wampum, see Frederick J. H. Merrill, "Wampum and Shell Articles," *Bulletin of the New York State Museum* 8, no. 41 (February 1901; repr., New York: AMS Press, 1978), 455–57; and George Hammel, "The Iroquois and the World's Rim," *American Indian Quarterly* 16, no. 4 (Fall 1992), 451–70. Carol Cornelius, director of Oneida Nation Historical and Cultural Department, agrees that white symbolized peace but could not confirm the cultural meanings of the use of black or red wampum. (Phone interview with author, November 2000.) Excellent histories and images of wampum belts are available on the web. See www.nativetech.org/wampum/wamphist.htm.

5. Edward Benton-Banai, *The Mishomis Book* (St. Paul: Red School House, 1988), 29–34.

6. Oneida Nation, from the pamphlet *The Iroquois Story of Creation* (Oneida, WI: Oneida Nation Culture and Heritage Department, n.d.).

7. Ho-Chunk Nation, from the pamphlet *Ca Worak [Deer Story]* (Mauston, WI: Ho-cak Wazijaci Language and Culture Program, 1997).

8. The notion that animals helped create the earth is a theme repeated in the origin stories of many Indian nations. Joseph Bruchac tells a particularly compelling version of the Fisher story in *Native American Stories* (Golden, CO: Fulcrum Publishing, 1991), 79–86.

9. Joseph Bruchac and Michael Caduto have a wonderful collection of stories about the relationship between Native people and plants and animals in *Keepers of the Earth* (Golden, CO: Fulcrum Publishing, 1988).

10. For more on the mound-building and Mississippian cultures, including the settlement at Aztalan, see *The Wisconsin Archeologist* 78, no. 1/2 (1997), 141–249 passim.; Robert A. Birmingham and Katherine Rankin, *Native American Mounds in Madison and Dane County*

(Madison: City of Madison and the State Historical Society of Wisconsin, 1996); and Robert A. Birmingham, "Ancient People of Monona" (unpublished paper, n.d.).

11. Benton-Banai, *The Mishomis Book*, 74–78.

12. Verna Fowler, "Creation Story," as cited in *Wisconsin Indian Literature*, edited by Kathleen Tigerman (Madison: University of Wisconsin Press, 2006), 11.

13. Robert Bieder discusses the Menominee and Ho-Chunk clan systems in *Native American Communities in Wisconsin, 1600–1960* (Madison: University of Wisconsin Press, 1995), 23–38. The origins of the Ho-Chunk Buffalo Clan are recounted in the informational sheet *The Ho-Chunk and Green Lake* (Black River Falls, WI: Hocak Wazijaci Language and Culture Program, n.d.).

14. Barbara A. Mann and Jerry L. Fields, "A Sign in the Sky: Dating the League of the Haudenosaunee," *American Indian Culture and Research Journal* 21, no. 2 (1997), 143.

15. Carol Cornelius, author interview, September 20, 1999, Oneida, WI.

CHAPTER 2

1. *Since 1634: In the Wake of Nicolet*, a videotape produced by Ootek Productions, the Educational Communications Board, and the Board of Regents, University of Wisconsin System, 1993. Dave Erickson wrote, produced, and directed the video with assistance from coproducers Lance Tallmadge of the Ho-Chunk Nation and Alan Caldwell of the Menominee Nation.

2. Jay Miller wrote a concise and very readable general history of the French fur trade era and its impact on the Indian nations of the Northeast and Great Lakes regions. See chapter 10, "The Northeast" in *The Native Americans*, edited by Betty Ballantine and Ian Ballantine (Atlanta: Turner Publishing, 1993).

3. Although some western historians speculate that the Ho-Chunk may have been ravaged by a smallpox epidemic, Randy Tallmadge, Hocak (Ho-Chunk) Wazijaci Language and Culture Program, states that the reference to "yellow sickness" was not consistent with tribal descriptions associated with pox. Randy Tallmadge, author interview, December 10, 1997, Madison.

4. For more on the fur trade and its effects on Indian nations in Wisconsin, see chapter 3 of Robert Bieder, *Native American Communities in Wisconsin, 1600–1960* (Madison: University of Wisconsin Press, 1995).

5. Richard White, *The Middle Ground: Indians, Empires, and Republics in the Great Lakes Region, 1650–1815* (Cambridge: Cambridge University Press, 1991). White argues that after encounter, Native communities did not merely assimilate European culture and values but rather intermingled with Europeans to construct "new systems of meaning and of exchange" (xxvi).

6. *Potawatomi Nation in Canada* (Mactier, ON: Keewatinosagiganing Potawatomi Nation Cultural Council, 33103 [1988]), 26, 47.

7. In his 1852 history of the Ojibwe, William Warren, the son of an Ojibwe mother and English father, complained about "chief making" by the English and Americans. Unlike the French,

whom Warren believed did not appoint chiefs "unless being first certain of the approbation of the tribe," the English and their successors awarded medals and presents "indiscriminately or only in conformity with selfish motives and ends." He alleged that this undermined the influence of the hereditary chiefs. William Warren, *History of the Ojibway People* (St. Paul: Minnesota Historical Society, 1885), 135.

8. Simon Pokagon was a Christian clan leader of the St. Joseph's Band of Potawatomi in Michigan. Although most Potawatomi unsuccessfully resisted efforts by the federal government to remove them west of the Mississippi River, Pokagon was able to establish a permanent reservation in Michigan. In a biography written by C. H. Engle, Pokagon issued a diatribe against the use of alcohol. See *O-gî-mäw-kwe mit-i-gwä-kî* (Hartford, MI: C. H. Engle, 1899).

9. Alice E. Smith, *The History of Wisconsin*, vol. 1, *From Exploration to Statehood* (Madison: State Historical Society of Wisconsin, 1973). Smith relies heavily on Reuben G. Thwaites, ed., *The Jesuit Relations and Allied Documents: Travels and Explorations of the Jesuit Missionaries in New France, 1610–1791*, 73 vols. (Cleveland: Burrows Brothers, 1896–1901), in particular volumes 18 and 23, as well as other nineteenth-century and early-twentieth-century accounts written by American, Canadian, and French historians.

10. Edward Benton-Banai, *The Mishomis Book* (St. Paul: Red School House, 1988), 106.

11. James Denomie, who has conducted genealogical research over the past decade, supplied the author with a Denomie (DeNomie) family tree during an interview in Milwaukee, Wisconsin, August 1986.

12. See Smith, *From Exploration to Statehood*, 51–56.

13. Thomas Vennum Jr. provides a fascinating account of the fateful lacrosse game in his fine book, *American Indian Lacrosse: Little Brother of War* (Washington, DC: Smithsonian Institution Press, 1994), 82–103. In summer 2000, Vennum helped establish a youth lacrosse program on the Red Cliff Ojibwe Reservation, where the game had not been played since the 1930s.

14. Reports of skirmishes between Native people and American frontiersmen likely reached Indian communities in what would become Wisconsin through the trade networks. Alice Smith writes that these frontiersmen, who were floating their goods down the Ohio River and moving their families over the mountain passes, were a "constant threat to the Indian way of life." In offering another explanation for why the tribes of the Great Lakes remained loyal to the British, she points out that the Indians "had few religious, language, or economic ties with the eastern colonists and little inclination to take the rebel side." Smith, *From Exploration to Statehood*, 69.

CHAPTER 3

1. David Beck, *Siege and Survival* (Lincoln: University of Nebraska Press, 2002), 7; and David Grignon and Rebecca Alegria, author interview, February 17, 2012, Keshena, WI.

2. Marshal Pecore, forestry manager, Menominee Nation. The author interviewed Pecore for "Nation Within a Nation," a documentary segment within *Looking for America*, which aired nationally on PBS, October 12, 1998.

3. For more detailed accounts of the Menominee's role in the American Revolutionary War, see Patricia Ourada, *The Menominee Indians: A History* (Norman: University of Oklahoma Press, 1979), 47–51; and Felix M. Keesing, *The Menomini Indians of Wisconsin* (Madison: University of Wisconsin Press, 1987), 87–90.

4. *Tomau* is the preferred Menominee spelling. It has also been spelled *Tomah*, as in the western Wisconsin city that bears the name, and *Tomaw*.

5. Menominee Tribal Historic Preservation Office, "Menominee Veterans: A Photo History of Our Land, Our Battles, Our Victories," *Menominee Indian Tribe of Wisconsin* (Keshena, WI: Menominee Tribal Historic Preservation Office, 2009), 12.

6. Tecumseh traveled to Green Bay in 1810 or 1811 and met with Menominee chiefs, including Tomau, one of the most important Menominee clan leaders at the time. Tomau told the Shawnee war chief that he would not prevent individual warriors from joining Tecumseh, but that he himself intended to stay neutral and counseled his tribe to do likewise. "These hands are unstained with human blood," Tomau told Tecumseh. James W. Biddle, "Recollections of Green Bay in 1816–17," *Wisconsin Historical Collections* 1 (1903), 52.

7. Grignon, interview.

8. Beck, *Siege and Survival*, 97.

9. The interpreter pressed into service spoke Ojibwe, the prevailing language of trade, not Menominee. His unfamiliarity with the Menominee language resulted in an accidental invitation to the Ho-Chunk to join the session, an invitation that complicated the treaty sessions. For more, see Beck, *Siege and Survival*, 92.

10. Grizzly Bear, "Minutes of the 1825 Treaty at Prairie du Chien, August, 1825," Documents Relating to the Negotiation of Ratified and Unratified Treaties with Various Tribes of Indians, 1801–1869, Record Group 75, Records of the Bureau of Indian Affairs, National Archives, Washington, DC; available at the Wisconsin Historical Society as microfilm P97-2750, reel 1 (hereafter cited as Ratified and Unratified Treaties).

11. Grignon, interview.

12. Grizzly Bear was also known as Mahkeemeeteuv and sometimes referred to as Kauskkau-no-naïve, which was also the name of his father. He was an outstanding orator who served under the leadership of Tomau. After Tomau's death, he was chosen as Speaker of the Chiefs. For additional information, see *Menominee Indian Reservation Historical Review* (Keshena, WI: Menominee Historic Preservation Department, 2004), 13.

13. *Indian Removal Records, Senate Document no. 512*, 23d Cong., 1st Sess., vol. 1, part 21 of 21, ed. Larry S. Watson, 36.

14. Treaty of February 8, 1831, Treaty of February 17, 1831, and Treaty of October 27, 1832 (all negotiated in Washington, DC), Ratified and Unratified Treaties.

15. Ourada, *The Menominee Indians*, 118.

16. Treaty of May 12, 1854, Falls of the Wolf River, Ratified and Unratified Treaties.

17. Treaty with the Menominee, 1856, in Charles J. Kappler, comp. and ed., *Indian Affairs: Laws and Treaties*, vol. 2, *Treaties* (Washington, DC: Government Printing Office, 1904), digital.library.okstate.edu/kappler/Vol2/treaties/men0755.htm.

18. Beck, *Siege and Survival*, 21–27.

19. Francis Paul Prucha, *The Churches and the Indian Schools* (Lincoln: University of Nebraska Press, 1979), 58.

20. H. H. Chapman, "The Menominee Indian Timber Case History" (proposal typed and bound by or for Chapman, 1957), p. 1. Chapman, a professor emeritus at Yale University, compiled a history of the legislation and administration of the Menominee timberlands and offered proposals for settlement. In his foreword, Chapman stated that the main purpose of the text was to "emphasize the unsettled character of the Menominee Timber problem and the need for enlightened and constructive action for the benefit not only of the Tribe but of the public and of conservation in Wisconsin." This document was instrumental in the $8.5 million judgment awarded to the Menominee by the US Court of Claims in 1952.

21. Deborah Shames, *Freedom with Reservation* (Washington, DC: National Committee to Save the Menominee People and Forests, 1972), 10. This is an excellent economic, political, and social history of the Menominee people during the termination years. It is told from the perspective of Determination of Rights and Unity for Menominee Shareholders (DRUMS), an activist group that opposed termination and agitated for restoration.

22. Ibid.

23. Ibid.

24. Nicholas C. Peroff, *Menominee DRUMS* (Norman: University of Oklahoma Press, 1982), 56. I am indebted to Ada Deer, former secretary of the Bureau of Indian Affairs and Menominee activist, who shaped my understanding of Menominee termination. Her seminar on American Indian issues was one of the first I took when I enrolled in graduate school at the University of Wisconsin–Madison in 1987. As the tribe's official representative in Washington during the termination years, Deer was intimately involved in the negotiations and resolution of Menominee termination and restoration.

25. Shames, *Freedom with Reservation*, 26–27.

26. Grignon, interview.

27. "Menominee County," Audit Summary, Wisconsin Legislative Audit Bureau, Report 93-3, February 1998, http://legis.wisconsin.gov/lab/reports/98-3tear.htm.

28. "Our Mission Statement," Menominee County Taxpayers Association website, www.legendlake.info/mcta.php.

29. "Menominee County's Taxpayers Ask for Relief," *Milwaukee Journal Sentinel*, December 26, 1995, 5B.

30. "Dispute over Property, Sovereign Tribal Rights Could End Up in Court," *Shawano Leader*, June 7, 2009, 12A.

31. "Association's Proposed Covenant Draws Tribe's Ire," *Shawano Leader*, June 7, 2009, 1A.

32. "Legend Lake Property Association Vote [*sic*] Yes on Restrictive Covenant," *Menominee Nation News*, June 22, 2009, 3A.

33. United States Code, 25:7, section 280, states that the secretary of the Interior is authorized to issue patents for up to 160 acres of land to religious organizations engaged in mission or school work. However, the code states that when "no longer used for mission or school purposes said lands shall revert to the Indian owners."

34. See Libby R. Tronnes, "Where Is John Wayne?: The Menominee Warriors Society, Indian Militancy, and Social Unrest during the Alexian Brothers Novitiate Takeover," *American Indian Quarterly* 26 (Fall 2002), 529.

35. Ibid., 548.

36. Menominee Tribal Historic Preservation Office, "Menominee Veterans," 17.

37. Ibid., 27, 35.

38. Ibid., 75–88.

39. "Answering the Call," *St. Louis Post-Dispatch*, July 6, 2008, A1.

40. J. Boyd, Menominee Vietnam veteran, author interview, September 7, 2005, Madison, WI.

41. "Phase One of Menominee Casino Resort Expansion Project Underway," *Menominee Nation News*, October 12, 2009, 1.

42. "History Clinic 20th Anniversary," Menominee Tribal Clinic www.mtclinic.net/history. htm; and "Services," Menominee Tribal Clinic, www.mtclinic.net/Services.htm.

43. "Culture Camp 2005," *Menominee Nation News*, July 25, 2005, 1.

44. Grignon, interview.

45. Hilary Waukau Sr., interview by Rebecca Alegria, July 27, 1997, Neopit, WI.

46. "Biologists Breathe New Life into Sturgeon's Ancient Habitat," *New York Times*, July 2, 2002, section F, 2.

47. Gordon Dickie, Menominee tribal chair, to Secretary John H. Herrington, Department of Energy, April 16, 1986. Gordon S. Dickie Sr. Papers, Menominee Historic Preservation Department. Private collection of Rebecca Alegria.

48. "Statement of Gordon Dickie, Chairman, Menominee Tribal Legislature, Before United States Senate Committee on Energy and Natural Resources Subcommittee on Energy Research and Development, 16 June, 1986, and Dickie to Secretary of Energy, 16 April, 1986," Gordon S. Dickie Sr. Papers, Menominee Historic Preservation Department.

49. Alegria, interview.

50. Menomineee Tribal Legislature Resolution No. 84-7, March 1, 1984. Private collection of Rebecca Alegria.

51. Foth and Van Dyke and Associates, Inc. Executive Summary, Crandon Mining Company Environmental Impact Report, vol. 1 (1995). Full text available at University of Wisconsin Digital Collections, Ecology and Natural Resources Collection, http://digicoll.library

.wisc.edu/cgi-bin/EcoNatRes/EcoNatRes-idx?type=turn&entity=EcoNatRes.EIR95v01.
p0099&id=EcoNatRes.EIR95v01&isize=M.

52. Waukau, interview.

53. "Preserving His People, Menominee Elder Dedicates His Remaining Years to Protecting the Environment," *Milwaukee Journal Sentinel*, April 30, 1995, http://nl.newsbank.com/.

54. Marshall Pecore, Menominee Forest manager, remarks to journalists during the Native American Journalists Association Eco-Tour, June 17, 2003, Keshena, WI.

55. John Kotar, UW–Madison forestry scientist, cited in "Forest Keepers: Menominee Have Been Practicing Sustainable Forestry for Centuries," *Wisconsin State Journal*, October 6, 2003, A1.

CHAPTER 4

1. Ho-Chunk Nation Heritage Preservation Department, *The HoChunk Nation: A Brief History* (Black River Falls, WI: Ho-Chunk Nation, n.d.). There is some disagreement about the translation of "Ho-Chunk." Ken Funmaker Jr., former director of the Hocak Wazijaci Language and Culture Program and a fluent Ho-Chunk speaker, stated that the literal translation is "People of the Sacred Language," a reference to Ho-Chunk being the parent language of many Siouan dialects. Ken Funmaker Jr. and Randy Tallmadge, author interview, November 18, 1997, Mauston, WI. The tribe has used alternate spellings in its various publications; these include Hocak, Ho-Chunk, and HoChunk.

2. Ho-Chunk Nation Heritage Preservation Department, *The Ho-Chunk and Green Lake* (Black River Falls, WI: Ho-Chunk Nation, n.d.). References to the Ho-Chunk origin stories are also made in *Thunder in the Dells*, a television documentary coproduced by Dave Erickson and Lance Tallmadge, which aired on Wisconsin Public Television in 1992. *Thunder in the Dells* (Spring Green, WI: Ootek Productions, 1992).

3. Letter by Joseph Street, Secretary of War, describing talks with Winnebago leaders, January 8, 1828, Office of Indian Affairs, Letters Received, Prairie du Chien Agency, Roll 696, quoted in *Winnebago Oratory: Great Moments in the Recorded Speech of the Hochungra, 1742–1887* by Mark Diedrich (Rochester, MN: Coyote Books, 1991), 27.

4. The Wisconsin Historical Society's Draper Manuscripts contain "The Tecumseh Papers, 1911–1931," a collection of letters, clippings, and other material assembled by Lyman Copeland Draper for his projected biography of the Shawnee leader. The papers indicate that as early as 1806, Tecumseh began traveling to Potawatomi, Menominee, Ojibwe, and Ho-Chunk communities in an effort to enlist their support for his pan-Indian alliance.

5. The 175 Ho-Chunk attending the council were represented by two leaders identified in treaty documents as "principal chiefs": Caramine and "De-ca-ri" (probably Decorah). Although the Ho-Chunk were concerned about incursions by white settlers, they appeared to be quite content to continue to share the land with other tribes. Caramine told the American delegation: "The lands I claim are mine and the nations here know it is not only claimed by us but by our brothers the Sacs and Foxes, Menominees, Iowas, and Sioux, they have used it in

common. It would be difficult to divide it, it belongs as much to one as the other." His remarks are contained in "Minutes of the 1825 Treaty at Prairie du Chien, August, 1825," Documents Relating to the Negotiation of Ratified and Unratified Treaties with Various Tribes of Indians, 1801–1869, Record Group 75, Records of the Bureau of Indian Affairs, National Archives, Washington, DC, and are available at the Wisconsin Historical Society as microfilm P97-2750, reel 1.

6. Treaty Journal, August 11, 1827, Winnebago file, Great Lakes–Ohio Valley Ethnohistory Archive, Indiana University, Bloomington, quoted in Diedrich, *Winnebago Oratory*, 23.

7. Thomas L. McKenney, *Memoirs, Official and Personal* (Lincoln: University of Nebraska Press, 1973), 107–8, quoted in Diedrich, *Winnebago Oratory*, 24.

8. Donald Jackson, ed., *Black Hawk: An Autobiography* (Urbana: University of Illinois Press, 1964), 114–15. Antoine LeClair, US interpreter for the Sacs and Foxes, wrote Black Hawk's "autobiography." Although LeClair maintained that he was "cautious" with the narrative and pronounced it "strictly correct," there remain questions about how much of the narrative was Black Hawk's and how much of it LeClair's.

9. Henry Dodge to Old Turtle, Spotted Arm, Little Black, Silver, and Man Eater (represented by his sister and her daughter) at Four Lakes [Madison], May 26, 1832, from an article by Milo M. Quaife, "Journals and Reports of the Black Hawk War," *Mississippi Valley Historical Review* 12, no. 3 (December 1925), 406.

10. In 1958, anthropologist Nancy Oestreich Lurie interviewed Mountain Wolf Woman, a Ho-Chunk elder, who told Lurie that "land matters were the exclusive concern of the Bear Clan people who would act in the interests of the entire group." Nancy Oestreich Lurie, ed., *Mountain Wolf Woman* (Ann Arbor, MI: Ann Arbor Paperbacks [The University of Michigan Press], 1961), 114.

11. Erickson and Tallmadge, *Thunder in the Dells*.

12. Baptiste, "Blue Earth & Crow Creek," from the pamphlet *The Ho-Chunk Removal Period* (Black River Falls, WI: Ho-Chunk Nation Heritage Preservation Department, n.d.).

13. Lurie, *Mountain Wolf Woman*, 3.

14. A few homesteads were also registered in Minnesota.

15. Ho-Chunk Nation, "Migrant Farm Workers," from the pamphlet *The Cranberry People* (Black River Falls, WI: Ho-Chunk Nation Heritage Preservation Department, n.d.).

16. Ho-Chunk Nation, "Protestant and Catholic," from the pamphlet *The Blackrobes* (Black River Falls, WI: Ho-Chunk Nation Heritage Preservation Department, n.d.).

17. Randy Tallmadge, Hocak Wazijaci Language and Culture Program, author interview, November 18, 1997, Mauston, WI.

18. *Since 1634: In the Wake of Nicolet* is an excellent documentary chronicling the histories of the Menominee and Ho-Chunk people from Nicolet's arrival to the early 1990s, produced by Dave Erickson and coproduced by Lance Tallmadge, Ho-Chunk, and Alan Caldwell, Menominee (Spring Green, WI: Ootek Productions, 1993).

19. Section 3, Powers Retained by the General Council, Constitution of the Ho-Chunk Nation, www.ho-chunknation.com/?PageId=180#art_4.

20. Erickson, *Since 1634: In the Wake of Nicolet*.

21. Population figures taken from "Ho-Chunk Nation Legislative Districts and Member Enrollment, August 2010," Ho-Chunk Nation map. Land-base figures are taken from "Ho-Chunk Nation at a Glance," *Ho-Chunk Nation*, May 2009. An additional 3,628 acres are held by Ho-Chunk tribal members as individually owned allotments.

22. "Ho-Chunk Nation to Close Bison and Organic Beef Operations," *Indian Country Today*, May 12, 2010, Business and Financial News.

23. Under terms of the 1934 Indian Reorganization Act, when federal property is declared "surplus," Indian nations in whose ancestral lands the federal property is located are prioritized for receipt of the land.

24. Ho-Chunk Nation, "BIA Denies Transfer of Badger Ammo Plant Land for Ho-Chunk Nation," media release, October 4, 2011. The Ho-Chunk tribal newspaper documented the tribe's struggle to acquire a portion of the decommissioned site. See "Ho-Chunk Nation Considers Badger Plant," *Hocak Worak* 12, no. 7 (March 31, 1998), 1; "HCN Receives Support in Badger Land Plan," *Hocak Worak* 12, no. 23 (November 25, 1998), 1; and "Ho-Chunk Blocked from Local RAB," *Hocak Worak* 13, no. 9 (May 10, 1999), 1.

25. The Ho-Chunk Ten-Year Plan, Ho-Chunk Nation, 27–28. Private collection.

26. Crystal Young, executive director, Ho-Chunk Department of Labor, phone interview with author, April 4, 2012.

27. In 2009, the Ho-Chunk Nation employed 3,354 workers, of which 74 percent were non-Indian, a percentage that most likely changed in 2011 when the Nation began a Ho-Chunk preferential hiring policy. According to the Wisconsin Department of Workforce Development, the Ho-Chunk Nation is the fourteenth largest government employer in Wisconsin. http://worknet.wisconsin.gov/worknet/largemp.aspx.

28. The Ho-Chunk Ten-Year Plan, 38.

29. The five sites are located in Indian Mission, Ahuco, Potch Che Nunk, Chakh Hah Chee, and Winnebago Heights.

30. "More Indians Owning Homes," *Wisconsin State Journal*, April 21, 2002, A1.

31. Roughly 1,500 Ho-Chunk children participate in Johnson O'Malley programs (the federal program that provides funds to public schools to address the unique cultural needs of Indian children) or pre-K–12 programs. An additional 120 children attend Head Start centers in five communities. An estimated 200 Ho-Chunk members are enrolled in postsecondary colleges and universities. See "Newly Confirmed Executive Director Shares Her Views," *Hocak Worak*, February 11, 2011, 4.

32. The Ho-Chunk Ten-Year Plan, 46.

33. Richard Mann, Hocak Wazija Haci Language Program, phone interview with author, April 4, 2012; "Hocak Language Apprentice Program Update," *Hocak Worak*, November 30, 2007, 1; http://ho-chunknation.com/UserFiles/File/2007_Issues/issue%2022.pdf.

34. Quoted in Cassandra Colson, "Ho-Chunk Striving to Preserve Language," *Jackson County Chronicle*, December 29, 2010, http://lacrossetribune.com/jacksoncochronicle/news/local/ho-chunk-striving-to-preserve-language/article_d9c4a823-b7f9-5f82-bcab-4025d40ae693.html.

CHAPTER 5

1. Edward Benton-Banai, an Ojibwe medicine man, recounts the Ojibwe migration story in chapter 14 of *The Mishomis Book*, a spiritual history of the Ojibwe people originally published in 1988 by Red School House in St. Paul, Minnesota. The book was written at the request of parents and educators in the Twin Cities area who recognized the need for culture-based educational materials. Still in print, *The Mishomis Book* is distributed by Indian Country Communications in Hayward, Wisconsin.

2. Josephine Denomie, a student at St. Mary's School in Odanah, discussed Tagwagane in her essay "History of Our Nation," in St. Mary's Industrial School, Odanah, Wis., *Noble Lives of a Noble Race* (Minneapolis: The Brooks Press, 1909).

3. For a more detailed description of Ojibwe spearfishing, see "Casting Light Upon the Waters, a Joint Fishery Assessment of the Wisconsin Ceded Territory," US Department of the Interior, Bureau of Indian Affairs, Minneapolis, 1991, 60.

4. For Ojibwe elder Archie Mosay's bilingual description of the seasonal activities of the Ojibwe, see "What They Did Long Ago" in *Living Our Language: Ojibwe Tales and Oral History* by Anton Treuer (St. Paul: Minnesota Historical Society Press, 2001), 25–29.

5. From 1936 to 1942, Sister Macaria Murphy of St. Mary's School in Odanah interviewed elders about traditional activities, such as ricing and sugaring, as part of a Works Progress Administration historical project. The compilation is available on microfilm in the Wisconsin Historical Society archives, wihv91-A679, reel 532. Another excellent source on Ojibwe ricing is Thomas Vennum Jr.'s *Wild Rice and the Ojibway People* (St. Paul: Minnesota Historical Society Press, 1988).

6. There is considerable debate about when the Ojibwe first inhabited the island or whether the early inhabitants were Ojibwe at all. The Ojibwe historian William Warren estimated that the Ojibwe had arrived in Chequamegon Bay in the late fifteenth century. He based this on stories he gathered from elders and a copper plate with eight incisions he saw in the 1820s, in which each incision denoted a generation since his ancestors had arrived in the bay. Other historians, including Theresa Schenck, who annotated a second edition of Warren's history, argue Warren erred in his calculations and interpretations. Schenk contends that the Odaawa and Huron settled the island first and that the earliest large Ojibwe village on Madeline Island was not established until the eighteenth century. Some anthropologists, including Robert Mazrim, counter that archaeological evidence supports an earlier Ojibwe presence on the island. See Theresa Schenk, *The Voice of the Crane Echoes Afar* (New York: Garland Publishing, 1997); William Warren, *History of the Ojibway People*, 2nd ed., edited by Theresa Schenck (St. Paul: Minnesota Historical Society Press, 2009); and "Reconsidering

the Antiquity of Trade on Madeline Island," *Midcontinental Journal of Archaeology* 36, no. 1 (Spring 2011), 29–71.

7. Lone Man's comments were included in the minutes to the 1825 treaty at Prairie du Chien. See Documents Relating to the Negotiation of Ratified and Unratified Treaties with Various Tribes of Indians, 1801–1869, Record Group 75, Records of the Bureau of Indian Affairs, National Archives, Washington, DC. Ron Satz provides the major Ojibwe treaties and minutes to the treaties as appendices in *Chippewa Treaty Rights: The Reserved Rights of Wisconsin's Chippewa Indians in Historical Perspective in Transactions of the Wisconsin Academy of Sciences, Arts and Letters* 79, no. 1, 1991. *Ojibway Oratory*, compiled by Mark Diedrich, is a fine collection of speeches delivered by Ojibwe chiefs and headmen between 1695 and 1889 (Rochester, MN: Coyote Books, 1990).

8. David Wrone, *Economic Impact of the 1837 and 1842 Chippewa Treaties* (Stevens Point, WI: D. R. Wrone, 1989).

9. See appendix 2, "Treaty with the Chippewa, 1937," and appendix 4, "Treaty with the Chippewa, 1842," in *Chippewa Treaty Rights* by Ron Satz (Madison: Wisconsin Academy of Sciences, Arts, and Letters, 1991), 155–76.

10. Ibid., 41.

11. The Ojibwe's understanding of the 1837, 1842, and 1854 treaties was detailed in the 1864 document "Statement Made by the Indians: A Bilingual Petition," which was published in 1988 by the University of Western Ontario as part of its series Studies in the Interpretation of Canadian Native American Languages and Cultures. The document is in the Wisconsin Historical Society archives, Madison, WI.

12. "Sandy Lake Tragedy and Memorial," *Great Lakes Indian Fish and Wildlife* (Ashland, WI: GLIFWC, 2003), www.glifwc.org/publications/pdf/SandyLake_Brochure.pdf.

13. The accuracy of Armstrong's account, written forty years after the visit occurred, has been questioned. Key features are corroborated in Indian office records, "though not always in the exact way or exact order in which Armstrong describes them." See chapter 10, "The Pleasure of the President," in *Fish in the Lakes, Wild Rice, and Game in Abundance*, comp. James McClurken (East Lansing: Michigan State University Press, 2000), 244–255.

14. Ibid., 267.

15. Benjamin Armstrong provided a fascinating account of the events leading up to and concluding with the 1854 treaty, including the Sandy Lake debacle, in *Early Life among the Indians* (Ashland, WI: Press of A. W. Bowron, 1892).

16. "St. Croix Chippewa Indians," letter from Franklin K. Lane, Secretary of the Interior, to the House Committee on Indian Affairs, December 7, 1914, 63rd Cong., 3rd sess., Document no. 1184, 59–64. See also McClurken, *Fish in the Lakes*, 84–85.

17. *Minutes of the Meetings, United States Board of Indian Commissioners, 1869–1917*, February 6, 1914, meeting, Washington, p. 424, Ayer Collection, Newberry Library, Chicago, Illinois.

18. Martin's evaluation of her Ojibwe servant is contained in a 1903 letter to Samuel Campbell, who served as Indian agent at La Pointe from 1899 until 1913. See Mrs. J. Martin to

Campbell, December 12, 1903, Samuel Campbell Papers, Wisconsin Historical Society Manuscript Collections, River Falls Area Research Center, River Falls, WI. Campbell's papers formed the basis for chapters on Ojibwe allotment and boarding schools in Patricia Loew, "Newspapers and the Lake Superior Chippewa in the 'unProgressive' Era" (PhD diss., University of Wisconsin–Madison, 1998).

19. David Bisonette, who teaches Ojibwe language at Lac Courte Oreilles Ojibwa Community College, provided this explanation. E-mail correspondence, October 24, 2011.

20. This account of the Lac Courte Oreilles was compiled from oral history the author collected in 1997–1998 for Celebrating Wisconsin's Native American Heritage, a public history project coordinated by the Great Lakes Intertribal Council as part of the Wisconsin Sesquicentennial commemoration. Source material also came from interviews I conducted with tribal members James Schlender, Jerry Smith, and others for *The Center of the Earth: The Chippewa Flowage after 75 Years*, an educational video produced in 1999 by the Institute for Environmental Studies, University of Wisconsin–Madison. Additional historical background came from Charlie Otto Rasmussen, *Where the River Is Wide: Pahquahwong and the Chippewa Flowage* (Odanah, WI: Great Lakes Indian Fish & Wildlife Commission Press, 1998).

21. Dozens of tribal members, including Headflyer, testified before a US Senate subcommittee that traveled to Wisconsin to take testimony during fall 1909. These accounts were published a year later in *Condition of Indian Affairs in Wisconsin* (Washington, DC: Government Printing Office, 1910). Headflyer's testimony is found on pp. 713–15 and 751–53.

22. This account of the Lac du Flambeau derives from the author's interviews with tribal elders, including Joe Chosa, George Brown Sr., and Tinker Schuman in 1997–1998 for the Celebrating Wisconsin's Native American Heritage project; from the Samuel Campbell Papers; Albert Cobe's recollections of the Lac du Flambeau Boarding School in the autobiographical *Great Spirit* (Chicago: Childrens Press, 1970); and *Reflections of the Lac du Flambeau, an Illustrated History of Lac du Flambeau, Wisconsin, 1745–1995,* compiled by Ben Guthrie, written and edited by Michael J. Goc (Friendship, WI: New Past Press, 1995).

23. The Red Cliff account is based on the author's interviews with Red Cliff tribal members Leo LeFrenier and Joe Bresette in September 1997 and Walt Bresette in May 1998 as part of the Celebrating Wisconsin's Native American Heritage project. Additional material came from the Campbell Papers; from *Condition of Indian Affairs in Wisconsin*; and from Edmund Danziger's *The Chippewas of Lake Superior* (Norman: University of Oklahoma Press, 1990).

24. The oral history in this section came from interviews with Dana Jackson, Bad River tribal historian, in August 1997 and September 1999, and with Joe Rose, Bad River elder and director of American Indian Studies at Northland College, in August 1997. Information about St. Mary's School was drawn from *Journal of Sister M. Cunigunda Urbany*, compiled by Sister Bonaventure Schoeberle, 1883, Franciscan Sisters of Perpetual Adoration archives, La Crosse, WI; letters from tribal members to the Bureau of Catholic Indian Missions, 1897–1915; the Samuel Campbell Papers; and *Condition of Indian Affairs in Wisconsin*. For more detailed citations, see Patricia Loew, "Natives, Newspapers, and 'Fighting Bob': Wisconsin Chippewa in the 'unProgressive' Era," *Journalism History* 23, no. 4 (Winter 1997–98); and Loew, "Newspapers and the Lake Superior Chippewa in the 'unProgressive' Era."

25. Oral history accounts for the Sokaogon section draw heavily from interviews with the hereditary chief of the Sokaogon, Charles Ackley, along with tribal members Fred Ackley and Fran VanZile, in Mole Lake, October 18–20, 1999. Additional material came from Satz's *Chippewa Treaty Rights.*

26. McClurken, *Fish in the Lakes*, 85.

27. Ibid., 282.

28. Ibid., 283.

29. Very little written information exists about the St. Croix Ojibwe, and much of the oral history is speculative. Most of the information I was able to collect on the St. Croix came from interviews with tribal historian Gene Connor in Hertel, Wisconsin, in September 1997 and in a telephone interview on September 29, 1999.

30. Alison Bernstein, *American Indians and World War II* (Norman: University of Oklahoma Press, 1991), 46.

31. Between 1992 and 1994, Wisconsin Historical Society researchers interviewed 115 Wisconsin women, including several Ojibwe, about their experiences during World War II. Some of the material in this section draws from these interviews, along with my article "Back of the Homefront: Oral Histories of Native American and African-American Wisconsin Women during World War II," *Wisconsin Magazine of History* 82, no. 2 (Winter 1998–99). Alison Bernstein provides a good general history of Native Americans during the wartime period in *American Indians and World War II* (Norman: University of Oklahoma Press, 1991).

32. Much of the material on the Chippewa treaty rights disputes is distilled from interviews the author collected while covering the boat-landing demonstrations during 1988–1994 as a news reporter for WKOW-TV (ABC) and WHA-TV (PBS). Also, see Patty Loew, "Hidden Transcripts in the Chippewa Treaty Rights Dispute: A Twice-Told Story," *American Indian Quarterly* 22, no. 1 (Winter 1998); and *Spring of Discontent* (WKOW-TV documentary produced by Patty Loew), which aired statewide on ABC affiliates in Wisconsin in May 1990. Two excellent resources on the topic are *Chippewa Treaty Rights* by Ron Satz and *Walleye Warriors* by Rick Whaley and Walt Bresette (Philadelphia: New Society Publishers, 1994).

33. "Mole Lake and Potawatomi Tribes Purchase Crandon Mine," press release, October 28, 2003, available at www.sacredland.org/PDFs/Crandon_Press_Release.pdf. For a concise history of the Crandon Mine issue, see Al Gedicks and Zoltan Grossman, "Defending a Common Home: Native/Non-Native Alliances Against Mining Corporations in Wisconsin," chapter 11 in *In the Way of Development: Indigenous Peoples, Life Projects and Globalization*, edited by Mario Blaser, Harvey A. Feit, and Glenn McRae (London: Zed Books, 2004).

34. Mike Wiggins, Bad River tribal chair, author interview, June 11, 2011, Bad River Reservation, Odanah, Wisconsin; "Tribe to Protect 21,300 Acres of Land," *Wisconsin State Journal*, October 2, 2003, B3.

35. Paul Hackerson, director, Bad River Housing Authority, personal correspondence, June 16, 2011; "Bad River Tribal Elder Center Open for Activities," *The Daily Press*, August 21, 2009, meyergroupduluth.com/resources/The+Daily+Press-+Elder+Center.pdf.

36. Mike Wiggins, Bad River tribal chair, remarks delivered at a celebration honoring the Mother Earth Water Walkers, Bad River powwow grounds, June 11, 2011. See "2011 Mother Earth Water Walkers Converge at Bad River," *Mazina'igan*, Great Lakes Indian Fish and Wildlife Commission, Fall 2011, 1.

37. "Sierra Club Opposes Taconite Mine Proposal in Penokee Hills," Sierra Club news release, October 11, 2011, www.wisconsin.sierraclub.org/About/documents/10112011_PR_SierraOpposesTaconiteMine.pdf.

38. Richard Ackley, technical assistant, Sokaogon Planning Department, phone interview with author, April 4, 2012.

39. Tom Maulson, Lac du Flambeau Band of Chippewa president, author interview, June 15, 2011, the National Congress of American Indians Mid-year Conference, Milwaukee; DSGW Architects, "First American-Portfolio," www.dsgw.com/portfolio_PCHealthClinic.html; and "Peter Christensen Health Clinic," Lac du Flambeau tribal website, www.ldftribe.com/department_details.php?departmentID=40.

40. Nicole Bowman, *Lakeland Union High School Native American Achievement Project: Final Report* (Shawano, WI: Bowman Performance Consulting, 2007), 16.

41. Patty Loew and James Thannum, "After the Storm: Ojibwe Treaty Rights Twenty-Five Years after the Voigt Decision," *American Indian Quarterly* 35, no. 2 (Spring 2011), 176.

42. Ibid., 177.

43. Maulson, interview. See also "Tribes Declare Spring Spearing Goals," *Daily Globe*, April 12, 2003, 12.

44. "Tribes start receiving settlement money," *Kalihwisaks*, www.oneidanation.org/newspaper/page.aspx?id=36434.

45. Mic Isham, phone interview and e-mail correspondence, January 12, 2013. See also "LCO Says It Is Not Near Bankruptcy," *Wisconsin Public Radio News*, August 12, 2012, http://news.wpr.org/post/lco-says-it-not-near-bankruptcy.

46. LCO Ojibwa Community College website, www.lco.edu/; and "Summarized History of Lac Courte Oreilles Ojibwe Community College," www.lco.edu/history.html. The spelling of "Ojibwa" is often intermingled with "Ojibwe," as it is on these two LCOOCC websites.

47. This web excerpt, written by Tribal Council member Mic Isham, displays the willingness of LCO to work cooperatively with other units of government to protect the flowage from environmental degradation and to consider the cultural interests of the tribe when making decisions about development. www.lco-nsn.gov/funding.htm.

48. The original name of the publication was *News from Indian Country: The Journal*. For a history of NFIC, see DeMain's account: www.ojibwe.org/home/pdf/Demain_Econ_NFIC.pdf.

49. Other publications include *The Ojibwe Sun*, *The LCO Times*, and *The Ojibwe Times*, published by Joe Morey, and *Explore Indian Country* and *Ojibwe Akiing*, published by DeMain. ICC's enterprises have grown to include an Internet shopping site, an electronic version of *News from Indian Country*, and the video web channel IndianCountryTV.com. For more on ICC,

visit indian countrynews.net; for more on IndianCountryTV.com, see indiancountrynews.net /index.php?option=com_content&task=section&id=42&Itemid=131.

50. *Montana v. United States*, 450 U.S. at 566, as cited in Paul M. Drucker, "Wisconsin v. EPA: Tribal Empowerment and State Powerlessness Under Sec. 518(e) of the Clean Water Act," *University of Denver Water Law Review*, Spring 2002. Full text of this article is available at www.lexisnexis.com.ezproxy.library.wisc.edu/hottopics/lnacademic.

51. *Wisconsin v. EPA*, 266 F.3d 741, 743 (7th Cir. 2001).

52. Sue Erickson-Truchon, public information director, Great Lakes Indian Fish and Wildlife Commission, e-mail correspondence, July 28, 2011. According to GLIFWC, Bad River and Sokaogon have TAS status for water and have set water quality standards. Bad River had already been granted TAS status for air quality in October 2011.

53. Larry Balber, Red Cliff historic preservation officer, e-mail correspondence, July 27, 2011. Also see "Iconic Peace Pipe Returns Home to Red Cliff," *The Daily Press* (Ashland), December 10, 2010.

54. 2010 Annual Report to the Membership of the Red Cliff Band of Lake Superior Chippewa, Red Cliff Band of Lake Superior Chippewa, 10.

55. The planning meeting resulted in a collaboration among Red Cliff; University of Wisconsin professor Susan Thering, University of Wisconsin Extension's Native American Task Force; and Design Coalition, a small architectural company that promotes "socially conscious and ecologically responsible design." For more on the project, see Susan Thering, "The Scholarship of Transdisciplinary Action-Research: A Case Study from Indian Country," *Landscape Journal* 30, no. 1 (2011), 166. Thering's and Design Coalition's websites offer interesting insights into the cultural protocols and green materials used in the projects, as well as photos and sketches of some of the designs used: http://affordablegreenhousing.org/admin/projects _programs/projects_programs.htm and www.designcoalition.org/projects/TSC/TSC.htm.

56. Tribal members make up 68 percent of Red Cliff's employees, 9 percent are people enrolled in other tribes, and 23 percent are non-Indian, according to the Red Cliff 2010 Annual Report to the Membership, 8.

57. "Public National Park Is a Tribal First," JSOnline (*Milwaukee Journal Sentinel*), December 26, 2011, www.jsonline.com/news/wisconsin/first-tribal-national-park -launched-vl3guoh-136240853.html.

58. "Red Cliff Redemption," *Wisconsin Trails*, March/April 2012, www.wisconsintrails .com/explore/nature/150013535.html.

59. "Brownfields 2004 Grant Fact Sheet, St. Croix Chippewa Indians of Wisconsin," United States Environmental Protection Agency, National Service Center for Environmental Publications, EPA website, nepis.epa.gov.

60. "Tribal Brownfields and Response Programs," United States Environmental Protection Agency, 2011. For more, see the EPA document at www.epa.gov/brownfields/state_tribal /tribalreport11.pdf.

61. Peter F. David, "Wild Rice (Manoomin) Abundance and Harvest in Northern Wisconsin in 2008," March 2010, Great Lakes Indian Fish and Wildlife Commission, http://glifwc.org /Reports/Administrative%20Report%2010-02.pdf.

62. "St. Croix Chippewa Indians of Wisconsin," Wisconsin State Tribal Relations Initiative, http://witribes.wi.gov/docview.asp?docid=5633&locid=57. According to the St. Croix Chippewa Indians of Wisconsin website, the tribe employs more than two thousand workers through its tribal center and government programs and at its three gaming facilities and hotels; www.stcciw.com.

63. "St. Croix Waters Fishery," *Midwest Tribal Aquaculture Network*, United States Fish and Wildlife Service e-newsletter, vol. 45b, September 2003, www.fws.gov/midwest/ashland /mtan_45_b.html. Also see "Tribe Plans to Get Fishery Running Again," *Eau Claire Leader-Telegram*, January 9, 2008, http://the-leader.net/tribe-plans-to-get-fishery-running-again -p8691.htm.

64. For the Ojibwe, Seventh Generation philosophy is a fundamental belief dictating that present plans must be weighed upon their perceived impact on future generations. This ontology places value on sustainable resource management and long-range planning.

CHAPTER 6

1. The Ojibwe and Odaawa refer to the three tribes as the Anishinaabe or Anishinaabeg Alliance. Much of the oral history included in this chapter came from Jim Thunder, a Potawatomi elder and former tribal chair, who guest-lectured in the author's American Indian Studies seminar on Wisconsin Indians (AIS 450), University of Wisconsin–Madison, on March 2, 1998.

2. In 1988, Shup-Shewana (Howard Lahurreau), an elder of the Keewatinosagiganing Potawatomi Nation (Canada), wrote a fascinating historical account of the Potawatomi. Shup-Shewana translated songs and scrolls of the Midewiwin, the Ne shna bek traditional religion, and described the medicinal usages of native plants by the Potawatomi. According to Shup-Shewana, "The Confederacy of the Three Fires Ojibwa-Odawa-Pottawatomie took place in or about 31899 [1200 BP, or 796 AD] at Michilimackinac, and was a loose unit of many bands of related people. As time went forward this group of bands became more distant and generally came together to fight off the thrusts of the Sioux and Iroquois." This little-known manuscript, written in Potawatomi with an English translation, also explained the clan structure and cultural activities of the tribe. *Potawatomi Nation in Canada* (Mactier, ON: Keewatinosagiganing Potawatomi Nation Cultural Council, 33103 [1988]), 120.

3. Clarice Ritchie, Potawatomi elder and historian, author interview, April 4, 2000, Crandon, WI.

4. R. David Edmunds has several excellent chapters on the Potawatomi role in the French fur trade in *The Potawatomis: Keepers of the Fire* (Norman: University of Oklahoma Press, 1978).

5. Richard Battin, "Early America's Bloodiest Battle," *News-Sentinel* (Fort Wayne, IN), 1994, reprinted on the Archiving Early America website, www.earlyamerica.com/review/summer /battle.html.

6. Lyman Copeland Draper, who intended to write a biography of Tecumseh, collected an impressive amount of material on the Shawnee leader, including notes, clippings, and letters about Tecumseh's visits to the Potawatomi and other Indian nations in Wisconsin. This material is part of the Draper Manuscripts, Tecumseh Papers 1811–1931, Wisconsin Historical Society archives, Madison, WI. Another good general source on Wisconsin's early history and the activities of the Potawatomi is Alice E. Smith's *The History of Wisconsin*, vol. 1, *From Exploration to Statehood* (Madison: State Historical Society of Wisconsin, 1973).

7. Edmunds, *The Potawatomis*, 220.

8. James Clifton, *The Potawatomi* (New York: Chelsea Publishers, 1987).

9. In 1998, Wisconsin Public Television coproduced an excellent documentary, *The Rush for Grey Gold: How Wisconsin Began*, which described the impact of lead mining on the Indian nations of southwestern Wisconsin and the resulting land loss (Madison, WI: Ootek Productions and Wisconsin Public Television, 1998).

10. Information about the treaty period came largely from *Potawatomi Tribe*, a historical pamphlet written by Jim Thunder (Cottage Grove, WI: Jim Thunder, 1993), and "Keeper of the Fire: Potawatomi Tribal History" in *Forest County Potawatomi Nation: Keeper of the Fire* (Crandon, WI: Forest County Potawatomi Nation, n.d.). Additional oral history and written materials came from Clarice Ritchie, Jim Thunder, and Billy Daniels during discussions for a public history exhibit sponsored by the tribes to commemorate the Wisconsin Sesquicentennial in May 1998.

11. Recounted by Jim Thunder, tribal historian and former tribal chair of the Forest County Potawatomi.

12. George T. Amour, "My Birthplace: The McCord Indian Village," unpublished memoirs, Office of the State Archaeologist, Wisconsin Historical Society, April 20, 1992. Big Drum, or Dream Dancing, as it is sometimes described, was a pan-Indian religion introduced to the Ne shna bek by the Sioux. According to oral tradition, a young Santee Sioux woman who survived the slaughter of her village by the US cavalry had a vision that directed her to carry a drum to other Indian nations in a spirit of peace and friendship. The Ne shna bek, traditional enemies of the Sioux, received the first drum sometime in the late 1870s. Today, many Potawatomi continue their memberships in Big Drum societies and the Midewiwin, even as they identify themselves as members of Christian religions.

13. In September 1909, Chief Kish-ki-kaam and other Potawatomi testified before a US Senate panel that included Senator Robert M. "Fighting Bob" La Follette of Wisconsin. After taking Ojibwe testimony in Shell Lake, Ashland, Lac Courte Oreilles, and Lac du Flambeau, the senators visited the Potawatomi who were living near Laona. A year after the hearings, the testimony of the Potawatomi was combined with that of other Wisconsin Indians and published as *Condition of Indian Affairs in Wisconsin* (Washington, DC: Government Printing Office, 1910). Kish-ki-kaam's testimony is on pp. 793–94.

14. Although there are no detailed postwar histories of the Indian nations in Wisconsin, there are several good general histories that contain chapters on termination and relocation. These include Peter Nabokov, *Native American Testimony* (New York: Viking, 1991); Frederick E. Hoxie, *Indians in American History* (Chicago: The Newberry Library, 1988); and Peter

Iverson, *We Are Still Here: American Indians in the Twentieth Century* (Wheeling, IL: Harlan Davidson, 1998).

15. More than half of the PBC workforce is made up of people of color: African Americans (27%), Native Americans (10%), Hispanics (9%), and Asians (7%). Caucasians represent 47% of PBC employees. "Social Responsibility at Potawatomi Bingo Casino," 2010 Annual Report, http://www.paysbig.com/business/social-responsibility/.

16. "A Vision for the Monomonee Valley," Menomonee Valley Partners, Inc., www.hankaaronstatetrail.org/pdf/MVPBrochure.pdf.

17. Laura Bray, executive director, Menomonee Valley Partners Inc., e-mail correspondence, October 26, 2011.

18. "PBDC Subsidiaries," Potawatomi Business Development Corporation 2003 Annual Report, 4.

19. "PBDC Investments," Potawatomi Business Development Corporation 2004 Annual Report, 4.

20. "A Letter from our CEO," Potawatomi Business Development Corporation 2010 Annual Report, 4.

21. Eugene Shawano, Forest County Potawatomi administrator, interview by Christina Rencontre, October 24, 2011, Crandon, WI.

22. Mission statement, National Indian Gaming Association website, www.indiangaming.org.

23. "Indian Community School in Franklin Is Nearly Complete," *Milwaukee Journal Sentinel*, September 30, 2006, 3B; "Indian School Offers a Design at Peace with the Earth," *Milwaukee Journal Sentinel*, May 3, 2004, 1B.

24. Shawano, interview.

25. Forest County Potawatomi Health and Wellness Center Family Assistance Plan, Forest County Potawatomi website, www.fcpotawatomi.com/patient-forms-a-documents/family-funding-forms.

26. Shawano, interview.

27. The *Potawatomi Traveling Times* is a twice-monthly publication and is available online: www.fcpotawatomi.com/media/traveling-times-news.

28. Brian Tupper, Forest County Potawatomi athletics director, interview by Christina Rencontre, October 24, 2011, Crandon, WI.

29. The Potawatomi received final TAS approval from the EPA in September 2010. 2010 Third Quarter Report, Forest County Potawatomi Community—Natural Resources Department, 3.

30. Billy Daniels Jr., interview by Patty Loew for Wisconsin Public Television program *Week-End*, October 12, 1999, Crandon, WI.

31. Harold "Gus" Frank, interview by Patty Loew for the Wisconsin Public Television program *WeekEnd*, October 12, 1999, Crandon, WI. Both the Daniels and Frank interviews are available at https://courses.cals.wisc.edu/cals/mod/resource/view.php?id=2999.

32. The act, which was passed in 1997, was signed by Governor Tommy Thompson in 1998. Under provisions of the bill, mining companies have to provide examples of similar mines that have operated safely for ten years without causing environmental damage, as well as mines that have been closed for ten years without causing environmental damage. Background on the mine and the moratorium can be found on the Wisconsin Department of Natural Resources website: www.dnr.state.wi.us/org/es/science/crandon/review/moratorium.htm.

33. "Mole Lake and Potawatomi Tribes Purchase Crandon Mine," press release, Martin Schreiber & Associates, October 28, 2003, www.sacredland.org/PDFs/Crandon_Press _Release.pdf.

34. Ibid.

35. "Planting Trees on the Reservation," *Potawatomi Traveling Times*, June 1, 2011, 1.

36. "Potawatomi to Expand Broadband Access in Northern Wisconsin," *Potawatomi Traveling Times*, January 15, 2011, 2.

CHAPTER 7

1. In deference to the Oneida who are uncomfortable with the term *Iroquois*, I have elected to use the terms *Haudenosaunee*, *Five Nations*, or *Six Nations* to describe the confederacy. Oneida scholars, including Carol Cornelius, author of *Iroquois Corn in a Culture-based Curriculum* (Albany: State University of New York Press, 1999), acknowledge the difficulty in avoiding the use of the word *Iroquois*, since its usage has become so widespread. During an interview, she said she preferred to use *On^yote:aka* or *Oneida* when referring to her nation or the terms *Five Nations* or *Six Nations* when referring to the confederacy. Carol Cornelius, author interview, March 9, 2000, Oneida, WI.

2. The story of Hiawatha and the Great Law of Peace is well known to generations of Haudenosaunee. One of the most popular versions is contained in *American Indian Myths and Legends*, edited by Richard Erdoes and Alfonso Ortiz (New York: Pantheon Books, 1984), 193–99.

3. William A. Starna, "The Oneida Homeland in the Seventeenth Century," in *The Oneida Indian Experience*, edited by Jack Campisi and Laurence M. Hauptman (Syracuse: Syracuse University Press, 1988), 19. *The Oneida Indian Experience* offers perspectives from contemporary scholars, including linguists, anthropologists, and historians as well as oral history accounts from Oneida elders and community leaders. Along with *The Oneida Indian Journey*, edited by Laurence Hauptman and L. Gordon McLester III (Madison: University of Wisconsin Press, 1999), it is an excellent resource on the Wisconsin Oneida.

4. Starna, "The Oneida Homeland," 13.

5. Loretta Metoxen, Oneida tribal historian, author interview, March 9, 2000, Oneida, WI.

6. The original source for the many good general and regional histories about the French fur trade era is Reuben Gold Thwaites's multivolume *Jesuit Relations* (1925). Thwaites used

mission accounts compiled by the Jesuit missionaries in North America from 1610 to 1791. The Wisconsin Historical Society has archived additional material collected but not used by Thwaites. See Jesuit Relations Papers, Wisconsin Historical Society Manuscripts Collection, Madison, WI.

7. Historian Loretta Metoxen, who has researched the Doxtator family history, says there is evidence that it may have been Sarah Montour, another of Doxtator's wives, and not Cobus, who fought at Oriskany. Loretta Metoxen, author interview, Oneida, WI, January 20, 2012. For more about the Oneida role in the American Revolution, see Barbara Graymont, "The Oneidas and the American Revolution," in Campisi and Hauptman, *The Oneida Indian Experience*, 31–42.

8. Loretta Metoxen, "Oneida Traditions," in Campisi and Hauptman, *The Oneida Indian Experience*, 145–46. The official website of the Oneida Nation of New York (a community separate but culturally related to the Oneida of Wisconsin) has a link devoted to Cooper that includes oral history written down by the nineteenth-century chief William Honyost Rockwell, www.oneidaindiannation.com/culture/shako/exhibits/27015199.html.

9. Hauptman and McLester, *The Oneida Indian Journey*, 23.

10. Laurence Hauptman and L. Gordon McLester III, *The Oneida Indian Journey* (Madison: University of Wisconsin Press, 1999), 64.

11. "Before the Indian Claims Commission," The Oneida Nation of New York, the Oneida Tribe of Indians of Wisconsin, the Oneida Nation by Julius Danforth, Oscar Archiquette, Sherman Skenandore, Mamie Smith, and Amanda Pierce, Petititoners v. The United States of America, Defendant, docket no. 301 (Claims 3–7), September 22, 1978, 43 Ind. Cl. Comm. 373, 408. Full text available at http://digital.library.okstate.edu/icc/v43/iccv43p408.pdf.

12. Interview with Carol Cornelius. For more information about this period in Oneida history, see Carol Cornelius, "Examining the Forces after the American Revolution Which Impacted Our Move to Wisconsin," and Judy Cornelius, "Eleazer Williams and Albert G. Ellis"; both papers were delivered to the Oneida History Conference, Oneida, WI, October 23, 1998 (copies in author's possession). The Oneida land loss and resulting migration are covered extensively in Hauptman and McLester, *The Oneida Indian Journey*.

13. Loretta Metoxen, "Subdivide and Conquer: The Dawes Allotment Act," *Oneida Cultural Heritage Department Newsletter*, no. 6 (n.d.).

14. Like most Indian nations reorganized under the 1934 act, the Oneida adopted a constitution that delineated legislative, executive, and judiciary branches within its "General Tribal Council." The Oneida constitution, which was revised in August 1998, continues to adhere to this trifurcated form of government.

15. Unnamed Oneida elder, quoted in Rosalie M. Robertson's "Oneida Educational Planning," in Campisi and Hauptman, *The Oneida Indian Experience*, 166. In September 1997, I spoke to several Oneida elders during a visit to gather research for a public history exhibit commemorating the State of Wisconsin sesquicentennial. One woman, who wished to remain anonymous, told me that while she made "some friends I stayed close to all my life . . . that first Christmas was really hard. I cried the whole day, I was so homesick."

16. Military records and oral history indicate that the Oneida participated in and supported the efforts in both world wars; however, no detailed history has yet been written. Two excellent general histories of Native Americans during the war years are *American Indians in World War I*, by Thomas A. Britten (Albuquerque: University of New Mexico Press, 1997), and *American Indians and World War II*, by Alison R. Bernstein (Norman: University of Oklahoma Press, 1991).

17. Jeff Metoxen, director of Tsyunhehkwa, interview by Reynaldo Morales, June 8, 2011, Oneida, WI.

18. Ibid. For more on Oneida Nation Farms, cannery operations, Tsyunhehkwa, and Oneida cultural heritage, visit the Oneida Community Integrated Food Systems website: www.oneidanation.org/ocifs/.

19. "KSG Announces Tribal Governance Award Finalists," *Harvard Gazette* archives, October 20, 2005, www.news.harvard.edu/gazette/2005/10.20/08-tribal.html.

20. Comments by John Echo Hawk, US Interior Department assistant secretary—Indian Affairs, in a news release, "Echo Hawk Announces SIPI and Oneida Nation High School as Featured Entries of the 2011 Indian Education Renewable Energy Challenge," July 15, 2011, www.bia.gov/idc/groups/public/documents/text/idc014293.pdf.

21. Laura Manthe, director, Oneida Environmental Resource Board, interview by Reynaldo Morales, June 8, 2011, Oneida, WI. See also "Oneida Nation to Build Biomass Plant in Green Bay," The BioenergySite.com, and "Oneida Seven Generations Corporation's Biomass Project Receiving Pushback," *Kalihwisaks*, www.oneidanation.org/newspaper/page.aspx?id=31927.

22. Sovereign immunity is a legal principle under which tribal nations, as with states and the federal government, cannot be sued.

23. Karen Lincoln Michel has written an excellent background article on the long-standing tensions between the Oneida Nation and the village of Hobart. See "Hobart, Oneida Tribe Share Complex Relationship," *Green Bay Press Gazette*, August 18, 2009, http://indigenews.kisikew.org/forum/viewtopic.php?f=2&t=2364.

24. Loretta Metoxen, tribal historian, interview by Reynaldo Morales, June 8, 2011, Oneida, WI.

25. Information about contemporary Oneida activities came from the tribe's promotional brochure; from "Development and Enterprises" in *Oneida Nation* (Oneida, WI: Oneida Nation, n.d.); and from the author's interviews with Carol Cornelius, Loretta Metoxen, Kirby Metoxen, and Keith Skenandore in September 1997 and May 2000.

26. Metoxen interview.

27. City of Sherrill, New York, Petitioner v. Oneida Indian Nation of New York et al, No. 03-855, March 29, 2005, www.law.cornell.edu/supct/html/03-855.ZO.html.

Chapter 8

1. Mohican Nation, Stockbridge-Munsee Band, *Brief History of the Mohican Nation, Stockbridge-Munsee Band* (Bowler, WI: Stockbridge-Munsee Historical Committee, 1996), 3.

2. This account comes from John Quinney, who explained that after Aupaumut wrote the oral account, "in the mid-1700s, a non-Indian took the manuscript to be published and it was reportedly lost." "Origin and Early Mohican History," Stockbridge-Munsee Community, Band of Mohican Indians website, www.mohican-nsn.gov/Departments/Library-Museum /Mohican_History/origin-and-early.htm.

3. In her history of the Mohicans (1852), Electa Jones described the Wi-gow-wauw, or chief sachem, as a leader, "chosen by the nation, whom they looked upon as conductor and promoter of their general welfare." The office was hereditary "by the lineage of a female's offspring, but not on the man's line, but on woman's part." When he died, a nephew (his sister's son) was appointed to the office, "not any of his sons." *Stockbridge, Past and Present* (Springfield, MA: Samuel Bowles & Company, 1854), 20.

4. Ibid., 22.

5. This account, attributed to Hendrick Aupaumut at an Indian conference in 1754, is quoted in both Patrick Frazier, *The Mohicans of Stockbridge* (Lincoln: University of Nebraska Press, 1992), 2–3, and Shirley Dunn, *The Mohicans and Their Land, 1609–1730* (Fleischmanns, NY: Purple Mountain Press, 1994), 18.

6. Relations between the Mohawk and the Mohican warmed after a Mohican chief married a Mohawk woman. Their son, Hendrick, became one of the most celebrated Mohawk leaders. In 1710, Hendrick and the Mohican sachem Etowaukaum traveled to England together to meet with Queen Anne. Frazier, *Mohicans of Stockbridge*, 9.

7. Ibid., 13.

8. Author's interview with the Stockbridge-Munsee Historical Committee, including Dorothy Davids, Sheila Powless, Bernice Miller Pigeon, and Ruth Gudinas in Bowler, WI, October 1997.

9. In a 1782 letter to the New York General Assembly, Johannis Mtohksin, Jacob Nanauphtaunk, Solomon Uhhaunauwaunmut, and the "sons of King Ben" asked that some of their ancestral land along the Hudson River and Lake Champlain be returned to them. "Brother," they wrote, "what I ask is that you resign to me that land, which is justly mine, which I have neither sold or given to you; or give me its value, that I may get food and cloathing for myself, my women and children and be happy with you as formerly." Quoted in Frazier, *Mohicans of Stockbridge*, 235.

10. Mohican Nation, Stockbridge-Munsee Band, *Brief History of the Mohican Nation*, 6.

11. Ibid.

12. Annie Paprocki, "On New Ground: The Life of Electa Quinney" (unpublished paper, 1999, in author's possession); and "Electa Quinney: Kaukauna and the State's First Female Schoolteacher," *Kaukauna Times*, April 7, 1994.

13. Nancy Oestreich Lurie, *Wisconsin Indians*, revised and expanded edition (Madison: Wisconsin Historical Society Press, 2002), 12.

14. Youth of the Mohican Nation, *Stories of Our Elders* (Gresham, WI: Muh-he-con-neew Press, 1999), 10.

15. A reprint of Eureka Davids's letter appeared in "Rambling through History with Dot Davids," *Mohican News*, September 1, 2001, 5.

16. "Rambling through History with Dot Davids," *Mohican News*, July 15, 2010, 5.

17. Davids, interview, October 1997; phone interview, June 2000.

18. Pigeon, phone interview, June 2000.

19. Davids, phone interview, June 2000.

20. "Origin and Early Mohican History," Stockbridge-Munsee Community, Band of Mohican Indians website, www.mohican-nsn.gov/Departments/Library-Museum/Mohican_History/origin-and-early.htm.

21. Ibid.

22. Davids, phone interview, June 2000.

23. Ibid.

24. Kim Vele, Stockbridge-Munsee Community tribal council president, interview by Reynaldo Morales, June 9, 2011, Bowler, WI.

25. Pigeon, phone interview, June 2000.

26. "$2 Million Housing Grant Approved for Stockbridge-Munsee," *Mohican News*, September 1, 2009, 1, www.mohican-nsn.gov/Departments/Mohican_News/issues/09-01-09.pdf.

27. Vele, interview.

28. Forestry web page, Stockbridge-Munsee Community, Band of Mohican Indians, www.mohican-nsn.gov/Departments/Forestry/index.htm.

29. Arvid E. Miller Memorial Library/Museum website, www.mohican-nsn.gov/Departments/Library-Museum/index.htm.

CHAPTER 9

1. Not all members of these tribes became Brothertown Indians. Many retained their identities in tribes that still exist today. The Mashantucket Pequot, Mohegan, and Narragansett, for example, are federally recognized Indian nations. Like the Brothertown, the unrecognized Montauk are also seeking federal acknowledgment.

2. The Puritans established the first Praying Town in 1646.

3. "Eoyamqittoowauconnuck," Brothertown Indian Nation website, www.brothertownindians.org.

4. Ibid.

5. Laura J. Murray, ed., *To Do Good to My Indian Brethren: The Writings of Joseph Johnson, 1751–1776* (Amherst: University of Massachusetts Press, 1998), 242–43.

6. Caroline K. Andler, "Brothertown Indian Nation Brief History," Brothertown Indian Nation website, www.brothertownindians.org.

7. Jack Campisi, "The Brothertown Indian Nation of Wisconsin Brief History" (Beaver Dam, WI: Brothertown History Committee, 1982), Wisconsin Historical Society Pamphlet Collection.

8. "Brothertown History," Milwaukee Public Museum website, www.mpm.edu/wirp /icw-157.html.

9. Ibid.

10. Charles J. Kappler, comp. and ed., *Treaty with the Menominee, 1831*, as reprinted in *Indian Affairs: Laws and Treaties*, vol. 11, *Treaties* (Washington, DC: Government Printing Office, 1904), 320. After the Menominee signed the treaty, the US Senate changed the boundaries in order to give the New York Indians better land. However, the Menominee refused to ratify the agreement until it was rewritten.

11. Some Brothertown did relocate to Kansas and were absorbed into other tribes or slipped quietly into mainstream society. Others returned to Wisconsin.

12. Campisi, "Brothertown Indian Nation Brief History."

13. "Brothertown History," Milwaukee Public Museum website, www.mpm.edu/wirp/icw -157.html. See also "Proposed Finding against Acknowledgment of the Brothertown Indian Nation (Petitioner #67), Prepared in Response to the Petition Submitted to the Assistant Secretary-Indian Affairs for Federal Acknowledgment as an Indian Tribe," August 17, 2009, *Federal Register* 74, no. 162, www.bia.gov/idc/groups/xofa/documents/text/idc-001523.pdf. It wouldn't be until 1924 that Congress passed the Indian Citizenship Act, conferring citizenship on all American Indians.

14. An Act for the Relief of the Brothertown Indians, in the Territory of Wisconsin. Statutes at Large 5:349, chap. 83.

15. The removal orders against the Menominee (1848) and Ojibwe (1850), signed by President Zachary Taylor, were rescinded by President Millard Fillmore.

16. Proposed Finding against Acknowledgment of the Brothertown Indian Nation, 3.

17. Craig Cipolla and Caroline Adler, "A Brief Historical Overview of the Brothertown Indian Nation," from the Brothertown Archaeological Project website, http://web.mac.com /craigcipolla/Brothertown_Archaeological_Project/Brothertown_Archaeological _Project.html.

18. Ibid.

19. Proposed Finding against Acknowledgment of the Brothertown Indian Nation, 58.

20. Kathleen Brown-Pérez, phone interview by Reynaldo Morales, April 18, 2011. Brown-Pérez, who has been active in the federal recognition effort, is an enrolled member of the Brothertown Indian Nation. She is chair of Five College Native American Indian Studies at the University of Massachusetts–Amherst and a federal Indian law attorney.

21. The names "Brothertown" and "Brotherton" have been used to describe the same people. On April 15, 1980, the Brothertown filed their petition under the name "Brotherton Indians of Wisconsin."

22. 83.7 Mandatory criteria for Federal acknowledgment, 25 CFR Part 83, Procedures for Establishing that an American Indian Group exists as an Indian Tribe, US Department of the Interior, Indian Affairs, Office of Federal Acknowledgment (OFA) www.bia.gov/cs/groups /public/documents/text/idc-001219.pdf.

23. "Federal Recognition Status," National Congress of American Indians, www.ncai.org /Federal-Recognition.70.0.html.

24. Statement of Glen Marshall, president of the Mashpee Wampanoag Tribe, during the Federal Recognition and Acknowledgment Process by the Bureau of Indian Affairs Oversight Hearing, Committee on Resources, US House of Representatives, 108th Cong., 2nd sess., March 31, 2004.

25. Statement of Hon. Nick Rahall (D-West Virginia). Federal Recognition and Acknowledgment Process by the Bureau of Indian Affairs Oversight Hearing, Committee on Resources, US House of Representatives, 108th Cong., 2nd sess., March 31, 2004.

26. Caroline Andler, e-mail correspondence, August 25, 2011. Andler is the tribal genealogist and in 2005 served as chair of the Brothertown Recognition Committee.

27. Ibid.

28. Statement of Wilford "Longhair" Taylor, tribal chief, Mowa Band of Choctaw Indians, Federal Recognition and Acknowledgment Process by the Bureau of Indian Affairs Oversight Hearing, Committee on Resources, US House of Representatives, 108th Cong., 2nd sess., March 31, 2004. Taylor and other representatives of petitioning tribes pointed out the irony of the BIA, an agency tasked with overseeing tribal affairs, not accepting oral tradition in its federal acknowledgment procedure. Testimony from anthropologists, ethnologists, and other scholars argued that the collection of interviews and other nonprint data from cultures having an oral tradition is not only an acceptable methodology but at times also the best and most reliable method of reconstructing their past.

29. Richard Schadewald, Brothertown tribal chair, interview by Reyaldo Morales, April 22, 2011, Green Bay, WI.

30. There are five Brothertown Peacemakers. Four are elected and one is appointed.

31. Brown-Pérez, interview.

32. Darren Kroenke, e-mail correspondence, August 31 and September 1, 2011. See also "Private Collection Dates Back to 1754," Kalihwisaks, October 21, 2010, 10A, www .oneidanation.org/uploadedFiles/October%2021%202010%20Kalihwisaks.pdf. According to Oneida oral history, Deganawida, also known as "the Great Peacemaker," unified the Haudenosaunee (Onondaga, Oneida, Mohawk, Seneca, and Cayuga) and guided the creation of their confederacy. A version of the Great Law of Peace can be viewed at www .indigenouspeople.net/iroqcon.htm.

33. "Private Collection Dates Back to 1754."

34. Brown-Pérez, interview.

CHAPTER 10

1. "Wisconsin Race by Population and Hispanic Origin, 2007 Estimate," *2009–2010 Wisconsin Blue Book*, compiled by the Wisconsin Legislative Reference Bureau, 810, http://legis .wisconsin.gov/lrb/bb/09bb/pdf/621-862.pdf. Note: The *Blue Book* reservation population figures were taken from the 2000 Census, while the *Blue Book* population figures were based on 2007 US Census data. The 2011 US Census figures show a 17 percent increase overall in the number of Native Americans statewide from 2000 to 2010; US Census, Profile of General Population and Housing Characteristics: 2010 Demographic Profile Data (Wisconsin), http:// factfinder2.census.gov/faces/tableservices/jsf/pages/productview.xhtml?src=bkmk.

2. Antonio J. Doxtator and Renee J. Zakhar, *American Indians in Milwaukee* (Charleston, SC: Arcadia Publishing, 2011), 11.

3. Native people were more likely to find work in positions vacated by whites, who took higher-paying jobs in the defense industry. For more, see Patty Loew, "Back of the Homefront: Oral Histories of Native American and African-American Women during World War II," *Wisconsin Magazine of History* 82, no. 2 (Winter 1998–99).

4. "Per Cent Increase of Population by Race, 1950 and 1960, Milwaukee City and State," *1964 Wisconsin Blue Book*, compiled by the Wisconsin Legislative Reference Bureau, 632.

5. The US Census Bureau makes a special effort to work with Indian nations to eliminate the underreporting of American Indians and Alaska Natives. See "Tribal Governments Liaison Program," http://factfinder.census.gov/home/aian/TGLH_43009.pdf. For population estimates of Milwaukee's urban Indian community, see Susan Applegate Krouse, "What Came out of the Takeovers: Women's Activism and the Indian Community School of Milwaukee," *American Indian Quarterly* 27, no. 3/4, special issue: "Urban American Indian Women's Activism" (Summer–Autumn, 2003), 534.

6. US Census Bureau, "State and County Quick Facts," http://quickfacts.census.gov/qfd /states/55000.html. Roughly 3,300 Oneida live on the reservation.

7. US Census Bureau, "The American Indian and Alaska Native Population in the United States," http://factfinder2.census.gov/faces/tableservices/jsf/pages/productview .xhtml?pid=ACS_10_1YR_B02005&prodType=table; and Donald Lee Fixico, *Urban Indian Experience in America* (Albuquerque: University of New Mexico Press, 2000).

8. Bernadine Vigue interview in DC Everest Area Schools, *Native Nations of Wisconsin* (Westin, WI: DC Everest Area Schools, 2009), 432.

9. Doxtator and Zakhar, *American Indians in Milwaukee*, 64.

10. See Chapter 5, "Education for the Concrete Reservation," in Edmund Danzinger's *Survival and Regeneration: Detroit's American Indian Community* (Detroit: Wayne State University Press, 1991).

11. Gail Guthrie Valaskakis, *Indian Country: Essays on Contemporary Native Culture* (Waterloo, ON: Wilfrid Laurier University Press, 2005), 246–47.

12. Ace Boxing Club continues to operate as a nonprofit organization. See "Fight's End Was What Mattered to Coach," JSOnline (*Milwaukee Journal Sentinel*), May 8, 2008,

www.jsonline.com/news/milwaukee/29521064.html; and "A Tribute to the Late Del Porter," Ace Boxing Club website, http://aceboxingclub.org/index.php?page.Del Porter.

13. Opal Skenandore, "Reminiscences of Oneida Life in Milwaukee, 1920–1975," in *A Nation within a Nation: Voices of the Oneidas in Wisconsin*, ed. L. Gordon McLester III and Laurence M. Hauptman (Madison: Wisconsin Historical Society Press, 2010), 84.

14. In 1968, a group of pan-Indians including Dennis Banks (Leech Lake Ojibwe), Clyde Bellecourt (White Earth Ojibwe), Herb Powless (Oneida), and Edward Benton-Banai (Lac Courte Oreilles Ojibwe) formed AIM to address issues of police brutality.

15. Krouse, "What Came out of the Takeovers," 534.

16. "Indian School Director Quits," *Milwaukee Journal*, December 29, 1976, Accent, 1.

17. Krouse, "What Came out of the Takeovers," 536.

18. Donald Fixico, *Urban Indian Experience in America* (Albuquerque: University of New Mexico Press, 2000), 120.

19. Krouse, "What Came out of the Takeovers," 539.

20. "Indian Community School in Franklin Is Nearly Complete," *Milwaukee Journal Sentinel*, September 30, 2006, 3B.

21. Founders mission, Indian Community School of Milwaukee website, www.ics-milw.org.

22. Rhonda B. Jeffries, Mary Nix, and Carson Singer, "Urban American Indians 'Dropping' Out of Traditional High Schools: Barriers & Bridges to Success," *High School Journal* 85, no. 3 (February–March 2002), 45.

23. Ibid., 46.

24. "Potawatomi to Start Remodeling Ex-Concordia Campus by Early 2011," blog post by *Journal Sentinel* business reporter Tom Daykin, November 23, 2010, www.jsonline.com /blogs/business/109951814.html.

25. "A Home for the Great Spirit," JSOnline (*Milwaukee Journal Sentinel*), October 18, 2008, www.jsonline.com/features/religion/31215909.html.

26. Lutheran Church of the Great Spirit Facebook page, www.facebook.com/pages/Lutheran -Church-of-the-Great-Spirit/114582671898123?sk=wall#!/pages/Lutheran-Church-of-the -Great-Spirit/114582671898123?sk=info. See also Congregation of the Great Spirit, www .congregationofthegreatspirit.org; and Update on Native American Ministries in the Wisconsin Annual Conference, www.wisconsinumc.org/content/Missions/Documents /Partnerships/WINativeAmericanMinistries.pdf.

27. Rob Odum, pastor, United Methodist Church Native American Ministry, phone interview with author, November 3, 2011.

28. The Harvard Project on American Indian Economic Development, 2003 Honorees, High Honors, http://hpaied.org/images/resources/general/Dir_web.pdf.

29. "Community Health Profile 2009, Gerald L. Ignace Indian Health Center Inc., Milwaukee, WI," Urban Indian Health Institute, www.uihi.org/wp-content/uploads/2009/11 /Milwaukee-Community-Health-Profile_Final-PDF.pdf.

30. The word *recreational* is used to distinguish this use of tobacco from ceremonial use, which is common in Native American traditional practices.

31. "Community Health Profile 2009, Amerindian Health Center, Green Bay," Urban Indian Health Institute, www.uihi.org/wp-content/uploads/2009/11/Green-Bay-Community -Health-Profile_Final-PDF.pdf.

32. "Native American Clinic Loses Contract," *Green Bay Press Gazette*, September 30, 2008, A3.

33. Phyllis Wolfe, director of Urban Indian Health Programs, Indian Health Service, phone interview with author, October 31, 2011. In September 2007, IHS awarded the United Amer-Indian Center a $276,000 "America's Dream" award with a one-year option to renew. Although the Indian population in the clinic's service area was about 6,800, the clinic saw fewer than two patients per day, according to Wolfe. When the center received just 57 out of 211 points in an IHS evaluation, Wolfe said she decided not to renew the contract.

34. Craig Anderson, executive director, American Indian Chamber of Commerce of Wisconsin, phone interview with author, September 27, 2011.

35. Disadvantaged Business Enterprise (DBE) Program, Wisconsin Department of Transportation website, www.dot.wisconsin.gov/business/engrserv/dbe-main.htm.

36. Anderson, interview.

37. Jeff Bowman, FACC president, phone interview with author, September 27, 2011.

38. Ibid.

39. Some Native Americans living on reservations do own their own land in fee simple (land owned that is subject to taxation), and some tribal governments have purchased land that has not been placed in trust.

40. "UIM History," United Indians of Milwaukee website, www.unitedindiansofmilwaukee .com/United%20Indians/History.html.

41. "Indians Feed the Poor on 'Day of Mourning,'" *Milwaukee Journal*, October 13, 1992, 5.

42. Shirley Hill, phone interview with author, September 30, 2011. Hill served as director of the United AmerIndian Center from 1976 until 1990, when she was elected to the Oneida Tribal Council.

43. David Webster, phone interview with author, September 30, 2011. From 2003 to 2005, Webster served as director of the United AmerIndian Center.

44. Head Start is a preschool program for all children. In Indian Country, TRAIL is an acronym for Together Raising Awareness for Indian Life.

45. Webster, interview.

46. "Native American Clinic Loses Contract," *Green Bay Press Gazette*, September 30, 2008, A3. See also "Federal Budget Cuts Could Shutter Native American Health Program," *Medill Reports*, January 28, 2008, http://news.medill.northwestern.edu/chicago/news .aspx?id=76597.

47. Webster, interview.

48. See "Regents to Vote on Business School Tuition Hike," *Badger Herald*, April 12, 2007, http://badgerherald.com/news/2007/04/12/regents_to_vote_on_b.php.

49. The American Indian Studies Summer Institute is a one-week program for educators in American Indian Studies, which meets licensing requirements for educators trained outside of Wisconsin. The Oneida Nation hosted the 2011 institute, which has been held on the Menominee Reservation in previous years. For more information, see the Fifteenth Annual American Indian Studies Summer Institute webpage, www.regonline.com/builder/site /Default.aspx?EventID=954096.

50. Lisa Poupart, UW–Green Bay professor and director, First Nations Studies, e-mail correspondence with author, September 30, 2011.

51. Milwaukee's reputation as "The City of Festivals" has evolved in large part because of its Summerfest celebration and the nine ethnic festivals, including Indian Summer Festival, that are held at Henry Maier Festival Park on the city's lakefront each summer. Summerfest is an eleven-day music event billed as the largest music festival in the world.

52. Judy Dordel, executive director, Indian Summer Inc., e-mail correspondence with author, October 21, 2011.

53. Butch Roberts, founder, Indian Summer Festival, phone interview with author, October 23, 2011.

54. Roberts, interview. Roberts was a member of the National Indian Youth Council for nineteen years and had served as its president. He took part in a number of AIM protests, including Wounded Knee, where he provided security outside the compound. A self-described "community organizer," Roberts said he was on the "other side" before being recruited by a Native detective into the Milwaukee Police Department.

55. Like the American flag, the Eagle Staff is a symbol of Indian Country. Veterans carrying Eagle Staffs, American flags, and tribal flags lead the dancers into the arena during a powwow.

56. Alice Loew, phone interview with author, September 27, 2011. Alice Loew is the author's mother.

57. Jim Denomie, phone interview with author, September 30, 2011.

58. Ibid. For more, see "Indian Summer's Silver Anniversary," ExpressMilwaukee.com, www .expressmilwaukee.com/article-16035-indian-summers-silver-anniversary.html.

59. Roberts, interview.

BEYOND

1. "Manna in the Form of Jobs Comes to the Reservation," *New York Times*, February 21, 1999, section 4, 6.

2. Ibid.

3. "Disappearing Languages," National Geographic website, http://travel.nationalgeographic .com/travel/enduring-voices/.

4. "Mining Moratorium Bill Still Hangs in Governmental Limbo," editorial, *Menominee Nation News*, March 19, 1998, 24.

RESOURCES AND FURTHER READING

BOOKS AND JOURNALS

Armstrong, Benjamin. *Early Life among the Indians*. Press of A. W. Bowron, 1892.

Beck, David. *Siege and Survival*. University of Nebraska Press, 2002.

Benton-Banai, Edward. *The Mishomis Book*. St. Paul: Red School House, 1988 (distributed by Indian Country Communications, Hayward, Wisconsin).

Bieder, Robert. *Native American Communities in Wisconsin, 1600–1960: A Study of Tradition and Change*. Madison: University of Wisconsin Press, 1995.

Campisi, Jack, and Laurence M. Hauptman. *The Oneida Indian Experience*. New York: Syracuse University Press, 1988.

Densmore, Frances. *Chippewa Customs*. Minneapolis: Ross & Haines, 1929. Reprint, St. Paul: Minnesota Historical Society Press, 1979.

Doxtator, Antonio J., and Renee J. Zakhar. *American Indians in Milwaukee*. Mount Pleasant, SC: Arcadia, 2011.

Edmunds, R. David. *The Potawatomis: Keepers of the Fire*. Norman: University of Oklahoma Press, 1978.

Frazier, Patrick. *The Mohicans of Stockbridge*. Lincoln: University of Nebraska Press, 1992.

Hauptman, Laurence M., and L. Gordon McLester. *The Oneida Indian Journey*. Madison: University of Wisconsin Press, 1999.

Jones, Electa F. *Stockbridge, Past and Present*. Salem, MA: Higginson Book Co., 1854.

Krouse, Susan Applegate. "What Came Out of the Takeovers: Women's Activism and the Indian Community School of Milwaukee." *American Indian Quarterly* 27, no. 3/4, special issue: "Urban American Indian Women's Activism" (Summer–Autumn, 2003): 533–47.

Loew, Patty, and James Thannum. "After the Storm: Ojibwe Treaty Rights Twenty-Five Years after the Voigt Decision." *American Indian Quarterly* 35, no. 2 (Spring 2011): 161–91.

Lurie, Nancy Oestrich. *Mountain Wolf Woman*. Ann Arbor: University of Michigan Press, 1961.

McClurken, James. *Fish in the Lakes, Wild Rice and Game in Abundance: Testimony on Behalf of Mille Lacs Ojibwe Hunting and Fishing Rights*. East Lansing: Michigan State University Press, 2000.

McLester, L. Gordon, and Laurence M. Hauptman. *A Nation within a Nation: Voices of the Oneidas in Wisconsin*. Madison: Wisconsin Historical Society Press, 2010.

Menominee Tribal Historic Preservation Office. *Menominee Veterans: A Photo History of Our Land, Our Battles, Our Victories*. Keshena, WI: Menominee Tribal Historic Preservation Office, 2009.

Ourada, Patricia. *The Menominee Indians: A History*. Norman: University of Oklahoma Press, 1979.

Satz, Ron. "Chippewa Treaty Rights." *Transaction* 79, no. 1, Wisconsin Academy of Sciences, Arts and Letters (1991): 1–251.

Shames, Deborah. *Freedom with Reservation: The Menominee Struggle to Save Their Land and People*. Washington, DC: National Committee to Save the Menominee People and Forests, 1972.

Tanner, Helen Hornbeck. *Atlas of Great Lakes Indian History*. Norman: Published for the Newberry Library by the University of Oklahoma Press, 1987.

Vennum, Thomas Jr. *Wild Rice and the Ojibway People*. St. Paul: Minnesota Historical Society Press, 1988.

Warren, William. *History of the Ojibway People*. 2nd ed. Edited by Theresa Schenck. St. Paul: Minnesota Historical Society Press, 2009.

Whaley, Rick, and Walter Bresette. *Walleye Warriors*. Philadelphia: New Society Publishers, 1994.

White, Richard. *The Middle Ground: Indians, Empires, and Republics in the Great Lakes Region, 1650-1815*. Cambridge, UK: Cambridge University Press, 1991.

MULTIMEDIA

Enduring Ways of the Lac du Flambeau People. Madison: Wisconsin Public Television, 2009.

Maawanji'ding: Gathering Together (CD-ROM). Brain-Box Digital Archives. Collinsville, CT: Hup! Multimedia, 1998

No Word for Goodbye. Writer/producer, Patty Loew. Madison: WKOW-TV, 1986.

Ojibwe History. Writer/producer, Mic Derks. Madison: Wisconsin Public Television, 2000.

Ojibwe Music. Writer/producer, Mic Derks. Madison: Wisconsin Public Television, 2000.

The Oneida Speak. Writer/producer, Michelle Danforth. Wisconsin Public Television, 2008.

The Rush for Grey Gold. Writer/producer, Dave Erickson. Spring Green, WI: Ootek Productions, 1998.

Since 1634: In the Wake of Nicolet. Writer/producer, Dave Erickson; Ho-Chunk co-producer, Lance Tallmadge; Menominee co-producer, Alan Caldwell. Spring Green, WI: Ootek Productions, 1993.

The Spring of Discontent. Writer/producer, Patty Loew. Madison: WKOW-TV, 1990.

Thunder in the Dells. Producers, Dave Erickson and Lance Tallmadge. Spring Green, WI: Ootek Productions, 1992.

Waasa Inaabidaa: We Look in All Directions. Writer/producer, Lorraine Norrgard. Duluth: WDSE TV, 2002.

Way of the Warrior. Writer/producer, Patty Loew. Madison. PBS, 2007.

WEBSITES

American Indian Chamber of Commerce of Wisconsin: www.aiccw.org

Brothertown Indians: www.brothertownindians.org

"Conditions on Wisconsin Indian Reservations 1909–1910" (full text, online government report of *Condition of Indians Affairs in Wisconsin, 1910* (Washington, DC: Government Printing Office, 1910); www.wisconsinhistory.org/turningpoints/search.asp?id=1101

Forest County Potawatomi: www.fcpotawatomi.com

Great Lakes Indian Fish and Wildlife Commission (with links to each Ojibwe Band in Wisconsin and member bands in Michigan and Minnesota): http://glifwc.org

Great Lakes Inter-Tribal Council (with links to each Indian Nation in Wisconsin): www.glitc.org

Ho-Chunk Nation: www.ho-chunknation.com

    Hocak Worak (Ho-Chunk online tribal newspaper): www.hocakworak.com

Indian Country TV (web channel featuring national Native news and public affairs, art, and culture, originating on the Lac Courte Oreilles Reservation): www.indiancountrytv.com

Menominee:

    Menominee Nation website: www.menominee-nsn.gov

    College of the Menominee Nation: www.menominee.edu

    Through Tribal Eyes: Change on the Menominee Nation (produced by CMN students): www.youtube.com/watch?v=Mu3i63YaBgk

    The Last Menominee (produced by Wisconsin Public Television), American Indian Film Gallery, 1959: www.jfredmacdonald.com/aifg/playaifg133_thelastmenominee_1.htm

News from Indian Country (national Indian newspaper published by Paul DeMain): www
.indiancountrynews.com

Ojibwe:

    Bad River Band: www.badriver-nsn.gov

    Lac Courte Oreilles Community College: www.lco.edu

    Lac Courte Oreilles Tribal School: www.lcoschools.bie.edu

    Lac du Flambeau Band: www.ldftribe.com

    Lac du Flambeau Public School: www.ldf.k12.wi.us

    Red Cliff Band: www.redcliff-nsn.gov

    Sokaogon Chippewa Community: www.sokaogonchippewa.com

    St. Croix Chippewa Indians: www.stcciw.com

    The Vision (St. Croix online newspaper): www.stcciw.com/theVision.php

Oneida Nation website: oneida-nsn.gov

    Kalihwisaks (Oneida Nation online newspaper): ww.oneidanation.org/newspaper

Stockbridge-Munsee Community, Band of Mohican Indians website: www.mohican.com

    Mohican News Online: http://www.mohican-nsn.gov/Departments/Mohican_News
/issues/indcx.htm

Wisconsin Tribal Communities (website maintained by Milwaukee Public Museum with
links to each of the Indian Nations): www.mpm.edu/wirp/ICW-05.html

INDEX